M000032757

THE SUICIDE FACTORY

SEAN O'NEILL joined *The Times* in 2004 after working for the *Daily Telegraph* for twelve years. He has covered the Matrix Churchill affair and the Scott Inquiry into arms to Iraq, the Soham murders and the trial of Ian Huntley, and has reported extensively from Northern Ireland. Since 2001 he has focused largely on the al-Qaeda terrorist threat in the UK.

DANIEL McGRORY has reported from conflict zones around the world including Iraq, Lebanon, Bosnia, Kosovo and Central America, and has covered major terrorist incidents in the UK and Europe including the Madrid and London bombings. He worked for the BBC and the *Daily Express* before joining *The Times* in 1997.

THE SUICIDE FACTORY

ABU HAMZA AND THE FINSBURY PARK MOSQUE

SEAN O'NEILL & DANIEL McGRORY

HARPER PERENNIAL

London, New York, Toronto and Sydney

HarperCollins*Publishers*
77–85 Fulham Palace Road,
Hammersmith, London W6 8JB
www.harpercollins.co.uk

Published by HarperCollins*Publishers* 2006

Copyright © Daniel McGrory and Sean O'Neill 2006

1

The authors assert the moral right to be
identified as the authors of this work

A catalogue record for this book is
available from the British Library

ISBN 13 978-0-00-723469-1
ISBN 10 0-00-723469-4

Set in Minion and Vectora

Printed and bound in Great Britain by Clays Ltd, St Ives plc

Contents

PART III: THE RECKONING

Illustrations

Valerie Traverso married Mostafa Kamel Mostafa, the man who became Abu Hamza, less than a year after he arrived in Britain from Egypt. *(Solo Syndication)*

When Valerie's daughter was born in September 1980 Mostafa Kamel Mostafa, then an illegal immigrant, was named on the birth certificate as her father.

Abu Hamza in Afghanistan in 1993, just months before he lost his arms in an explosion near Jalalabad.

The North London Central Mosque on St Thomas's Road, Finsbury Park. *(Times Newspapers)*

After his injuries – he lost both arms and suffered a damaged eye – Abu Hamza was fitted with a leather-and-metal prosthetic limb. *(Empics)*

Haroon Rashid Aswat from Dewsbury, Yorkshire, became one of Abu Hamza's most loyal aides at Finsbury Park. *(Times Newspapers)*

Nizar Trabelsi, who was jailed in Belgium after being convicted of plotting a suicide attack on a NATO base.

The Palestinian Abu Qatada, described by a Spanish judge as 'al Qaeda's spiritual ambassador in Europe'. *(TopFoto)*

The Syrian-born Omar Bakri Mohammed ran the al-Muhajiroun group in London before going into exile in Lebanon after the 7 July 2005 bombings. *(Reuters/Toby Melville)*

Reda Hassaine, an Algerian journalist, risked his life to gather information about Abu Hamza and his associates for the intelligence services in Algiers, Paris and London.

Abu Hassan, leader of the Islamic Army of Aden, who led the kidnap of sixteen Western hostages in December 1998. *(Times Newspapers)*

The remote spot in the Yemeni desert where four of the hostages died after the kidnappers used them as human shields when soldiers mounted an armed rescue operation. *(Times Newspapers)*

The trial of some of the young Britons, including Abu Hamza's stepson Mohsen Ghailan, sent from Finsbury Park to train for jihad in Yemen. *(Times Newspapers)*

Grenades, explosives and a rocket-propelled grenade launcher, all allegedly found in the British men's car. *(Times Newspapers)*

Mohammed Mostafa Kamel, Abu Hamza's eldest son, arrives at Heathrow airport in January 2002 after spending three years in prison in Yemen. *(Reuters/Stephen Hird)*

Richard Reid from Brixton, south London, pictured minutes after being taken off a transatlantic airliner which he had tried to blow up with a bomb hidden in his shoe in December 2001. *(Empics)*

Zacarias Moussaoui, the only person to have been convicted in the United States of involvement in the 9/11 conspiracy. *(Empics)*

James Ujaama, a civil rights activist who left the United States to become Abu Hamza's webmaster in London. He was involved in plans to set up a jihad camp at an Oregon ranch. *(Neil Doyle)*

Feroz Abbasi, a computer science student from Croydon who was sent from Finsbury Park to train in Afghanistan, where he was captured in December 2001. *(Empics)*

Kamel Bourgass, an Algerian who lived at the Finsbury Park mosque, plotted to make ricin, cyanide and explosives to carry out terror attacks in London.

Detective Constable Stephen Oake, stabbed to death by Kamel Bourgass as he tried to escape arrest.

Following the discovery of the ricin plot and the connections to Abu Hamza's headquarters, police staged a dramatic raid on the Finsbury Park mosque. *(Times Newspapers)*

Police search officers discovered dozens of false and stolen passports in the mosque. *(Metropolitan Police Authority 2006: Source MPS DPA)*

A stash of knives and army-surplus field-kitchen equipment was hidden in the mosque. *(Metropolitan Police Authority 2006: Source MPS DPA)*

After his mosque was closed in the January 2003 raid, Abu Hamza continued to preach to hundreds of his followers on the street outside the barricaded building.

Scotland Yard's bill for policing Abu Hamza's Friday open-air gatherings came to almost £900,000. *(Paul Grover)*

Shehzad Tanweer, Jermaine Lindsay and Mohammed Siddique Khan at Luton railway station on a reconnaissance mission just weeks before they carried out suicide bombings on London tube trains on 7 July 2005. *(Metropolitan Police Authority 2006: Source MPS DPA)*

Hasib Hussain, the fourth 7/7 bomber, detonated his suicide bomb on a number 30 bus in Tavistock Square.

Jermaine Lindsay with his wife Samantha and their first child. Lindsay's suicide bomb on a Piccadilly Line train killed twenty-six people.

ABU HAMZA'S WORLD OF TERROR

1. **Bly, Oregon**: A group of Abu Hamza's followers accused of attempting to set up a jihad training camp in 1999

2. **Washington DC**: Zacarias Moussaoui has admitted being part of an al-Qaeda plot to hijack an airliner and fly it into the White House

3. **Miami**: Richard Reid tried to blow up flight from Paris to Miami in December 2001, with a bomb in his shoe

4. **Guantánamo Bay**: Records show many Finsbury Park graduates incarcerated at the detention camp

5. **Paris**: France considered kidnapping Abu Hamza; several Finsbury Park extremists now in jail in Paris, including Djamel Beghal

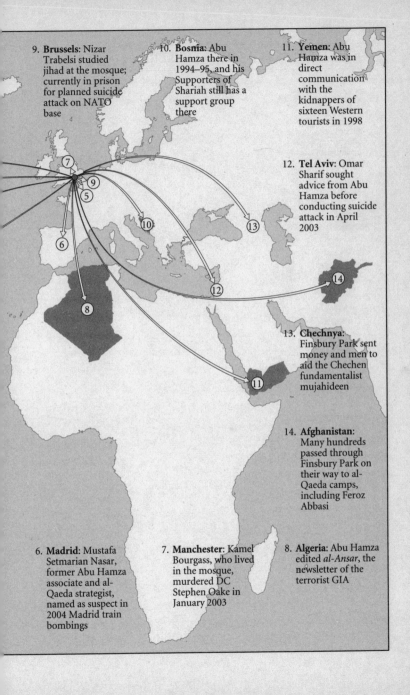

9. **Brussels**: Nizar Trabelsi studied jihad at the mosque; currently in prison for planned suicide attack on NATO base

10. **Bosnia**: Abu Hamza there in 1994–95, and his Supporters of Shariah still has a support group there

11. **Yemen**: Abu Hamza was in direct communication with the kidnappers of sixteen Western tourists in 1998

12. **Tel Aviv**: Omar Sharif sought advice from Abu Hamza before conducting suicide attack in April 2003

13. **Chechnya**: Finsbury Park sent money and men to aid the Chechen fundamentalist mujahideen

14. **Afghanistan**: Many hundreds passed through Finsbury Park on their way to al-Qaeda camps, including Feroz Abbasi

6. **Madrid**: Mustafa Setmarian Nasar, former Abu Hamza associate and al-Qaeda strategist, named as suspect in 2004 Madrid train bombings

7. **Manchester**: Kamel Bourgass, who lived in the mosque, murdered DC Stephen Oake in January 2003

8. **Algeria**: Abu Hamza edited *al-Ansar*, the newsletter of the terrorist GIA

Chronology

1958:
April: Abu Hamza is born Mostafa Kamel Mostafa in Alexandria, Egypt

1979:
January: Shah of Iran flees in face of Islamic revolution
July: Abu Hamza arrives in Britain on a one-month tourist visa
December: Soviet Union invades Afghanistan

1980:
May: Abu Hamza marries Valerie Traverso, although she is still legally married to her first husband
September: Valerie gives birth to daughter
October: Abu Hamza and Valerie Traverso claim on birth certificate that he is the father of her daughter; he applies for permission to stay in Britain indefinitely
December: Abu Hamza arrested as an illegal immigrant while working as a Soho doorman

1981:
February: Abu Hamza pleads guilty to illegal overstaying and is given a conditional discharge
August: Abu Hamza given leave to remain until May 1982 on grounds of marriage to British citizen

October: Valerie gives birth to Abu Hamza's son Mohammed

1982:
August: Abu Hamza granted indefinite leave to remain in Britain

1984:
August: Abu Hamza divorced from Valerie Traverso
October: Marries second wife, Nagat Chaffe
November: Applies for British citizenship

1986:
April: Abu Hamza granted full British citizenship
October: Begins civil engineering degree at Brighton Polytechnic

1987:
July: Goes on haj and meets Abdullah Azzam, father of modern jihad

1989:
February: Soviet withdrawal from Afghanistan
June: Abu Hamza graduates with second-class honours degree from Brighton

1990:
Abu Hamza working at Sandhurst Royal Military Academy as construction engineer and volunteering to help wounded Afghan mujahideen receiving treatment in London

1991:
Abu Hamza emigrates with family to Afghanistan

1993:
August: Abu Hamza loses both hands and an eye in an explosion near Jalalabad; he and family return to live in London

1994:

March: North London Central Mosque opens

Abu Hamza founds Supporters of Shariah movement

1995:

Abu Hamza makes three visits to Bosnia, ostensibly as an aid worker; changes name by deed poll to Adam Ramsey Eaman to get a second passport

February: Reda Hassaine begins working undercover at Finsbury Park mosque, spying on Algerian extremists for the French and Algerian secret services

1996:

Abu Hamza installed as preacher at mosque in Luton; allegations of attempted takeover of Luton Central Mosque

1997:

March: Abu Hamza appointed khateeb, or Friday preacher, at Finsbury Park mosque

1998:

May: First Charity Commission inquiry into Abu Hamza after complaints from trustees of Finsbury Park mosque

October: Legal attempt to oust Abu Hamza by former trustees is settled out of court; he retains control of mosque

November: Reda Hassaine working for British intelligence gathering information on Abu Hamza

December: Ten men sent from Finsbury Park for training arrested in Yemen; sixteen Western tourists kidnapped in retaliation; Abu Hamza in direct contact with the kidnappers; four hostages shot dead in rescue operation

1999:

January: Finsbury Park recruits tried and convicted of terrorist offences in Yemen; they allege torture; Abu Hamza named by Yemen as the mastermind behind the plot

March: Abu Hamza arrested in London and questioned about the Yemen kidnappings; held for four days then released without charge

November: Two emissaries sent from Finsbury Park to meet James Ujaama and inspect potential jihad camp in Bly, Oregon

2000:

April: Reda Hassaine's cover blown

December: Feroz Abbasi from Croydon travels to Afghanistan to train at jihad camp, accompanied by James Ujaama

2001:

July: Djamel Beghal, Finsbury Park recruiter, arrested in Dubai; Europe-wide plot for series of bomb attacks begins to unravel

September: 9/11 attacks in USA; former Finsbury Park worshipper Zacarias Moussaoui in custody accused of being part of the conspiracy. Abu Hamza says the hijackers were martyrs who acted in self-defence

December: Richard Reid from Brixton attempts to detonate a shoe bomb on a transatlantic airliner. Abbasi captured in Afghanistan and flown to Camp X-Ray, Guantánamo Bay

2002:

April: The Charity Commission says Abu Hamza is to be suspended for abusing the charitable status of Finsbury Park mosque by making political statements; he appeals, and continues preaching

September: Abu Hamza marks 9/11 anniversary with a conference entitled 'A Towering Day in History' at Finsbury Park mosque; British police begin Operation Springbourne, an inquiry into terrorist fundraising linked to Finsbury Park; they discover recipes for making poisons and explosives

2003:
January: Terrorist kitchen-sink laboratory found in Wood Green, north London; chief suspect Kamel Bourgass murders DC Stephen Oake in Manchester; Finsbury Park mosque raided by police who find military equipment, false documents and material linked to the ricin investigation; Abu Hamza begins to preach his Friday sermons on the street outside the closed mosque
April: The Home Office orders that Abu Hamza be stripped of his British citizenship
May: Asif Hanif and Omar Sharif, both linked to Finsbury Park, carry out a suicide bombing in Tel Aviv
July: The Charity Commission removes Abu Hamza as agent of the mosque

2004:
April: Abu Hamza appeals against removal of UK citizenship; case adjourned
May: US issues extradition warrant; Abu Hamza arrested and jailed
August: Re-arrested and questioned over content of taped sermons
October: Abu Hamza charged with incitement to murder and soliciting racial hatred

2005:
April: Kamel Bourgass, who lived in the Finsbury Park mosque, is convicted of plotting to make ricin poison for an attack in London; he had previously been found guilty of the murder of DC Oake
July: Suicide bombers attack the London Tube and bus network; Abu Hamza's trial postponed

2006:

January: Abu Hamza goes on trial at the Old Bailey

February: Judge sentences Abu Hamza to seven years in prison after a jury convicts him of inciting murder and race hate and one terrorism offence

Prologue

Ciaran Cassidy knew the streets of Finsbury Park well. He was a north London boy, the son of Irish parents, born, reared and completely at home in this bustling neighbourhood with its many creeds, faces of all shades and multitude of voices. This was where he played childhood games and ran errands for his mother, where he walked to school and to Mass on Sundays. As a young man he came to know the smoky, friendly pubs that adorn so many of the street corners, and looked forward to his weekend drink.

On match days Ciaran and his mates would walk down Stroud Green Road, turn right by the garish red-and-white souvenir shop, nip between the cars choking the Seven Sisters Road and pass the towering redbrick mosque to join the throng heading for Highbury stadium. Arsenal Football Club was his passion; he was a Gunner to his core.

Ciaran was twenty-two years old when he died. The man who killed him was just nineteen, and knew only one street in Finsbury Park.

Jermaine Lindsay came here no more than a handful of times to kneel on a tarpaulin laid on St Thomas's Road, and join in Friday prayers after the mosque had been closed and barricaded by police. He had listened intently to Abu Hamza al-Masri's message of hatred, bigotry and violent intolerance.

Men like Abu Hamza, skilled weavers of words and manipulators of minds, convinced Jermaine – a convert to Islam – that he would be doing God's work if he were to blow himself up and kill as many unbelievers as he could. He would be a martyr, and would be welcomed into paradise where his sins would be forgiven and he would take seventy-two wives.

On the morning of 7 July 2005 Ciaran Cassidy boarded a Piccadilly Line train at Finsbury Park Underground station to go to work at a printing shop in Chancery Lane. A twenty-minute trip on a good day; six stops to Holborn and then a walk. He was saving his wages for a six-month adventure in Australia.

Jermaine Lindsay boarded the front carriage of Ciaran's train when it stopped at King's Cross. On his back was a bulky rucksack in which was packed a crude concoction of high explosives and nails. The train left the station, and almost immediately Jermaine detonated his bomb. He killed himself. He murdered Ciaran, a young man with the warmest smile who friends said was the life and soul of any party. And he took the lives of twenty-five other people. This, Jermaine had been taught to believe, was what God wanted him to do.

At exactly the same time, on Circle Line trains at Edgware Road and Aldgate, Mohammed Sidique Khan and Shehzad Tanweer – who had also visited Finsbury Park mosque to listen to Abu Hamza and the advocates of jihad (holy war) gathered around him – exploded identical bombs. Almost an hour later their accomplice Hasib Hussain set off a fourth device on the top deck of a bus in Tavistock Square. In all the four bombers killed fifty-two innocent people and injured hundreds more – men and women, young and old, of many faiths and none; typical Londoners who hailed originally from all parts of the world.

Why they chose 7 July may never be explained. It could have been because on that day Tony Blair was hosting the most powerful men in the world at the G8 summit in Scotland. Perhaps they chose that morning because, the day before, London had held a spontaneous party to celebrate being declared the host city for the 2012 Olympics.

But maybe there was another motive. At the moment the first three explosions occurred beneath the streets of London, Abu Hamza was arriving at the Old Bailey courthouse to stand trial for inciting his followers to kill and be killed, to carry out what he liked to call 'martyrdom operations'.

The case of The Crown vs Abu Hamza was one of just two trials to sit that day in the historic old courthouse. When the news of the terrorist attacks on London became known, all legal business was abandoned and lawyers, jurors and court staff left the building quickly to join the millions of people walking home, like columns of refugees fleeing a stricken and frightened city. It was an eerie scene: London empty of traffic and its accompanying roar. Strangely quiet save for the ghostly wail of sirens, the clatter of helicopters and the steady footfall of the legions of walkers.

Abu Hamza was sitting in the dock as news filtered through to the court of the carnage that had occurred in the city outside. The trial judge decided that it would be simply impossible to find a jury that week or in the immediate future to conduct a fair trial of Abu Hamza. The preacher was taken back to the cells, knowing that holy warriors had brought the bloody jihad he advocated to London. The case was adjourned for six months.

A panel of jurors was finally assembled in January 2006 to hold the infamous hook-handed cleric to account for his role in fomenting terrorism in Britain and around the world. But that jury would be told only a fragment of the story. This book is an attempt to explain the role played by this extraordinary figure in the global jihad. Abu Hamza seized control of the Finsbury Park mosque, which had been built with the support of the Prince of Wales and cash from the Saudi royal family, and turned it into an al-Qaeda camp in the heart of London. He provided a safe haven for experienced terrorists and jihad veterans who came from around the world to meet one another, engage in ideological debate, spread the word and plan terrorist attacks. His mosque was a place where impressionable young minds were imprinted with the theology of religious conflict and willing young bodies were recruited to train for death in battle. It was a centre for organised crime, in the shape of lucrative frauds, counterfeiting and identity theft, on an industrial scale. It produced propaganda, recruits, cash and forged documents – all essential components for the smooth running of a worldwide terrorist network. 'I don't know what was more dangerous, Abu Hamza himself or the environment he created around him,' reflected one high-ranking counter-terrorist investigator. 'It was a magnet for jihadis. It had a reputation far and wide as a place of sanctuary for like-minded people.'

But the great scandal of Finsbury Park is that the British authorities knew that all this was happening, and allowed it to go on happening. Politicians, spy chiefs, police officers, immigration officials and many other state agencies were told again and again – most often by frightened members of the Muslim community – what Abu Hamza was doing and why he should be stopped. Foolishness and fear prevented Britain's rulers from taking action. Their foolishness lay in believing that Abu Hamza and his ilk could be monitored, watched and kept under control. The shadowy figures from the world of intelligence spoke to him regularly and thought they had him tagged as a 'harmless clown'. He delighted in pulling the wool over their eyes. A senior government minister told the authors: 'It took a very long time to realise that monitoring him was not very productive. It took even longer to realise that far from leading us in the direction of dangerous men, he was the dangerous man.'

Errors were made, admitted a highly-placed security source: 'In the 1990s especially, people didn't really have a handle on the insidious radicalisation that was going on. We in Britain had no appreciation that young, impressionable people were being subjected to an intellectual onslaught of propaganda to turn them into extremists.'

More crippling, however, was the fear of acting against a religious leader and a place of worship, especially when they were of a minority faith. Those in positions of power dreaded being accused of racism, discrimination or the new buzzword, Islamophobia. Great Britain was only too quick to send soldiers to Afghanistan and Iraq to fight the so-called 'war on terror', but slow to tackle the very real threat lurking in London.

When they did get round to dealing with Abu Hamza, it was too late. Too late for Ciaran Cassidy and the other victims of 7/7. And too late for many others who have died and have yet to be killed at the hands of fanatical adherents to the message of Abu Hamza.

PART I

The Rise of Abu Hamza

1
Mostafa

'We are all under the feet and the heavy boots
of the kuffar [unbeliever].'

ABU HAMZA

The young Egyptian held the sheet of paper in both hands and, in his heavily accented English, read the words in front of him carefully: 'I, Mostafa Kamel Mostafa, do solemnly and sincerely affirm that I will be faithful and bear true allegiance to Her Majesty Queen Elizabeth the Second, Her Heirs and Successors, according to the law.'

Mostafa then signed the official form bearing the same pledge; his signature was formally witnessed by his solicitor and the document placed in the out-tray to be posted to the Immigration and Nationality Directorate of the British Home Office.

Just ten days later a certificate of naturalisation, declaring him to be a citizen of the United Kingdom of Great Britain and Northern Ireland, dropped through the letterbox of Mostafa's London council flat.

For the man who would become known as Abu Hamza al-Masri – possibly the most hated man in Britain and someone who would angrily despise British values – this was quite an achievement. Citizenship of the United Kingdom of Great Britain and Northern Ireland was a goal he had pursued almost from the day he stepped off a flight from Cairo seven years before.

Abu Hamza had accomplished his aim with a display of ruthless and cynical dishonesty. Had his applications for refugee status been properly scrutinised by immigration officials, he could have been deported from Britain as an illegal immigrant and a fraudster long before he caused the trouble that he went on to stir up. Those investigations were never undertaken. Instead, on Tuesday, 29 April 1986, he swore allegiance to the Crown and won the right to stay in Britain for ever.

Ironically, he took that oath of allegiance as he was on the cusp of his conversion to a brand of political and religious fanaticism that would lead him to regard his adopted country as a godless, decadent land whose Queen deserved the sword rather than his allegiance. England, he became fond of proclaiming, was 'a toilet'.

But Abu Hamza, the fanatical preacher of hatred, was a completely different person from Mostafa, the twenty-one-year-old student who disembarked at Heathrow airport on 13 July 1979. Tightly clutching his new Egyptian passport, number 172167, issued in Alexandria less than a fortnight before, he arrived in Britain in the middle of a year of revolutionary change. Margaret Thatcher had been swept into Downing Street, heralding an era of right-wing free-market radicalism that would shatter Britain's post-war political consensus. The most feared terrorist organisation of the day, the Provisional IRA, struck that summer at the very heart of the British establishment, blowing up Lord Mountbatten, a senior member of the royal family, as he pottered around in a boat off the west coast of Ireland. In Europe, Pope John Paul II toured his native Poland, drawing massive crowds and throwing down the gauntlet to Eastern Bloc communism. On the other side of the world, Sandinista guerrillas seized power in Nicaragua and set about creating peasant socialism in America's backyard.

But the changes that would have the longest-lasting global impact were happening in the Muslim world that Mostafa was leaving behind. 1979 began with the Shah of Iran fleeing into exile in the face of the modern world's first Islamic revolt, and Ayatollah Khomeini returning to Tehran to seize power. The year drew to an end with the mighty Red Army of the Soviet Union pouring into Afghanistan to shore up its puppet government. The events that followed in poverty-stricken Afghanistan would change the world by reviving the Islamic concept of physical jihad in defence of the Muslim religion and lands. They spawned not just war without end for the Afghan people, but the brand of global terrorism that would be propagated by Osama bin Laden's al-Qaeda.

Such things could not have been further from the mind of the young Mostafa Kamel Mostafa when he left his family's comfortable middle-class home in Alexandria to travel abroad for the first time. There was a fashion among young Egyptians that year for visiting London, and almost from the moment he arrived, he wanted to stay. Although he was three years into a five-year degree course, he decided to abandon his engineering studies at Alexandria University. A powerful incentive for staying in England was the chance to avoid national service in the military back home.

He was a powerfully-built young man with a thick mop of curly hair, golden brown skin, an infectious smile and a mischievous twinkle in his eye. London offered things he hankered after more than a degree in engineering and years in the army – most especially women and wealth.

'He had this huge chest, huge broad shoulders and big biceps, he had awesome genetics,' remembered a friend. 'He just had to look at a weight bar and he'd put on more muscle. He wore jeans and T-shirts and usually had a gold chain around his neck. He was cool and, yes, he was a womaniser – he was an Egyptian after all, what do you expect?'

Although his one-month visitor's visa specifically ruled out working, the young man who would later be known as Abu Hamza quickly found a job, and he liked the feel of English pound notes in his pocket. A month after his arrival he applied to extend his stay by another month. Permission was granted without question, on the same 'no work' condition that he – like many others – was blissfully ignoring.

'He was just like the rest of us,' remembered Zak Hassan, another of the five or six hundred young Egyptian men having a youthful adventure in London that year. 'We used to hang around in coffee shops in Queensway to talk and chat and eat. Everyone wore jeans, no one had a beard and nobody talked politics or religion, it wasn't an issue any of us was interested in. Abu Hamza sat in the corner and joined in with everybody else. We talked about work, women and football. We were nearly all supporters of Al Ahly, Cairo's biggest team, who play in red. So a lot of us started supporting Liverpool, because they played in red and they were the team of the moment in England. We were just ordinary young men looking for work. At night a lot of us went to pubs, not to drink but to chat up girls. But the priority was work. We had no families to support us, no mothers to go back to, so we had to earn money to rent our rooms and have enough food to eat.'

One of the future Abu Hamza's several jobs was as night porter in a bed and breakfast hotel in Gloucester Place, not far from Paddington rail station. These establishments were often more hostels than hotels, with most of the residents living in cramped conditions as they waited to be housed in council accommodation. Here, in the spring of 1980, he met Valerie Traverso, a single mother of three young children who was pregnant by Michael Macias, her first husband, from whom she had recently separated.

Valerie, who was twenty-five at the time, felt an immediate attraction to the young Egyptian, and her feelings seemed to be reciprocated. He was a hunk, he paid her attention, and he made her laugh. She remembers his 'nice, big hands', his eyes and his coffee-brown skin; as a single parent, down on her luck, Valerie was flattered that the exotic young foreigner was interested in her.

But Abu Hamza's interest in Valerie seems to have been more than just a physical one. He was an illegal immigrant. He had not renewed his visitor's visa when it expired the previous September. Instead he blended into the black-market world of cash-in-hand casual work. Valerie's pregnancy presented him with an opportunity which he could exploit. If he could marry her and persuade her to let him claim that he was the father of her child, his immigration status would be vastly improved.

He acted quickly. As night porter, Abu Hamza allowed Valerie to use the staff kitchen in the hotel to warm up milk for her toddler son. One night, not long after they first met, she was alone in the kitchen when he came straight up to her and kissed her passionately. He was direct and physical, and she found him hard to resist.

'He made the first move,' she said. 'I'm not the sort of person to do that kind of thing. It was there in the kitchen. I was surprised, I didn't think it would happen so soon because I hadn't long come out of a long relationship and was surprised with myself more than anything. Things moved pretty fast. We became very close very quickly. But he was also a romantic man, quite tender and softly spoken. We laughed a lot.'

The sex was good, but when Abu Hamza suggested they get married, Valerie turned him down. He had proposed as they sat in the reception of the Four Seasons Hotel, Queensway – another of his places of employment – late one night. She was four years older than him, and felt that she would not be able to trust him.

There were lots of women after the young night porter, drawn by his rugged looks and ready charm. Valerie did not trust Abu Hamza to stay faithful when there were so many other women who would not encumber him with a brood of young children. Other women who lived or worked in the hotel were interested in him; one in particular, called Tracy, made no bones about the fact. She was always hanging around the reception desk or butting in when Valerie was chatting to her new man.

Regardless of what Tracy wanted, Abu Hamza had set his sights on Valerie. He persisted with his marriage proposal, and it was not long before she relented. They were married in Westminster Register Office on 16 May 1980, just ten months after he had arrived in Britain. Around twenty guests were present; acquaintances rather than friends. None of his family attended. His father was an Egyptian navy officer and his mother a schoolteacher and later a schools inspector. They were disappointed that he had decided to stay in Britain rather than return to Alexandria to complete his degree course.

Valerie has repeatedly insisted that the marriage was the result of a genuine love affair. But she can hardly have been unaware of Abu Hamza's immigration status. Significantly, when they wed she spelt her name on the marriage register incorrectly, as 'Traversa' and not 'Traverso'. At the time of her marriage to Abu Hamza she and her first husband were separated but not divorced. They did not divorce until July 1982. Her marriage to Abu Hamza was bigamous. Valerie has protested in interviews since that there was no intent on her or Abu Hamza's part to marry illegally. It was a mix-up, a simple confusion. But just a few months later a second false entry was being made on an official register.

On 26 September 1980, Valerie gave birth to the child with whom she had been pregnant when she met Abu Hamza. Her daughter was born in the South London hospital in Clapham. Within four days of the baby's birth, Abu Hamza instructed lawyers to write to the Home Office stating that the young Egyptian immigrant had married an Englishwoman and become a father. He had been living in Britain illegally, but now that he had a wife and child here he wanted to 'regularise' his stay. He wanted to remain in the country indefinitely.

Such a claim would have to be supported by documentary evidence, namely marriage and birth certificates. The wedding document the couple already had. On 22 October the birth of Valerie's daughter was recorded at the office of the Registrar of Births, Deaths and Marriages in Lambeth. The child's name was entered as Nahed

Donna Mostafa, and the name of her father was registered as Mostafa Kamel Mostafa. He gave his birthplace as Egypt and his occupation as 'labourer'. Abu Hamza signed the register 'Mostafa'. The name of the child's mother was recorded as Valerie Olga Macias – using the surname of her first husband, to whom she was still married, albeit bigamously. She gave her maiden name as Traverso – spelling it correctly on this occasion. Beside Mostafa's signature, the name 'V. Macias' was signed.

The marriage of Abu Hamza and Valerie Traverso was not legal. It appears that the registration of Valerie's daughter's birth was also carried out illegally. Valerie insists to this day that she was pregnant when she met Abu Hamza – she is '150 per cent on that'. If that is true, the birth certificate for the child, which states that he is the father, is a fraudulent document. Now registered as both a husband and a father under British law, Abu Hamza had a strong claim to be allowed to live legally in Britain. But his claim was based on a double deception.

Abu Hamza seemed firmly set on the path to citizenship, but it was not to run as smoothly as he had hoped. On the night of 12 December 1980, police carried out a series of raids on clubs in Soho, the centre of London's sex industry. They were looking for unlicensed premises and illegal workers from overseas. At Jan's Cinema Club on Archer Street, a seedy porn-and-prostitutes joint owned like much of Soho at the time by a Maltese family syndicate, officers arrested a number of people, including the Egyptian doorman.

Abu Hamza's muscular frame had made him ideal for work as a bouncer. It was relatively well-paid, strictly cash, no questions asked, and involved little more difficult than warding off drunks and protecting the club's strippers and hostesses from the over-enthusiastic attentions of some of the clientele. The clubs operating on the wrong side of the law always employed security to keep the punters in order and reduce the chances of attracting any police attention. Jan's Cinema Club was shut down, albeit temporarily, and the employees rounded up. The doorman was quickly identified as an illegal immigrant and charged.

The following February he was brought before Great Marlborough Street magistrates' court, where past defendants have included Oscar Wilde and Mick Jagger. As Mostafa Kamel Mostafa he pleaded guilty to the offence of overstaying his visitor's visa by fifteen months. But he had an effective sob story of love, marriage and fatherhood to tell the court. Furthermore, the magistrates were told, the doorman had already applied to 'regularise' his immigration situation and the file was being considered by the Home Office. On 3 February 1981 the magistrates handed down a conditional discharge and sent him on his way. Six months later, Abu Hamza was granted official permission to stay in Britain until May 1982 on the grounds of his marriage to a citizen. His request for permission to stay indefinitely was kept under review.

No one could have known it at the time, but the Great Marlborough Street bench had been presented with the opportunity to deport a man who would become one of the most potent recruiters for a brand of worldwide terrorism that was then unimaginable. Much has happened since: the grand old courthouse has become a fashionable hotel, restaurant and bar; Jan's Cinema Club is long gone and Archer Street is down to its last sex shop; and Mostafa the doorman somehow transformed himself into a designated international terrorist.

Valerie Traverso's life has changed greatly too. She has married two more husbands, but still denies adamantly that Abu Hamza used her as his fast track to British citizenship. She has insisted in interviews that they were in love, and that the relationship was cemented in early 1981 when she fell pregnant by him. Her then husband, she said, was 'thrilled to bits'. When their son Mohammed was born in October 1981, Abu Hamza was every inch the doting father. 'You couldn't fault him with the kids. He took them everywhere, looked after them, provided us with money,' she told *The*

Times in 2006. He was 'determined to be a brilliant father and a good husband', she said in the *Mail on Sunday* in 1999. Family snapshots from the time seem to support her story. They show Abu Hamza, dressed in the fashions of the time, proudly holding his baby son or rolling about on the carpet, playing with the boy.

But the image of the family man was hard to maintain. Abu Hamza's work in Soho took him to brothels and bed shows, and onto streets ripe with temptation for a young male. The working girls were often grateful for the protection of their musclebound guardian. Abu Hamza began at least one affair. He has always been coy about this period of his life, bemoaning the men who came 'to fantasise' at these places, but adding: 'I was a very undisciplined Muslim.'

Back home, busy with nappies and night feeds and waiting for the scrape of his key in the lock each night, Valerie became increasingly suspicious of her husband's nocturnal activities. He seemed to be arriving later and later at their flat in Putney, south-west London. And he would not tell her where he had been or, when he left home, where he was going. Eventually, after a noisy confrontation, he admitted that he had had an affair with a girl he met through the club. The *Sun* newspaper has reported that her former husband's lover was a prostitute.

This confession was to be one of the key turning points that would put Abu Hamza onto the path of radical Islam. Until that moment he had shown little interest in being a Muslim. The Egypt he grew up in was Muslim in name but secular and nationalist in much of its outlook, although he followed some traditions, such as having men and women dine separately whenever his friends visited.

But when Abu Hamza admitted the affair, Valerie threatened to leave him. He could not afford to be deserted. His immigration status was not secure. 'I told him that things had gone too far and I was leaving,' she said. 'He responded by saying that he would change and he would dedicate himself to Islam. He swore that he would never do it again. He was going to be religious, he was going to pray and ask for God's help.'

Valerie, who had been born into a family of Spanish Roman Catholics, decided that she too would investigate this religion with her husband: 'We would sit and read it [the Koran] together. When he started to study, I started to study. I started to learn Arabic. I tried to learn to write it too but it was pretty tough.'

The alien language was not the only tough aspect of her conversion. Walking on the street in Putney one day, Valerie and a friend were attacked because they were wearing the hijab, or headscarf. 'A few lads came along, jumped out of their car and pulled our scarves off our heads and threw them in the road,' she said. 'Our friends were very troubled. They had wreaths put outside their door, their car was attacked and their children were bullied at school. My reaction was to stop wearing the hijab. Mostafa asked me why I had stopped. I told him it was my own choice, that I had started wearing it and that I could stop wearing it if I so wished.'

Despite the prejudice his wife had encountered, Abu Hamza was still keen on staying in Britain, and continued to pursue a resolution of his immigration situation. In April 1982 the Home Office informed him that he had to extend the validity of his Egyptian passport before it could consider his case further. The passport had expired, rendering him in a stateless limbo. He responded in June, claiming that the Egyptian embassy in London had refused to renew his passport because he was a young man of army age. He was supposed to return home for national service. Two months later, perhaps because the threat of conscription was considered oppressive, the Home Office decided to give Abu Hamza permission to remain in Britain indefinitely. He was now just one short step way from his goal of citizenship.

With his position in Britain secure, Abu Hamza's marriage to Valerie began to go off the rails. He was angry about her decision not to wear the hijab, while after his infidelity, she still felt she could not trust him. They separated, and Abu Hamza took custody of their son. He says the arrangement was by 'mutual consent'. She says she agreed to let him take Mohammed on a six-month visit to Egypt to meet his parents, his brothers and sisters and extended family. Whatever the truth of the arrangement, Valerie would not see her son again until 1999, when he was put on trial in Yemen and convicted of terrorist offences. When she met him again, Mohammed said that his father had told him that his mother was dead.

It was Abu Hamza who petitioned for divorce in June 1984, naming Valerie as respondent and referring to an unknown co-respondent. The divorce was uncontested and the decree absolute, ending their marriage, was issued at Wandsworth County Court, south London, on 15 August 1984.

A little more than two months later, Abu Hamza married his second wife in an Islamic ceremony in London. Nagat Chaffe, a Moroccan national, was also divorced with a young child. The couple are said still to be devoted to one another. As he became a notorious public figure, she remained firmly in the background, the dutiful and veiled wife and mother.

Their first child, Mostafa Kamel Hamza, was born in 1986, and it was his birth that gave his father the kunya, or nickname, of Abu Hamza, by which he would become known around the world. Abu Hamza al-Masri is translated as 'the father of Hamza, the Egyptian'. Abu Hamza and Nagat would go on to have five more children – three sons and two daughters – the youngest of whom was born in 1997. Like their father, all the children are British citizens. Having obtained his leave to remain in the country indefinitely, Abu Hamza formally applied for full citizenship in November 1984. It was granted in the spring of 1986, on the basis of five years' continuous residence. All Abu Hamza had to do in return was pledge allegiance to the Crown.

*   *   *

His second marriage made Abu Hamza a more reflective man. He was still involved in 'security' and had a commercial interest in a restaurant in west London, but he was increasingly curious, if not terribly well-informed, about Islam. He also had a sense that he had been wasting these years in London, and that the time had come to return to his engineering studies and devote himself to his faith.

He applied to study civil engineering at Brighton Polytechnic, and was admitted to a place on a degree course at the seaside college. A few months before he enrolled in October 1986, however, Abu Hamza finally achieved his aim of becoming a British citizen and swore that oath of allegiance to the Queen.

Not long after becoming a British national, Abu Hamza knocked on the front door of the mosque in Dyke Road, Brighton – a distinguished-looking Edwardian house set back from the traffic – and asked if he might have lodgings there in return for performing some caretaking duties.

'We had eleven beds in a room on the top floor and we let Muslim students stay there; they would eat, cook and pray together and they looked after the building,' said Dr Abduljalil Sahid, who was then imam. 'Mostafa, because that was what his name was then, was just like all the others. He was an ordinary young man, fun-loving and not very religious. He stayed here from Monday to Thursday, then he would go back to London to his wife and family.'

While at Brighton Polytechnic, Abu Hamza became acquainted for the first time, through some of his fellow students, with ideas and discussions of jihad and militant Islamism. In 1987 he went on the haj pilgrimage to Mecca – an obligation of the Islamic faith – and while there he met the Palestinian Islamic scholar Sheikh Abdullah Azzam, a leading pioneer of radical Islam. It was a meeting that would change the course of his thinking and of his life.

Azzam was already a heroic figure in fundamentalist circles, and arrived in Saudi Arabia that year fresh from writing and publishing a pamphlet entitled *Join the Caravan*. The text is still regarded in the jihadi movement as the most important rallying call for militant Islamism. Azzam had taught in Saudi Arabia's leading universities, but had abandoned academia to go to Afghanistan and fight the Soviet infidels. His most famous protégé was Osama bin Laden, the son of a mega-rich Saudi family, who also moved to Afghanistan to fight and to organise the Arabs flocking to join the mujahideen. Thousands from the Arab countries followed Azzam and bin Laden to the Afghan war; it was an exodus of idealistic young men that has been compared to the formation of the International Brigades that fought Franco during the Spanish Civil War in the 1930s.

Azzam's example in taking up arms was an inspiration, but his lasting contribution to the worldwide jihad lay in his writings and teachings. In polemical tracts like *Join the Caravan* and *In Defence of the Muslim Lands* he argued that fighting jihad was not a noble option for Muslims, but a religious duty. 'Jihad must not be abandoned until Allah alone is worshipped,' he preached. 'Jihad continues until Allah's word is raised high. Jihad until all the oppressed peoples are freed. Jihad to protect our dignity and restore our occupied lands. Jihad is the way of everlasting glory.'

He prayed that Allah would make the mujahideen sincere and steadfast, and 'bring us our end in martyrdom'. Azzam was the first to articulate the jihad cause in language that ordinary Muslims could understand. His message was one of holy war until Islam dominated the earth, a conflict in which it would be a privilege to kill and be killed. To this day his didactic beliefs remain at the core of the al-Qaeda ideology.

This was the blood-soaked creed that Abu Hamza imbibed at the feet of Azzam in 1987. His curiosity about Islam was being stoked into a burning passion fuelled by the injustices committed against Muslim peoples around the world that called out for redress. The Azzam theology made a deep impression on him, not least because the teacher both taught it and fought for it.

The fact that he spent time in the company of Azzam has given

Abu Hamza real credibility in the jihad movement. It carries far greater weight than the boasts of thousands of jihadis that they have met bin Laden. 'The West always makes a big deal about people meeting bin Laden,' said one British veteran of the training camps. 'Anybody could meet bin Laden, it was easy. I know a guy who was having a cigarette when bin Laden walked into the room. Bin Laden turned to him and said, "It's a long time since I've had a cigarette," and the guy was really embarrassed and threw it down. I don't think Abu Hamza ever met bin Laden, but he had met Sheikh Abdullah Azzam, and that really counted for something.'

Two years after that meeting in Mecca, the widely revered Azzam was assassinated in the Pakistani border town of Peshawar, the headquarters of the Arab fighters. His enemies – in all likelihood another mujahideen faction – killed him and two of his sons by detonating a huge bomb buried under the road. The story goes that despite the force of the blast Azzam's body was left 'totally intact and not at all disfigured'.

But Abu Hamza was able to say that he had met Azzam and prayed with him and listened to him preach. He would recall: 'I sat with Sheikh Abdullah Azzam and he said, "We need you there." He had an agenda to take the people, train the people, to make people mujahids.'

'Azzam liked Abu Hamza too,' said a friend of the Egyptian. 'He recognised him as a very charismatic man who could be a good scholar and could arouse others to follow the path. A lot of people will tell you that Abu Hamza did not do any fighting, but he had another role to play.'

Despite his personal meeting with Azzam, Abu Hamza did not go to war. He returned instead to England and to Brighton, where he resumed his engineering course. But Dr Sajid noticed that the young lodger was a changed man: 'He told me he had met Sheikh Abdullah Azzam and that he was a great man who represented the future of Islam,' the imam remembered. 'He said Muslims must go and fight the corrupt rulers and the Russian invaders, and we must apply God's law. He was criticising me because I was a magistrate in Brighton, and he asked how could I apply British law and preach Islam at the same time.

'He started to become aggressive, and I thought this man will end up causing trouble. He also started to bring magazines about jihad and the mujahideen into the mosque, but I gathered them up and threw them away. I used to tell him, "This is not a political place, this is a mosque." He was not educated, he was only learning about Islam. He kept on arguing about the hijab, about my sermons, about jihad, about international issues. I used to say our problems here are about racism, unemployment and equality. But he would not listen.'

Dr Sajid was frightened and intimidated by Abu Hamza's threats, and reported his fears to police in Brighton. He was told that unless his lodger physically attacked someone at the mosque there was nothing they could do. This was just the start of a familiar pattern of community concern that was met with official inaction. Over the next twenty years many respectable figures in the Muslim population would also go to the police to raise the alarm about Abu Hamza, and would have their worries ignored.

For all his warlike talk, however, when the Soviet army fled Afghanistan in 1989, defeated by the guerrilla armies of the mujahideen, Abu Hamza was studying for his final exams. He graduated from Brighton Polytechnic that year with a second-class honours degree in civil engineering.

As Abu Hamza left the south coast to return to London, Dr Sajid noted that he had changed from being an uneducated Muslim into one who was arrogant and aggressive in argument. 'I thought his views were obnoxious, I predicted that he would not be a peaceful man.'

In London Abu Hamza immersed himself in radical Islam. He attended political and prayer meetings hosted by radical groups, and several talks given by a fundamentalist Egyptian cleric, Sheikh Omar

Abdel-Rahman. The sheikh was criss-crossing the world promoting and recruiting for the Afghan jihad. His travels were reportedly funded by the CIA, the US intelligence agency, in its anxiety to drum up support for what it mistakenly believed was an old-fashioned Cold War conflict against the Soviet Union.

Abdel-Rahman had been blind since childhood, studied the Koran in Braille and became a fervent advocate of violent jihad. He was charged in Egypt with issuing the fatwa for the assassination in 1981 of President Anwar Sadat. Today he is serving life imprisonment in the United States, convicted of plotting bomb attacks; he was investigated in the wake of the 1993 bombing of the World Trade Centre by some of his disciples.

His dedication to the jihadi cause, regardless of his disabilities, made a huge impression on Abu Hamza, as did the example of injured mujahideen receiving medical treatment in London. Rich Saudis were paying for many of the veterans to be treated at expensive Harley Street clinics. Abu Hamza volunteered to act as a translator for them, and was in awe of their determination to return to the battlefield: 'When you see how happy they are, how anxious just to have a new limb so they can run again and fight again, not thinking of retiring, their main ambition is to get killed in the cause of Allah ... you see another dimension in the verses of the Koran,' he enthused to a Yemeni newspaper interviewer. He later said that the injured mujahideen 'invited me to go to Afghanistan, they said they needed lots of people to help rebuild the country'.

Yet he was still reluctant to answer the call to arms. Instead, and quite bizarrely, he became a senior engineer on a construction project at the British Army's elite officer training school, the Royal Military Academy at Sandhurst. The man who would one day indoctrinate young men who would go to Afghanistan possibly to shoot at British soldiers, spent the best part of a year rebuilding car parks for British military vehicles. Soldiers going in and out of the academy every day used to salute him.

The job required Abu Hamza to have in his possession detailed surveyor's plans of the Sandhurst site, and he kept the papers for years after the work was completed. When his home was raided by police many years later, in May 2004, they were on his bookshelves. The police chose not to confiscate them.

While still working at Sandhurst, Abu Hamza started for the first time to teach his views on jihad and Islam. He was one of a number of hardliners attending the Regent's Park mosque in London, who gathered young men together into small study circles and lectured on the teachings of Azzam and the obligations of holy war. The elders suspected that Abu Hamza and his cronies were trying to seize control of the mosque, the Friday sermon and the collection boxes. It was a warning of what was to come some years later in Finsbury Park, where the giant new mosque was still only in the planning stage.

Fazli Ali, the estates manager at Regent's Park mosque at the time, recalled: 'Our mosque has always been a peaceful, non-political place and Abu Hamza wanted to turn it into a political arena. He and his cronies threatened me several times, they even threatened to kill me. It was difficult to get rid of him, but we managed it.'

They did so with the help of a High Court injunction banning Abu Hamza and several other radicals from the premises. But the engineer was planning to leave anyway. In late 1990 he paid a short visit to Peshawar and Afghanistan as he finalised his plans to move his family to Afghanistan. He also went to Egypt to see his ailing father, but his family were alarmed by the extremist views he was now espousing. While they lived their quiet lives in Alexandria, their relative from London had adopted the extreme views of Abdel-Rahman and the terrorist group Egyptian Islamic Jihad. They asked him to leave before everyone in the family fell under suspicion from the secret police. His father died eleven days after he left Egypt.

Back in London, Abu Hamza undertook one more major engineering project – working on the refurbishment and cladding of the underpass that runs underneath The Strand from Waterloo Bridge to Kingsway. He was learning techniques and skills that he hoped to be able to deploy to help in rebuilding the shattered country of Afghanistan.

Then, in 1991, Abu Hamza packed his and his family's entire life into a shipping container and set off for Afghanistan. 'I emigrated,' he said. 'I went there never intending to come back.'

2
The Man and the Myth

'Take what you want, Allah, whenever you want, we are happy, we are not resigning from this, from this thing and we've still got to do jihad. You take our hands we do it with the tongue.'

ABU HAMZA

The legend of Abu Hamza, hero of the jihad, was forged in the war-torn wreckage of Afghanistan and is etched in the scar tissue on the short, fleshy stumps which are all that remain of his muscular arms. These damaged limbs, to one of which he straps a leather and metal hook-handed prosthetic, have given him his distinctive public image and fuelled his notoriety.

With his hook, his damaged, unopening left eye and his wild rhetoric, he would become exactly the kind of villain that headline writers love. He was easily dismissed as some sort of cross between a Shakespearian fool and a James Bond villain, a ranting madman with visions of world domination. The problem was that others saw only the caricature and not the threat behind it. Embattled moderate Muslims said he was on the lunatic fringe and had no followers, and too many people in authority in Britain, who had little or no other contact with the community, were happy to accept that assessment.

The headlines too played their part. They were unkind, and would not have been directed at any other disabled person. He was referred to simply as 'Hook', and the sub-editors lapped up the chance to write front pages that screamed 'Sling Your Hook'. Privately, Abu Hamza revelled in the publicity and the attention. He made a collection of the newspaper headlines he relished most, and joked with reporters about his disfiguring injuries. 'Don't bring a photographer,' he answered one interview request, 'they always make me look ugly.'

He used to complain that his old-fashioned artificial limb chafed his skin and he had to frequently apply ointment to it. At the beginning of his preaching career he was usually seen without the hook. But as his infamy spread he took to wearing it more often, especially if he was likely to be photographed or filmed. He liked to show off his skill with the lethal-looking prosthetic, using it to answer the mobile phone that he kept on a cord around his neck. Tellingly, he refused offers of more advanced, less fearsome artificial hands.

But the story of how he lost his arms and gained his hook is one that Abu Hamza has preferred to keep shrouded in the mists of half-truth. When he stood trial at the Old Bailey in London in early 2006 – giving evidence from the witness box for five days – the question of his injuries was quickly passed over. Save for the statement that the incident occurred in Afghanistan in 1993, the subject was not mentioned.

The date appears to be true. Nevertheless, it is contradicted by a classified report by the Algerian intelligence service, the Département de Recherche et Sécurité (DRS). Written around 1997, it alleged that Abu Hamza lost his eye and arms in Bosnia in 1995 when a grenade exploded in his hands somewhere well behind the front line. That report may, however, have been written in a deliberate attempt to discredit the cleric by undermining his reputation as an Afghan veteran at a time when he was regarded as the spiritual authority behind the Armed Islamic Group (GIA), which was conducting a brutal guerrilla war in Algeria.

There remain two other versions of the story. One has been told by Abu Hamza himself, but only to Western reporters and interviewers. It appears to be a sanitised account, containing no suggestion that he was involved in any kind of military or terrorist activity; according to his followers, it is not an account that they are familiar with. They have heard – and prefer to believe – a different tale, told to them not by Abu Hamza but by Afghan veterans who were with him in Nengarhar province in the summer of 1993.

The media-friendly version of events was first heard in early 1999, when Abu Hamza originally attracted the attention of Fleet Street. His son and stepson were part of a group of young men sent by Abu Hamza for jihad training in Yemen, but found themselves on trial in Aden. The British press was desperate for information about the comic-book cleric and what he was doing behind the doors of Finsbury Park mosque, north London.

After a press conference on events in Yemen, Abu Hamza was approached by an eager young reporter from the *Daily Mail* who asked for an interview. He agreed to talk to the reporter, but only on one condition. The man from the *Mail* could have his interview if he paid for a taxi to take the cleric to the studios of the BBC, where he was to be interviewed on an evening news programme. The reporter could speak to him in the back of the taxi as it negotiated the slow-moving London traffic.

There are many photographs of the scene, some of the first to appear in print of Abu Hamza. He is seen sitting in the back of the black cab, the windows misted with condensation on a winter's day. Alongside him, but often cropped out of the shot, is Haroon Rashid Aswat, at the time his favourite lieutenant. Since July 2005 Aswat has been a prisoner, and is facing extradition from Britain to stand trial on terror charges alongside his emir (leader) Abu Hamza in the United States, although he maintains his innocence. The story Abu Hamza told that day, and which he has repeated to other reporters since, is one of an engineer nobly engaged in post-war reconstruction work who was blown up by one of the hundreds of thousands of landmines that have killed, maimed and injured so many in Afghanistan.

It was 1 August 1993, shortly after sunset. Abu Hamza was doing one of two things. He was either at a building site with a group of workmen, indicating how he wanted something done by drawing lines in the dusty roadway with a stick, or he was using the stick to try to mark a path through a minefield for a group of mujahideen. As the end of his stick scored the ground he felt, rather than heard, a big explosion. It was, he said, as if someone had hit him in the face with a shoe. His head and body were numb, and he seemed to recall wandering around his workmen asking if they were all OK. When they began to grab his arms he had no idea what was happening. Later, he said, he learned that they were trying to bind them up to stop the massive blood loss. There had been blood everywhere, but he had not realised it was his blood. His colleagues were fetching water and pouring it over his face, trying to clean and save his wounded eye. He couldn't see anything.

Abu Hamza collapsed, and when he regained consciousness three days later he was in a hospital across the border in Pakistan. He still could not see, and there was no feeling in his arms. He thought his hands were still numb from the blast and tried rubbing them together, sensing that something should be there beneath the bandages. It was only when he had a visitor and asked what had happened to his hands that he was told they had been blown off in the explosion. Abu Hamza says he experienced a sense of happiness. After all the suffering and pain of the ummah (Muslim nation), he was now taking his share of the burden. If this was Allah's will, then he was glad to serve.

The story has a ring of truth. In 1991 Abu Hamza, now a registered member of the British Institute of Civil Engineers, had moved with his family to Pakistan, and later to Afghanistan. He was appointed as chief engineer for a series of rebuilding schemes in and around Jalalabad, capital of the province of Nengarhar. The position carried with it the privilege of residence in the home of the former mayor of Jalalabad.

In early 1993 he gave an interview to the editor of a small

Pakistani magazine – called *Mine* – about the work he was involved in. 'We have been working on the reconstruction and building of schools, mosques, mini-bridges, on the restoration of old agricultural canals and the building of new ones,' he said. 'We rebuild hospitals and give life to new clinics. We build deep wells, protective walls against flooding and water facilities.'

New industrial complexes were being built, young men were being trained to be carpenters, electricians, mechanics, tailors and farmers. Abu Hamza and his team supplied water, clothing, tents and blankets to refugee camps; their work was funded through the generosity of King Fahd of Saudi Arabia. Unknown to Abu Hamza, the Saudi king was being approached at the same time by Muslims in Finsbury Park, north London, who were raising money to build a new mosque. In spite of his generosity, Fahd would later be vilified by Abu Hamza as an evil apostate and corrupt ruler who had betrayed Islam.

Abu Hamza's activities would seem at first glance to have been a model of peacetime rebuilding. But the war in Afghanistan was not over. The Red Army had withdrawn, defeated, but the communist regime of President Mohammed Najibullah remained. He fled Kabul in 1992, leaving behind a power vacuum and conditions which were ripe for civil war and power struggles between the various mujahideen factions. It was not long before warlords and ideological groups turned their Kalashnikovs on each other. When the Taliban finally triumphed in that conflict they found Najibullah, tortured and executed him.

Osama bin Laden had left Afghanistan and in 1993 was running his al-Qaeda organisation from Sudan; but many fighters loyal to him were still in the region. Abu Hamza met some of these men through his own associations with Kashmiri militants who were involved in battles in Afghanistan as well as for the 'liberation' of Kashmir from Indian rule. According to Abu Hamza, these mujahideen told him that he could never be a fighter. He had enormous physical strength, but he was too big and too heavy to fight in the mountains of Afghanistan. He would get left behind on treks over high, rough terrain; he would not survive, he might endanger his brothers in arms. But as an engineer he had skills that could be put to uses other than rebuilding dams and bridges and schools.

It was while turning his hands to such an alternative use at a mujahideen training camp, friends of Abu Hamza say, that he lost them. The second account of how he suffered his horrific injuries comes from a former member of Abu Hamza's inner circle. It describes how he lost his limbs as he manufactured a batch of high explosives.

The camp where the explosion occurred is said to have been the Darunta complex near Jalalabad, which was under the command of another Egyptian, Abu Khabbab al-Masri. The stern, red-bearded Abu Khabbab would go on to become al-Qaeda's number-one poisons expert and bomb-maker, and would have a $5 million bounty placed on his head by the United States. In the later 1990s he ran a specialist course in explosives and toxins inside the Darunta training complex to which only an elite few, selected for high-profile missions, were admitted. One of those was Richard Reid, an aspiring British suicide bomber, who first heard the doctrine of jihad from the mouth of Abu Hamza in London, but was taught how to make a bomb by Abu Khabbab in Afghanistan.

A disciple of Abu Hamza recounts in admiring tones the tale of the day the cleric lost his hands: 'Abu Hamza was in Abu Khabbab's training camp and he was mixing the ingredients to make a batch of explosives. The problem with Abu Hamza is that he has always been a bit reckless. He was getting the mixtures and the ratios all wrong and he had been told to be careful, he had been told he had it wrong. But he is a headstrong man and he wouldn't listen. He just carried on mixing and there was this explosion.

'Abu Hamza was sent flying backwards through the air and landed about twenty feet away against a wall. There were bits of his meat all over the place. People were shouting and running to get help, there was blood everywhere, pumping from his arms and pouring out of his eye. But he didn't make a sound. There was no screaming or crying from him, not a whimper. He just looked down at his arms, totally calm, and said: "I did a lot of bad with these hands and Allah has taken them away." Now when he said that, the people all around started crying. They were completely overwhelmed by his bravery and his courage and the fact that he dedicated himself there and then to Allah.

'I have never heard Abu Hamza speak of that day. He has never discussed it again. A lot of the veterans are the same, they do not like to talk of personal heroics or bravery. But what happened that day is what made him the man he became and is the reason why he is so loved and revered. He could not be an engineer or a fighter, so he became a preacher. He has often said he speaks the way he does – without fear and without compromise, tackling the difficult verses in the Koran that other scholars will ignore – because that is what he can do. Abu Hamza says it like it is in the holy book, he does not shy away from the verses about jihad and fighting that the other scholars pass over. When Allah took his hands away that was what he meant him to do.'

This account comes from a man who still holds Abu Hamza in high regard. It smacks of some embellishment, to add a strand of self-sacrificing heroism to the life story of the hook-handed preacher. But the story is supported by testimony that has been provided to the US courts by the FBI, which has devoted years to building a case to lock him up for the rest of his life. The evidence was given by Special Agent Fred Humphries, who had spent months debriefing the first significant al-Qaeda supergrass, an Algerian who had been involved in a plot to attack Los Angeles International Airport on 31 December 1999. The informant gave the FBI extensive and detailed accounts of his experiences in al-Qaeda camps in

Afghanistan, and long lists of the people he trained with and heard about. One of the names he had become familiar with was that of Abu Hamza al-Masri from London. He had never met the cleric, but had heard many stories about him in Afghanistan. Abu Hamza was known as someone who had the power to refer recruits to senior al-Qaeda figures. The supergrass was able to offer a lurid description of the London imam's appearance, and knew the tale of how he suffered his injuries. Special Agent Humphries told the US District Court in Seattle, Washington, that the prisoner 'described Abu Hamza as having lost his hands and an eye, purportedly while conducting explosives experiments in Afghanistan'.

Although he never spoke directly about his injuries, there have been heavy hints in Abu Hamza's sermons and lectures which suggest that the story from the training camp is the true one. Addressing an audience in London four years after the date of the explosion, he exhorted them to do whatever they could for the jihad, alluding strongly to his own experience and claiming that his injuries had been willed by God. 'Allah is talking about sincere people,' he once preached. 'About people who know what about it, they know they can get killed, they can be maimed, they can lose an arm, they can lose an eye, they can lose a leg, they can lose a half of it they can. Allah takes their body as he wishes, all of it, some of it, some today, some tomorrow, he blows them up, so there's nothing left of it. Take what you want, Allah, whenever you want, we are happy, we are not resigning from this, from this thing and we've still got to do jihad. You take our hands we do it with the tongue, you take our tongues we do it with money.'

Abu Hamza's life was saved by emergency treatment in Pakistan, but the doctors there advised him to return to England to ensure continuing care for injuries which would cause him severe pain and discomfort for the rest of his life. Initially he was reluctant to leave. His supporters say that he only quit Pakistan when he fell foul of the Inter-Service Intelligence (ISI), which was at that time trying to kick

out the legions of foreigners who had come to fight the Soviets but
had stayed, and now threatened to destabilise the region.

The story of his alleged expulsion added further credibility to Abu
Hamza's growing status in the jihadi movement. His followers claim
that he was approached by the ISI and asked to hand over to its
agents a stash of passports he was keeping safe for a group of Arab
mujahids who had crossed into Afghanistan to fight. Abu Hamza
refused to do so, and risked his own safety in order to save the
fighters. When he had successfully secreted the passports with other
sympathisers, he and his family left Pakistan, probably in late 1993.

Abu Hamza's return to Britain coincided with the arrival in the
country of Omar Mahmoud Othman Omar, a radical cleric better
known as Abu Qatada, who sat on al-Qaeda's religious rulings committee. Jordan sought Abu Qatada's extradition from Britain because
of his involvement in a series of car bombings, but Britain refused
the request. Instead it granted the cleric political asylum.

Unwittingly, Britain had given shelter to one of the fiercest
advocates of the global jihad. Abu Qatada lived and breathed the al-
Qaeda ideology, issued religious decrees (fatwas) allowing Algerian
terrorists to commit mass murder in the name of God, and raised
hundreds of thousands of pounds for Islamists to carry on the war
against Russia in Chechnya. He was also a well-read and controversial scholar of the Koran. Abu Hamza, no longer able to be an
engineer, became his pupil as he sought to turn himself into a jihadi
preacher.

'Abu Qatada used to say that Abu Hamza was the best student he
ever had,' recalled a follower. 'He was very impressed how quickly
Abu Hamza had memorised the Koran and the Hadith [the sayings
of the Prophet Mohammed]; he said Abu Hamza was a keen and
quick learner and had an exploratory mind.'

At mosques where he prayed and talked, Abu Hamza appealed for
people to donate books to him to help him build up a scholarly and

religious library. He could not go to libraries often because of his disabilities, so he needed to have a comprehensive collection of the works of the great Islamic scholars at home. One morning an Afghan veteran arrived on his doorstep in west London with a present for Abu Hamza. It was the eleven-volume *Encyclopaedia of the Afghani Jihad*, an extraordinary manual of guerrilla warfare written by veterans of the war against the Soviet Union and produced by the Makthab al Khidemat (Services Bureau) in Peshawar, Pakistan – the body which recruited foreign fighters to the Afghan cause, and from which al-Qaeda would spring. The encyclopaedia, each volume the thickness of a telephone directory with a picture of the Koran, a poppy field and a machine gun on the cover, was dedicated to Sheikh Abdullah Azzam and Osama bin Laden. The volumes bore titles such as *Security and Intelligence*, *Handguns*, *Explosives*, *Landmines*, *Tanks* and *Combat*. Their pages were packed with information and diagrams on how to make and use booby traps and bombs. Landmark buildings such as the Statue of Liberty in New York, the Eiffel Tower in Paris and Big Ben in London were held up as targets which, if struck, would gravely wound Islam's enemies. Abu Hamza placed the books – which were to become al-Qaeda's main operational manual – on his shelves alongside his growing library of works.

Although he was now quite badly disabled, Abu Hamza's hankering for the jihad experience had not diminished, and in 1995 he made three trips to Bosnia to see for himself the condition of the Muslim people battling with the Serbs. After his return to Britain from Afghanistan he had mixed exclusively in radical circles. In 1994 he had set up his own group, the Supporters of Shariah (SoS), to promote his views, recruit young followers to the cause, and above all so that he could be a leader.

Fearing that his activities might have attracted the attention of security agencies, Abu Hamza decided to enter Bosnia using a false name. In early 1995 he obtained a British passport in the name of Adam Ramsey Eaman, after paying £25 to change his name by deed poll. Using the new passport he journeyed to Bosnia as a relief worker with an aid convoy, even driving trucks carrying supplies with his hook. The regular road convoys carrying food, clothes and medicines to Bosnian Muslims were frequently exploited by would-be holy warriors who wanted to see what was happening in the Balkans. Once inside Bosnia, and issued with an identity card in the name of Eaman, Abu Hamza would leave the relief workers and seek out the mujahideen. He spent most of his time with Algerian factions, experienced fighters who had been in conflict with the military regime in their homeland.

The conflict was in its violent death throes – the massacres in Srebrenica occurred that year. But the Dayton Peace Accord was on its way, and the Arab fighters were in turmoil as ideological debate raged about whether or not they should stop fighting. Some believed they should use Bosnia as a base for the global jihad, establishing secret training camps in the Balkans. The new regime in Sarajevo was weak and they could operate as they pleased; there was a plentiful supply of weaponry and borders that were easy to cross. The most extreme religious fanatics wanted to turn their guns on the Westernised Muslim Bosnians, who were lax in the practice of the faith, and Islamicise the country. During the war the Arab mujahideen had smashed up bars and pizza parlours where ordinary Bosnian fighters relaxed during leave from the battles with the Serbs. The Afghan veterans – including close associates of bin Laden – felt Bosnia could be a bridgehead for the spread of radical Islam across Europe. Others argued that the conflict in Bosnia had gone as far as it could, the Bosnian Muslims were not ripe for conversion, and the efforts of the mujahideen could be put to better use elsewhere.

Abu Hamza threw himself into this debate. He lacked the authority of a fighter, but had all the arrogance and recklessness that had led him to blow himself up in Afghanistan. Convinced that he was a scholar, he believed he spoke with the authority of the Koran, and argued for small groups of fighters to take themselves into the

hills and continue to operate as independent mujahideen units. He
warned against a repeat of mistakes made in Afghanistan, and urged
the fighters not to surrender their arms when the peace deal was
agreed. Some of the commanders regarded him as divisive and
seditious. His life may even have been in danger.

Later, Abu Hamza would deny that he had created unrest: 'I
admired the brothers, the Algerian brothers. I said, "Look, you are
vulnerable, if you are there you are vulnerable, you cannot go out of
Bosnia and the situation of Afghanistan is going to be repeated …
don't hand over your weapons." The news reached Sheikh Anwar
[the commander] and he said Abu Hamza wanted to do a group
inside a group. I said no, I didn't. I said I wanted to do a group when
there is no group. And Allah as my witness, I had to leave Bosnia
straight away after the last battle finished.'

Back in Britain, Abu Hamza would retain the view that he was
right about what should happen in Bosnia, and those who had
fought in the war were wrong. 'They are very good brothers,' he said
in one of his lectures. 'They are fighting the best fighters, they are the
best people to sacrifice but when it came to management they
reached the wrong conclusions.'

Abu Hamza re-entered Britain as Adam Ramsey Eaman in late
1995. If the authorities knew who he was, they did not quiz him.
During those months hundreds of Britons were returning from the
conflict in the Balkans without hindrance. They had left seeking
adventure and a worthy cause; many returned equipped with the
ideology and military skills that would form a springboard for the
rise of Islamic militancy in Britain. For a lot of these fighters, Abu
Hamza had assumed a kind of heroic status. He was a veteran of two
jihad battlefields, although it was not widely known that he had
fought on neither. He had made a decision – or a decision had been
made for him by a higher power – that he should become a full-time
preacher and teacher.

A group of jihad veterans in the town of Luton, just north of

London, invited Abu Hamza to preach at the small mosque where they prayed. It seemed an unlikely place for the phenomenon of Abu Hamza to begin to take root. Luton was known for its airport – the starting point for so many cheap package holidays – its Vauxhall car factory and a mediocre football team that had once played on a plastic pitch. But its small band of militants offered Abu Hamza the platform he had been craving. He had tried and failed before to seize control of mosques. Luton gave him a base, and he launched himself like a hurricane on the Islamic circuit. Young men flocked to hear him and his reputation grew, drawing students from the Islamic societies of London universities to his Friday sermons.

One student who went there out of curiosity emerged as a committed radical. In a matter of an hour Abu Hamza had changed his view of the world: 'Beforehand I was told we were going to see this guy who was a veteran of the Afghan war, who was very brave, very humble, wasn't interested in money and was a great, great speaker. It was all true. If you were new to Islam, like I was, he was the way into so many other things. He set the fire.'

For Abu Hamza himself, Luton was just a stopping-off point on the way to bigger things. A new opportunity was soon to present itself which would offer him a position of real influence in the militant network that was fanning out around the world.

3
The Takeover of Finsbury Park

'If the people know you are firm they will back down. They all back down … you give him a couple of slaps, you give him a flat tyre outside, then the police take you and make you, give you a record, somebody else next day, finish, finish, they will all surrender, give me the keys for the mosque.'

ABU HAMZA

The religious lesson was nearing its end, and the thirty youngsters who sat cross-legged on the floor of the basement of Finsbury Park mosque in March 2000 were packing up their books. The soft-spoken imam, Shafiullah Patel, was explaining what they would do next time when a tall, masked figure loped into the room without warning. It was impossible to tell the intruder's age: the hood of his dark jacket was pulled low over his forehead, hiding his eyes, and a striped scarf was wrapped around his nose and mouth. He hopped from foot to foot as though he was using stepping stones to cross a river, and some of the children clapped.

Patel was not unduly concerned, as some of the young men who used the makeshift gymnasium next door would often drop in to amuse the kids. The imam stood with his arms folded across his chest as the interloper moved towards him, grunting at the young audience, who seemed grateful for the distraction from their studies. Without saying a word, the masked man threw a punch at the imam, who was at least a foot shorter than his assailant. The punch caught Patel on the side of his head, powerfully enough to rock him back on his heels.

The children still weren't sure if this was all part of some make-believe scrap for their amusement, and sat frozen in their places. Before Patel could speak, the trespasser swung his arms in wide arcs, pummelling his fists into his victim's face. Patel was defenceless, and as he felt blood oozing from his nose and his mouth he was aware that some of his young pupils were scampering from the room. The next thing he knew he was being revived by a couple of worshippers who had heard the commotion from the basement and seen the stampede of children charging up the steps to the front of the mosque. The imam had been knocked unconscious; he had no idea how long he had been lying there. Two ambulance men were wrapping a collar around his neck and asking him a series of questions he couldn't grasp as nausea was rising in his throat.

Patel could not give the police much help in identifying his attacker. But there was little doubt that he had been set upon by one of the young thugs from the private militia of Abu Hamza, the so-called scholar who was attempting to seize control of the mosque through intimidation and violent force.

Patel was neither the first nor the last to be attacked. Several of the mosque's trustees and elders were set upon: one man was clubbed as he worked in his shop by a youth wielding a baseball bat. Many of the older Muslims in this corner of north London were so afraid of Abu Hamza's goon squad that they had stopped coming to the mosque.

The mob would elbow their way to the front of the top-floor prayer room to harangue whoever was delivering a sermon, heckling and insulting the speaker. When Abu Hamza spoke they closed in around him like courtiers flattering a dictator, applauding his every sentiment and screaming 'Allahu Akhbar' at the end of each sentence.

Abu Hamza was running the mosque as though it were his own empire. He was never seen without his entourage in tow, and behaved more like a mafia godfather than a religious scholar. It was completely different from the situation in the early months of 1997, when senior members of the North London Central Mosque Trust – the charity which governed the affairs of the Finsbury Park mosque – first encountered the ample figure of Abu Hamza.

The management committee had been riven for months with petty disputes over who should have the prestigious post of khateeb, the person whose job it was to deliver the main Friday sermon. The character of Finsbury Park and its surrounding suburbs was changing. The Bengali and Pakistani communities which had dominated the congregation in its infancy were moving out of the area, to be replaced by an influx of asylum seekers and refugees from North Africa and the Arab world who agitated for a preacher who spoke Arabic, not Urdu. Younger worshippers, born and bred in north London, wanted someone who could explain their faith to them in English.

One of the selection committee, an Algerian-born butcher whose shop was close to Finsbury Park, first suggested Abu Hamza's name. He had heard good reports from friends in Luton who enthused about the Egyptian's energy and ability to engage an audience with his easy style and wit. This was self-evident at his first interview with the trustees. Acutely aware how his appearance could sometimes scare those not forewarned of his disabilities, Abu Hamza joked about the metal hook he had to replace his severed hands, and the loss of his eye.

There is no clerical hierarchy in Islam that can vouch for a candidate's scholarship, but Abu Hamza had prepared well for his interview. His command and knowledge of the Koran were impressive, he appeared modest and humble, and his passion for encouraging more of the Muslim youth to take an interest in their religion appealed to the trustees. So what if he had embellished the extent of his studies?

He also struck a resonant chord over money. The trustees had originally wanted to employ the Jordanian-born Palestinian cleric Abu Qatada. Back then the selection team knew nothing of Abu Qatada's radical background, and it wasn't something he was about to advertise on his CV, believing his reputation as a scholar and author preceded him. Abu Qatada told his interviewers they should be grateful he was willing to take the job, and thus that he should be amply rewarded. Shafiullah Patel was stunned when Abu Qatada demanded to see the mosque's balance sheet and, with his half-moon spectacles slipping off the end of his nose, insisted that 50 per cent of everything collected at Finsbury Park should go into his pocket.

In contrast, Abu Hamza told the trustees he was flattered to be considered by such an esteemed mosque. All he wanted financially was for the trustees to pay for his lunch after his Friday sermon, and to provide for a couple of helpers who would accompany him, as obviously he couldn't drive or carry his religious books himself.

There was no contest for the trustees, who frankly were short of funds. On 6 March 1997 they sent 'Dear brother Mostafa [sic]' a written offer. As well as delivering the Friday sermon, he was expected to organise tuition classes for adults and children 'in accordance with the policy agreed mutually by your Goodselves [sic] and the Trustees'. It was a two-year contract, but could be 'extended, altered or adapted by mutual agreement'. The key paragraph in the contract, which would come back to haunt the selection panel, warned: 'The trustees would, however, expect you not to engage in any activity which may be contrary to the Objects of the North London Central Mosque Trust.'

Abu Hamza signed the deal and sent it back by return post. The trustees were soon to learn to their cost, however, that his charm offensive had been a charade. Abu Hamza was a cunning master of deception no matter what audience he was addressing. Just as he had wormed his way to British citizenship or exaggerated his credentials as a fighter, he had now tricked his way into a position of power and influence at a major mosque.

Abdul Kadir Barkatullah, who was on that selection committee, cannot believe now that he and his friends were so readily conned. 'How were we duped by this monster? He lied to us; he was an organised criminal masquerading as a scholar. We were fooled by him.'

It was not until several years later, when the trustees sought help in getting rid of Abu Hamza in 1998, that they learned from police that other mosques – including one in Luton and the prestigious Central London Mosque in Regent's Park – had taken legal steps to thwart his attempts to take over their premises. Imams from Brighton in the south to towns in Lancashire and Yorkshire had reason to loathe him and his intimidating supporters. Largely because of the Abu Hamza experience, leading Muslim organisations in the UK have begun to argue for the establishment of a body that would vet imams and assess their fitness to preach at mosques in Britain.

Barkatullah, a respected scholar who runs the Islamic Cultural Centre and mosque in Finchley, north London, is troubled that at hundreds of mosques in the UK, sermons and teaching are not provided in English. He says that many of the imams at these mosques, brought from abroad, have simply learnt the Koran by heart: 'They lived in dormitories, they never leave these places to talk to people or learn about their society. They haven't got a clue. They live in a cloud cuckoo land, but what they teach our youth is misleading and dangerous.' Abu Hamza had seemed quite different. He came to the trustees as an English-speaker, who had lived in Britain since 1979, though predictably his application for the post made no mention of his days working as a Soho bouncer.

Finsbury Park was a coveted post. The hulking redbrick mosque with its towering minaret and dome shares the skyline in this corner of north London with Arsenal FC's famous old Highbury stadium. Its windows are a strange shade of bright green, and its four floors of prayer rooms can hold more than a thousand worshippers. It had taken years to build.

Forty years earlier, in the mid-1950s, a devout Muslim donated a room in his guest house at Woodfall Road in Finsbury Park to be used as a prayer room. As the immigrant population rose steadily in the late sixties and early seventies, with newcomers from Pakistan, India, Bangladesh, Malaysia, the Middle East and Mauritius, there wasn't room in the guest house for Friday prayers; and nobody had thought about educating the children of these arrivals.

The guest house was acquired under a compulsory purchase scheme by the local authority as it tried to redevelop this rundown quarter of London, blighted by unemployment, wretched housing and crime. Muslim community leaders set up the Muslim Welfare Centre (MWC), a registered charity, found new premises, and began to plan for a new mosque building which – they dreamed – would rival anything in Europe. In the mid-1970s the MWC bought up five terraced houses on the corner of St Thomas's Road which they planned to demolish and use the site to accommodate their vision.

They did not choose the most restful of locations. The site sits just south of the busy Seven Sisters Road, wedged between a railway line and a permanently congested traffic intersection. The adjacent streets today teem with cafés serving Arabic coffee and sweet cakes, bookshops, and cheap internet centres and phone bureaux.

Diplomats and dignitaries from various faiths lent their weight to the project, and in March 1987 the MWC found a new champion when the Prince of Wales visited the area and cast an appreciative eye over the novel architectural plans which allowed the mosque to stay within the planning laws. The prince was impressed by the designers' idea to get around height restrictions by having a five-storey building look like four from the outside, so blending in with the rest of the local council's rejuvenation scheme. All the community needed now was the £812,000 to pay for the construction.

Prince Charles played a pivotal role here too. Realising that he was due to greet King Fahd of Saudi Arabia on his forthcoming state visit to Britain, the trustees implored the heir to the throne to float the idea past his guest. When the two men shook hands on the platform at Victoria Station on the king's arrival on 25 March 1987, the prince lost no time in presenting the Finsbury Park scheme. The Saudi ruler quickly approved, and wrote a cheque for £12 million to fund a number of mosque-building projects around Britain, beginning with the North London Central Mosque in Finsbury Park. The Saudi ambassador to Britain and Bangladesh's high commissioner both served as trustees of the mosque for several years.

For all the civic goodwill and local enthusiasm, the project was mired by delays and disputes. The secretary's progress report in April 1991 makes disturbing reading, as trustees are warned that the project is hopelessly behind schedule and will cost far more than they had budgeted for. Contractors claimed they weren't being paid, surveyors were criticised for not keeping control of the site, and allegations were made that some of the management were being too lavish in their demands for luxuries like a terrazzo floor in the lobbies and in spending £90,000 on carpets. The building eventually opened its doors in March 1994.

But the arguments about overspending and building delays were nothing compared to the rows between rival ethnic groups over who should be their imam. The Bangladeshis, who regarded themselves as the majority voice, wanted one of their own, and a debate over who should get the post ended in a fist fight. One proposal was to postpone the appointment of an imam and settle instead for recruiting a muezzin and teacher to lead the call to Friday service and five daily prayers until some charismatic figure could be found.

Influential figures like Barkatullah argued that the trustees couldn't cope with running the mosque, which opened two years late and around £250,000 over budget. He urged the appointment of a twenty-five-strong management committee drawn from all nationalities using the mosque – which did little to end the internecine strife disfiguring Finsbury Park.

There were rows over how much to spend on classes for children, and inevitably over which language should be used for teaching.

Urdu was the dominant tongue in the mosque, but that offended Arabic-speakers, and Barkatullah concedes that there were racial tensions among worshippers. Ironically, they turned to Abu Hamza as a peacemaker.

In his first weeks as imam he proved an admirable choice. He was by turns passionate and reasonable, calm and engaging. He preached about the plight of Muslims around the world and the need for unity among people of the faith. He also suggested that as Britain was the adopted home for Muslims of all persuasions in north London, they should make the effort to speak English as often as they could.

But to his own band of followers, who had followed him to north London, he had another message. He told them stories of how much money had gone missing, and pointed the finger of blame at senior figures among the trustees. They had been given permission to convert a row of houses into flats with the intention of raising income for the mosque; but in his attempts to smear them Abu Hamza claimed that either rents had not been paid, or the cash had disappeared.

He was at his rabble-rousing worst when he suddenly launched into a tirade in front of his young followers during one of their private get-togethers in an upstairs prayer room, claiming that one of these flats was being used as a brothel. His voice quivering with outrage, he reported how a 'brother' had discovered that the girl was leaving her business cards in telephone boxes around the area, and disreputable men were pestering tenants at all hours. Worse, if there could be any greater shame, he added with a theatrical flourish, was the fact that someone among the mosque's old management was taking a cut of the woman's immoral earnings. He was careful not to identify the alleged culprit, but it didn't matter. He got the reaction he wanted. Mehdi Achiou, who was there, recalled how some of his followers wanted to burn down the flat and throw the woman out into the street.

Achiou, London-born but whose parents had emigrated from

Algeria, was one of the new generation appearing at Finsbury Park. He recalls the electric charge running through the prayer room. 'It felt exciting to be stopping corruption,' said the twenty-seven-year-old computer analyst who had amassed a tidy sum in the City during the latter years of the Thatcher boom. 'Mosque was boring. The sermons didn't strike a chord with my generation who were restless. We wanted something but weren't sure what it was. Then along comes this preacher who is speaking our language, and we wanted to follow him.'

Posters began appearing for Abu Hamza's movement, the Supporters of the Shariah. Achiou and his like had no idea what it was, but if Abu Hamza was involved, then they wanted in. At every meeting the cleric would rail against the old guard, who he called 'the greybeards'. The language was uncompromising; word soon spread, and the numbers showing up for his Friday sermons doubled, then quadrupled to over a thousand, until there was barely room to accommodate all those who wanted to see what the fuss was about. Others would stand outside as his sermon was played over loudspeakers from the minaret.

Abu Hamza always had a sense of the dramatic. He would flourish bits of paper, gripped between the two prongs of his hook, claiming that they were the mosque's accounts that showed £225,000 was missing. Once he flung a receipt out into the prayer group, showing a bill for £70,000 for hanging doors in the building. The histrionics were a triumph. Within weeks of taking over he was portrayed as the 'corruption buster'. He sent a couple of his most trusted – and heaviest built – acolytes to call on local businessmen to query a dubious account. Their approach was so menacing that some of these tradesmen, shop owners and builders telephoned the police to protect them; but local commanders were reluctant to get involved.

Abu Hamza had a particular rapport with his younger audience. When couples wanted to marry against their families' objections, it was Abu Hamza who would go to speak to the parents, and if that did not work he would conduct the wedding ceremony privately in the mosque. He sided with the youth against their old-fashioned parents. He too had lived in the West as a young man; he understood the temptations and the traps, and he could reach out to them with his vision of Islam – so much livelier than that of their parents' generation. Many young worshippers were enthralled, and came in growing numbers to hear him speak.

The larger crowds meant bigger revenues from Friday collections. Abu Hamza opened a shop just inside the mosque's main entrance, where tapes of his sermons were on sale along with videos which included graphic footage of the mujahideen putting their enemies to death in Algeria, Bosnia and Chechnya. Alongside this violent fare were cardboard boxes full of cheap plastic toys, heaps of household utensils and cut-price toiletries. The goods had been amassed from donors and were offered as bargains to entice local families into the mosque.

The trustees had no idea what was happening to any of this income from collection and commerce. Abu Hamza made it clear that it was none of their business. Financial matters were dealt with in his simple, rectangular first-floor office that overlooked the main street. He always told visitors they had the free run of the mosque, but this office was off limits. He had a combination lock installed on the door, which he said was done reluctantly after infiltrators had been caught in the mosque.

Abu Hamza's takeover was greatly assisted by the fact that a large number of Islamist radicals – many of them veterans of the bloody conflict in Algeria – had already infiltrated the mosque. They supported and facilitated his arrival, adding their muscle to that of his youthful followers from Supporters of Shariah.

But wherever the radicals were, there were spies and informants too. The Algerian-born Reda Hassaine, who was to spend five years inside Finsbury Park supplying information to Algeria, France and Britain, reported back to his handlers that the new preacher had made an impressive and sinister start: 'On the first day he came it was obvious he was a guy who was at war. He was at war with the secular state, at war against Arab governments. His first sermon was "prepare yourself", now is a new era of Islam, a new era in the mosque. After, the talk in the coffee shops was all about the new imam. People were saying, "He is great, we must listen to him." Before he turned up the mosque was for old people.'

Hassaine was keeping a special watch on the influence of a gang of sharp-featured Algerians who included key figures in the GIA guerrilla movement. Tumultuous events in Algeria almost led to Abu Hamza's downfall before he had secured control of Finsbury Park. There had been bloody massacres in the Algerian countryside early in 1997, in which hundreds of civilians had had their throats cut. Islamists tried to blame government death squads, but the GIA had been responsible, and finally admitted so in September that year in a communiqué issued by its leader. The notice was pinned to the wall inside Finsbury Park mosque, with a claim by the organisation that the population of Algeria had been excommunicated from Islam and was therefore a legitimate target.

As worshippers arrived at the mosque, their murmurs of discontent boiled over into anger which was directed at Abu Hamza, who had set himself up as the GIA's spiritual adviser and the editor of its newsletter *al-Ansar* (The Supporters). The cleric and his henchmen found themselves surrounded and jostled by several dozen men demanding that he leave the mosque. Copies of the GIA communiqué were torn up, punches were thrown and Abu Hamza was threatened. A couple of vanloads of police turned up in St Thomas's Road, but, in what would become their standard response, senior officers baulked at intervening inside the mosque. They were loath to send uniformed police into a place of worship.

Abu Hamza was forced to back down, and managed to worm his way out of the crisis. In what would be his final edition of *al-Ansar* he published a denunciation of the GIA's actions. And he began his

Friday sermon by apologising. According to Reda Hassaine, who was present that day, Abu Hamza said: 'It was not me that did it; it is the groups that did it. I have been their mouth but I do not agree with what they did.' He announced that he was resigning as spiritual guide to the GIA, saying he would pray to God for forgiveness.

His condemnation of the GIA was well-timed. The group was already splintering and losing ground among the jihadi faction in London. They increasingly favoured newer associations with groups that would form alliances with other jihad organisations, especially the leadership of al-Qaeda, now returned to Afghanistan and closely allied with the Taliban regime there.

But the strategy of offering a gateway to al-Qaeda and other terror groups had to wait until Abu Hamza had consolidated his hold on Finsbury Park mosque with the help of the chosen men in his kitchen cabinet. The powerful figure of Shahid Butt shadowed Abu Hamza everywhere, playing the role of minder, his obvious bulk an ample deterrent to anyone who voiced dissent in this dictatorship. This was the Taliban in miniature. Abu Hamza wanted to control every aspect of his subjects' lives, from their fitness and their diet to the books they should read and the length of their beards.

He redesigned the mosque, halving the size of the women's basement prayer room so he could build a makeshift gymnasium. He opened up a kitchen so followers could take their meals there, and he invited them to bed down in prayer rooms and offices so his lieutenants could keep an eye on them and spot those who might be ripe for 'special tuition', the phrase used for brainwashing the more gullible or fanatical into signing up for jihad training.

Of all his disciples the favourite was a young Yorkshireman, Haroon Rashid Aswat, whose skinny frame was in marked contrast to most others in Abu Hamza's company. The shrill-voiced Aswat had been born in Dewsbury, and studied at local schools until at the age of nineteen he told his father Rashid that he wanted to attend a Muslim madrassa, or religious college, near their home. Rashid

Aswat, who ran his own bathroom business and was on the committee of the mosque near his home in this Gujarati Indian community, was not concerned at his son's choice. That changed within a few months when Aswat became argumentative at home, criticising his family for their failure to live like 'good Muslims'. In 1995 he left for London, telling his parents he wanted to find like-minded young Muslims to share his life and advance his study of the Koran. He eventually found the ideal refuge at Finsbury Park. With his long, pointed nose, pinched chin and tight, narrow eyes he was not the most impressive of figures, and he was certainly much shorter than the cleric's usual crop of recruits, but followers say Abu Hamza treated him like a son.

Aswat had memorised the Koran, and because of his obvious devotion Abu Hamza left him to lead daily prayers, despite his youth. He was also the man asked to counsel troubled or confused recruits as Abu Hamza proudly looked on. During disagreements in the mosque the cleric would lean back in his seat, lower his eyes and point to Aswat to settle the conflict. Older supporters and those who had been at Abu Hamza's side a lot longer were jealous of Aswat's influence, but they dared not challenge him. Abu Hamza was temperamental. As his experience in Afghanistan and Bosnia showed, he liked to lead and dictate rather than be led or advised. Anyone doubting his judgement might find themselves excluded from his immediate circle. Those who stayed obedient basked in the warm glow of his charm, received cards for the festival of Eid from him and were delighted to be asked by him about their families.

The trustees fought a losing battle to control Abu Hamza's increasingly erratic behaviour at the mosque. Barkatullah felt impelled to say something when Abu Hamza used a Friday sermon to curse King Fahd of Saudi Arabia, whose money had built the mosque, and then to praise and pray for suicide bombers who had walked onto a rush-hour bus in Jerusalem. 'I said, "How dare you celebrate other people's misery?" but from the look on his face I suddenly realised he was on a different frequency and there was no point arguing,' Barkatullah recalls. Abu Hamza didn't need to reply. The ever-present gang of minders edged in around Barkatullah, making it abundantly plain that such insolence would not be tolerated. These men had no qualms about beating a religious scholar, and Barkatullah suffered facial injuries after one attack by Abu Hamza's militia.

The trustees arranged a meeting with the troublesome cleric at Barkatullah's office in St Thomas's Road in January 1998, hoping to thrash out some sort of truce. Abu Hamza turned up with his usual muscular posse and told them, 'If you want trouble, I am ready.' Trying to hide how intimidated they felt, Barkatullah and the others warned him that if he didn't behave they would terminate his contract. Abu Hamza just sneered at them and drew his hook across his throat.

Scared of where this violence might lead, Barkatullah and six other grandees of the North London Central Mosque agreed that they had no option but to resort to the High Court to try to get rid of Abu Hamza. They say that they again approached local police commanders, asking for their help and describing how this interloper was running the mosque like something out of Al Capone's reign in Chicago. Once more they were sent away by officers who said it was 'a private matter'.

At 9.45 p.m. on 29 October 1998 a deputation led by Barkatullah turned up at the gates of Finsbury Park to serve an injunction on the occupiers. The reception committee at the entrance included Abu Hamza's seventeen-year-old son Mohammed and two other men, including an Algerian who was jailed five years later under a Home Office control order as a 'threat to national security'. As Barkatullah tried to serve the court order and explain that Abu Hamza and his entourage should vacate the premises by eleven o'clock the following morning, the cleric's son strode forward, snatched the legal papers, rolled them into a bundle and threw them into the air.

The following morning young Mohammed was waiting in the entrance hall with up to thirty men as the trustees returned. Barkatullah remembers thinking he had never seen most of the muscle blocking his path, and wondered where Abu Hamza had found these men. The cleric was on the second floor, and as the five men tried to climb the stairs they were ambushed by the mob, yelling that they were 'infidels' for taking on their hero. Two of them were thrown down the stairs, and the secretary of the trustees, Mohammed Ashiq Asghar, ran to the police standing on the street in front of the metal gates. The officers heard the commotion, and could see these elderly men limping out of the door cut and bruised, but said that the court injunction gave them no power to arrest any of the mob inside.

The trustees appointed their own imam, a Pakistani preacher, but when he tried to lead prayers he was grabbed by three of Abu Hamza's supporters, manhandled into the street and told that their leader had given orders that neither he nor any of the trustees was allowed to enter the mosque.

Abu Hamza turned the confrontation to his advantage, telling his followers that the trustees were spending £80 an hour on lawyers, and adding, 'We are not going to give them peace. We will not leave the mosque and will fight to the end.'

In desperation the trustees asked local police commanders what to do, which is when they learned that Scotland Yard had been aware that Abu Hamza was the subject of previous injunctions from other mosques. The officers' solution was for the Finsbury Park trustees to go back to court to seek an eviction order. The police conceded that this would be costly and time-consuming, and that in the meantime they could do nothing to impede Abu Hamza's takeover.

Like a medieval monarch, Abu Hamza wasn't satisfied with just Finsbury Park, and wanted to expand his fiefdom. His first step was to take his roadshow around the country, poisoning other mosques with his hateful creed then leaving it to hand-picked locals and some of his Supporters of Shariah hard men to complete the takeover at mosques such as that in Stockwell, south London. He roamed the country with a convoy of cars, always with an entourage of minders in tow to whip up the crowd. Videos were shown of mujahideen violence that turned most people's stomachs, but Abu Hamza didn't care about that. He didn't want such timid souls in his sight anyway, so good riddance to them.

Teenagers in the audience were lectured that even though they lived in Bradford or Burnley, Birmingham and the Black Country, or by the seaside in holiday resorts like Brighton and spa towns such as Tunbridge Wells, they were still on the front line of the new war against the unbelievers and those who stood in the way of their aim of imposing Shariah law. They were fighters, the same as those in Chechnya, Afghanistan and other hot spots on the terror map.

Abu Hamza boasted of his own experiences in the lands of jihad, and recited the sacrifices of his volunteers slain on some foreign field. The incentive for the more enthusiastic among his audience was an invitation to Finsbury Park, and for hundreds of them the long march to the al-Qaeda training camps would begin from there. It was seductive stuff, recalled Mehdi Achiou, who for several months formed part of this travelling circus.

Abu Hamza was well rewarded for these trips when the collecting buckets were handed around, along with opportunities for the audience to buy his merchandise – tape recordings and videos of the great man's sermons. He was like a TV performer on a promotional tour, and these shows boosted his income and standing among the radical Muslim set.

He could afford the time to make these guest appearances as he had left Aswat in charge of business back at Finsbury Park, though he recognised that he had to deal with the legal action from the trustees. In November 1998 he finally replied in a sworn affidavit to the Chancery Division of the Royal Courts of Justice, the regal English courts which he was forever telling his followers had no power over them and should be destroyed. The tone he adopted in his twenty-five-page statement was a model of restraint and politeness. In short, he was shocked and horrified at the terrible accusations levelled against him, all of which he of course denied.

He told the justices that the trustees were trying to 'hoodwink' them with their interpretation of what a preacher like him could and could not do in a mosque, and insisted that he had never received a single complaint about any of his sermons. His legal team produced petitions from worshippers grateful that he had brought peace to the troubled mosque. There were letters from the Inland Revenue showing that the trustees were in breach of their duties, together with unpaid utility bills they had left him.

He enclosed affidavits testifying that on the days when the trustees came to serve the injunction he wasn't even at Finsbury Park but was leading prayers at other London mosques – so how could he have ordered them to be beaten up? At one point, when denying ever banning anyone from entering the mosque, he said, 'I am not able to physically restrain anybody as I do not have any hands to restrain anybody. I am a disabled person.'

Abu Hamza argued that the trustees were hated locally for renting out the adjoining flats at 13–15 St Thomas's Road, meant for Muslim students, to people who left 'condoms, alcohol, pork in the premises which were used for praying', adding that neighbours were upset by the drug-taking and loud music of these occupants. He also claimed that these flats were siphoning off electricity from the mosque that accounted for 90 per cent of the bill.

He said local authorities had given £160,000 in various grants to the trustees, and that he did not have a clue where that money had gone. He was particularly outraged at slurs that he himself had pocketed cash, insisting that he had nothing to do with handling funds as he was too busy with his other tasks, teaching Islam and delivering sermons. He only came to Finsbury Park, he protested, as 'I was informed that if I did not assist then there would be bloodshed'. As to allegations that he had a private army living at the mosque, he expressed dismay, saying that there were only a few homeless refugees seeking shelter, and he didn't know what they did under the roof of Finsbury Park, as he could only stay for two hours at a time 'due to my physical needs'.

He ended by saying it was the community who ran Finsbury Park, not him, and swore: 'I have never taken any money for my own personal use.' In a concluding remark which the trustees found particularly hard to swallow, he stated: 'I merely wish to continue my humble teachings.'

Abu Hamza signed this protestation of innocence at about the same time as a group of hand-picked recruits from Finsbury Park were preparing to travel to a terrorist training camp in Yemen to rehearse a bomb attack on British targets in Aden, planned for Christmas Day 1998.

By the time the trustees and the rest of the country became aware of Abu Hamza's involvement in terror activities in Yemen in the early weeks of 1999, he was, says Barkatullah, a changed man. In an unusually cooperative mood he contacted the trustees, suggesting that they should meet to end the legal stand-off, which was to nobody's advantage. As a gesture he offered to preach on only two Fridays a month, leaving the trustees to appoint their choice for the remaining ones, and insisted that they could all happily share the mosque. The trustees, who had spent £14,000 on legal injunctions and got nowhere, and who realised that it was going to cost a great deal more money if they were going to get the courts to evict Abu Hamza, willingly embraced the truce.

Barkatullah claims that the management committee were duped again. The legal actions were dropped, but when the trustees tried to re-enter the mosque, Abu Hamza's militia were still there, their very presence making it clear that 'outsiders' were not welcome. Exhausted, broke and scared, most of the old guard chose to walk away.

'Abu Hamza had unleashed these savage dogs on the Islamic community, and the authorities just stood by and watched and nobody came to help us,' Barkatullah said. 'Abu Hamza had won. Finsbury Park was all his.'

4
The Orator

'It must be said that the jihad of the word is important so that people can wake up from the Muslims and the non-Muslims.'

ABU HAMZA

Put simply, the core of Abu Hamza's appeal to thousands of young Muslims was that there had never been anything or anyone quite like him. Yes, there were other charismatic speakers, uplifting orators, fiery men of the jihad and holy men of the Koran. And yes, they were much better than the whiskery old Pakistani imams who didn't understand a word of English, regarded the British-born generation of young Muslims as wayward and thought that Muslims should be eternally grateful for factory jobs, corner shops and council houses. But none of them was Abu Hamza. The big Egyptian did not just talk the talk – he walked the walk. He swaggered, the stumps of his injured arms thrust in the pockets of an army-green raincoat, a Taliban-black turban on his head, a pair of shades hiding his damaged eye and an entourage of bodyguards – burly lads who meant business. And the word was that he had done the deeds himself.

There were hints in his sermons – wistful memories of meetings with Abdullah Azzam, the father of modern jihad, reminiscences of time spent with the mujahideen in Bosnia, and mentions of dear brothers who were brave warriors. But Abu Hamza never boasted about his own experiences. His disciples thought that was because he was modest, self-effacing and learned; the true scholar and mujahid would never be a blowhard. 'What happens on the front line is between you and Allah,' said one former fighter.

Of course, the truth was that Abu Hamza had no real war stories to tell. But to the young listeners who were fired up and captivated by him, it was part of the attraction that he was known in Afghanistan, Kashmir and Bosnia, he had been to the battlegrounds of the jihad and he seemed to have the scars to prove it.

When he talked about the jihad there was no mistaking his meaning. He didn't bemoan the plight of the Palestinians, the Chechens and the Kosovo Muslims then say that everybody must dig deep and give more to charity or get down on their knees and pray harder. Abu Hamza told his listeners that they should fight back. It was their obligation, outlined, he said, in the Koran, to train, to be fearless, to be ready to die in giving the kuffar a taste of his own medicine. Spill your blood, show the enemies of Islam that you are not afraid to give up your life in the cause of Allah.

Perhaps most importantly, he said all this in a language that everyone could understand. To hear Abu Hamza preach was to be assaulted by a machine-gun hail of florid rhetoric and London street talk. It was Osama bin Laden meets Alf Garnett. He mangled the English language, punctuating the torrent with frequent supplications, prayers and verses, recited at breakneck speed in the Arabic flourishes of the holy book. Yet at the same time he mixed this with the idiom of the man in the street – bristling with one-liners, putdowns and withering mockery – establishing a rapport with his young audience.

In the middle of a denunciation of the United Nations he might break off to poke fun at Boutros Boutros Ghali, the former Secretary General – 'Boutros, Boutros, Boutros, Boutros Ghali', he laughed, copying a joke from the hit TV programme *The Fast Show*. As for Diana, Princess of Wales, he was appalled at the heroine-worship that followed her death: 'After a while she will have her own Koran, have mosques and churches in her name.' People, he joked, would worship her cat if they had the chance. Years later, the same flashes of the London street would show when he was cross-examined for days in Courtroom Number Two at the Old Bailey. Pushed by lawyers to list the many places he had travelled to preach to willing and receptive audiences, he snapped back: 'I dunno, I'm not an A-to-Z, chief.'

In full flow Abu Hamza was irresistible and unstoppable. Ear-splitting and passionate, his commitment seemed to banish any doubts that lingered in impressionable minds. He radiated a sense of complete certainty in his creed; there were no questions or mundane concerns to stand as obstacles in his way. Abu Hamza knew what was right. He knew it was right because it was in the Koran, and he could recite from memory each and every verse of the holy book to support his claim that every word he spoke was actually the word of Allah. Just to make sure, the most important points were hammered home with a series of jabs, powerful punches in the air delivered with the stump of his right arm or, if he chose to wear it, his infamous hook.

To take one example, on 13 October 2000 the intifada in the Palestinian Territory was in the headlines, and was Abu Hamza's chosen topic for his Friday sermon at Finsbury Park mosque. The three floors of prayer halls were crowded with more than a thousand men. In the basement a handful of women also listened as the voice of Abu Hamza – who was on the top floor of the building, standing in front of the wood-panelled wall that faces Mecca – reverberated through loudspeakers. The intifada, with its images of children throwing stones at heavily armed Israeli soldiers and tanks, was a powerful tool with which to inflame his audience. But it was not just the intifada. The Palestinian struggle was merely one battle of many facing the ummah around the world. Muslims were being oppressed by the kuffar in Kashmir and Chechnya, and by apostate rulers in Egypt, Yemen, Saudi Arabia and throughout their own lands.

There could be only one solution: jihad. Muslims must rise up and fight their oppression. When the oppressor was defeated the jihad could continue until the Islamic state – the utopia of the khilafah – was established. It would be ruled by a caliph, who would have the trust and goodwill of his subjects. Muslims could then leave the decadent West and return to live in their own lands. Or they could fight on until the caliph was sitting in the White House, from where he would govern the world. But such dreams could only be achieved if the Muslims took up arms.

'You must increase your action, you must increase your jihad, because when you wake up you wake the scholars up and when you and the scholars are woken up the tyrants are shaking,' Abu Hamza told his congregation. 'And when the tyrants are shaking, their allies are shaking and Islam flourishes and Islam [is] becoming stronger and you will give your children a good Islamic manner, a good Islamic land, a good Islamic atmosphere. It's time for you and me and everybody to sacrifice, it's a time to prove that we are not here in the West just for the honey pot, just to take and not to give anything.'

By now Abu Hamza was sweating heavily. He wiped his forehead with the rolled-up sleeve of his tunic, leant forward, swayed a little, then, with a change of tone, beseeched his people to join the struggle with him in any way they could: 'My dear brothers, if you can go then go. If you can't go, sponsor. If you can't sponsor, speak. If you can't do all of this, do all of that. If you can send your children, send them, you must help, you must have a stand. You must have a stand with your heart, with your tongue, with your money, with your hand, with your sword, with your Kalashnikov, anything you think will help. Don't ask for so many fatwas, you are very clever with your business, you know how to get money out of the stone, don't ask "Shall I do this, shall I do that?" Just do it. Anything that will help the intifada, just do it. If it is killing, do it. If it is paying, pay, if it is ambushing, ambush, if it is poisoning, poison. You help your brothers, you help Islam in any way you like it, anywhere you like it. They are all kuffar and they are all acting and fighting us as one body and we should give them back as one body.'

Stop, rewind a second, and listen again. Abu Hamza was not just talking Palestine or the old jihad battlefields of the past. This was eleven months before the World Trade Centre would be demolished and three thousand people killed in the worst terrorist atrocity the world had ever seen, and here was one of al-Qaeda's most potent mouthpieces telling a congregation at Friday prayers in London to help their oppressed brothers, 'in any way you like and anywhere you like. They are all kuffar, and can all be killed. Killing a kuffar who is fighting you is OK. Killing a kuffar for any reason, you can say it is OK, even if there is no reason for it.'

The preacher is afire, he is overheating and the words are coming out of his mouth probably faster than his brain can think of them. But this is no one-off exhortation to global jihad. It will be repeated again and again, in sermon after sermon and talk after talk, all around Britain. The dark heart in the make-up of this powerful orator is the relentless bloodlust in his words. There is no charity, no compassion, no tolerance.

On this day the Supporters of Shariah video camera was running; hundreds of video and audio copies would be made for distribution around Europe, in the United States and further afield. Once the English-language sermon was finished, Abu Hamza would take a break then rise and deliver the same message with the same passion in Arabic. Again the recording machines would be running and the tapes made available to those refugees who had not yet learned English, or smuggled into the Arab world.

This is an extract from a sermon delivered in autumn 1999, again at Finsbury Park, shortly before the beginning of the fasting month of Ramadan. On this day Abu Hamza was preaching in Arabic.

'When the forbidden months are past, it is a timed period, then fight and kill the infidels wherever you find them. He [Allah] did not say only here or here or here. Wherever you find them, except where it is forbidden like the Sacred Mosque. Wherever you find them, the kuffar is killed. Wherever you find them, take them and seize them, beleaguer them and lie in wait for them in every stratagem.'

Listen again. 'In every stratagem'. Back in 2000 in Blackburn, Lancashire, one of his audience asked if every means possible included suicide bombings. Was it OK, the voice of a young man asked, to blow himself up in the cause of the jihad? Abu Hamza, squatting on the floor in the front room of a house, his back to the radiator for warmth, said it was: 'It is not called suicide, it is called shahid operation. It is not called suicide, this is called shahada, martyring, because if the only way to hurt the enemies of Islam except [sic] by taking your life for that then it is allowed.'

Such martyrs would be glorified, exalted above all when they reached paradise. They had sacrificed their souls to Allah, and in return He would grant them passage to paradise, where they would intercede on behalf of their families, have all their desires fulfilled, and take seventy-two virgins for their wives. 'If he is a person who actually wants to go to paradise, if he's sincere about the beautiful women of paradise which one day, *insha'Allah*, he will go to paradise and have a walk with all his wives in paradise and she will tell him "I used to watch you" ... This religion quenches this thirst with the blood of the martyrs. This religion fires the people with the blood of its sons and if it wasn't for those minority few, the weak in their armoury, strong in their blood and their faith, without them the world wouldn't have shook.'

Since Abu Hamza spoke these words the world has been shaken by the Islamist tactic of suicide bombing. But six years later the imam who once spoke so fearlessly would try to persuade a judge and jury that he did not always mean what he said. His command of the English language was not so good. 'I'm not Shakespeare, I make a hundred mistakes in one sentence,' he protested. 'You cannot hold me to account for phrases.'

But in that front room in Blackburn he revealed that he knew exactly what he was saying and its implications. When a member of his audience arrived late and made to sit down close to him, the wisecracker in Abu Hamza warned against it: 'Don't sit beside me, you'll get twenty years in prison.'

Visits to Blackburn were a regular feature of Abu Hamza's routine in the years before he became notorious. His roadshow went to everywhere in Britain with a sizeable Muslim community. He lectured all over London, returned to his former pitch in Luton, drew crowds in Birmingham and frequented mosques in Lancashire and Yorkshire. The Lancashire mill town of Burnley was a haunt until local Muslim elders realised with a shock what the visiting imam from London was really saying to their children.

Abu Hamza visited the town in 1998 with his entourage from Finsbury Park and preached to a number of gatherings. Cassettes entitled 'Abu Hamza in Burnley' went on sale in a local Islamic bookshop. The speaker on the cassette was not always Abu Hamza; he was joined on the platform by one of his closest followers at the time, a man from Birmingham who had fought with mujahideen forces in both Afghanistan and Bosnia. With his leader sitting alongside him the man delivered a chilling speech demanding violence and 'blood sacrifice' in Britain.

'Get training,' he told the audience. 'There must be some martial arts brothers amongst yourselves. You have to pump into the brothers what you are training for. It's so you can get the kuffar and crush his head in your arms, so you can wring his throat, so you can whip his intestines out. That's why you do the training, so you can rip the people to pieces. Forget wasting a bullet on them, cut them in half.'

He lacked the oratorical flourishes of Abu Hamza, but together the pair of them had a major impact on young Muslims who had not heard such fiery talk before. Not long after Abu Hamza's visit, seven youths from Burnley left the town for Pakistan. They told their parents they were going to study Islam in madrassas. A few months later news reached Burnley that two of the group, Afrasiab Ilyas and

Arshad Miaz, had been killed. Far from being in Pakistan studying, they were reported to have died when an artillery shell fired by Northern Alliance forces landed on a mosque inside which they were praying. The mosque was in Kabul, the capital of Afghanistan. Both the dead were educated and devout young men, teetotal and non-smoking. Ilyas had a degree in accountancy, while Miaz was a university undergraduate.

Rafique Malik, a leading figure in Burnley's Muslim community, said it emerged that young men in the town had been approached to go to help the Taliban: 'It was up to them what they did – go to war or do administrative work, helping to build a purely Islamic state. Nobody knew, not even their parents, that they were going to Afghanistan. They went to Pakistan and the next thing their parents hear is that they are dead.' The Burnley mosques united to ban Abu Hamza from preaching on their premises ever again. But he continued to tour Britain, disseminating what he believed was his message of the one and only truth.

His talks seethe with hatred and intolerance. The Abu Hamza repertoire was not restricted to preaching about the jihad of the battlefield. The struggle to establish his particular brand of fundamentalism encompassed every aspect of life. As he ranged over the world of the late twentieth and early twenty-first centuries, he revealed himself to be a man filled with suspicion. There was sin and conspiracy to be found everywhere, and all of it directed against his people. Food additives, for example, were part of a plot to trick Muslims into eating pork fat. Universities were preventing Muslim students from doing useful degrees.

As he raged and ranted against the world Abu Hamza put on display his rampant misogyny and violent homophobia. Although all Muslims had to fight, women could not. Their role was to show their children propaganda videos and prepare them for training from the age of ten. There was great danger in idle women: 'It is very important to have prudent women because women nowadays they

[are] doing nothing but sitting and talking and some of this talk is evil and some of this talk hurts … [Women must learn] the discipline of sitting, the discipline of tongue, the discipline of family interaction. But if she cannot memorise she should learn sewing. Why? To help her husband financially and to give herself something to do.'

Of course, women who stepped out of line could be assaulted by their husbands. It was the man's right to control his woman: 'Bring up your daughters to that manners [sic], otherwise they [are] going to be divorced in the first week of their marriage or slapped in the face. We teach our wives through television how to answer back.'

For gays and lesbians Abu Hamza reserved particular hatred. The punishment for such a grave sin as homosexuality was execution. Addressing the subject of homosexuality, or indeed of heterosexual sex, always seemed to bring out a particular prurience in his preaching: 'What would be the next thing if a man puts on a lipstick and he wear a skirt, the next thing another man will pick him up … Now if a woman is also trying to build muscles and decide to grow a moustache or cut her hair short or she wears suits from Lord Jones, what would be the next of it? She will be picked up by another woman. That is not allowed and people who do these kind of things are cursed.'

Gay people are, according to Abu Hamza, to be thrown off high buildings and then stoned to death. Aids was sent to punish them. If the state did not outlaw homosexuality, then 'some people have to stop it – people will be killed, no problem'.

Some of these sections of his sermons also expose a huge amount of self-loathing. Abu Hamza seems to be constantly trying to cleanse himself of the man he was before he found Allah. He appears to hate the fact that he was once married to a white Western woman, that he lives in the decadent West and that he once worked as a bouncer in Soho. This is him raging against Western women who flirt with Islam: 'As troubles happened in this country, religion is like a fashion,

fashion! Today she wears the veil and tomorrow she would wear the bikini or any other thing like that. She has no problem with that, she would say that this dress is nice and I would look like Batman or Zorro I would wear it for a bit and take it off, what is the problem?'

The problem, according to the Abu Hamza doctrine, was that in Europe such flighty women could not be punished by their husbands. His first wife, Valerie Traverso, had abandoned the veil after an incident when she was assaulted on the street while wearing it. She told Abu Hamza bluntly that it had been her choice to put it on in the first place, and it was her choice to take it off.

But what, he asked, can you expect if you have to live in England? The country which he tried so hard to become a citizen of, and where he has collected some £300,000 in welfare benefits, was nothing more than 'a toilet'. Its churches were full of child abusers and devil worshippers, its schools were snatching Muslim children and corrupting their minds, and its streets were lined with video shops selling pornography, brothels and stores that sold alcohol. Some of these were 'legitimate targets' to be ranked alongside banks and courts: 'Every place of iniquity, every brothel, every video shop which is selling naked is a target. If anybody protect these kuffar places and these fisq [sinful] places is a target. Anybody who propagate these kinds of things amongst Muslims is a target.' Mostafa Kamel Mostafa, the Soho strip-club doorman whose marriage to a Western woman got into trouble because he had an affair with a prostitute, might well have been a target for such righteous religious anger.

There were many more targets for Abu Hamza's ire. Magistrates who granted licences for the sale of alcohol 'should not be allowed to exist upon the earth.' Cinemas and video shops were all in the line of fire. As were tourists, like those killed in terrorist incidents in Egypt in 1997 or Yemen in 1998. Tourists went to Muslim lands to defile them. They kissed and fondled in hotel corridors, they had crack cocaine and whisky in their pockets, they sunbathed naked on Nile cruisers and they forced Muslim widows to debase themselves by serving them coffee and cleaning their hotel rooms. Tourism was 'haram', or forbidden.

But Abu Hamza's bitterest and most violent condemnation is reserved consistently for the Jewish people. The Jews – not Israelis or Zionists – were the bitterest of enemies, and it was a requirement for Muslims to kill them. Abu Hamza's lectures on the subject of the Jewish people are among his most frightening and vitriolic. The violence of his language makes the anti-Semites of the fascist far right seem almost tame. He knows, believes and regurgitates the same conspiracy theories so beloved of the white supremacist and the fascist far right. The accusation of Holocaust denial cannot be laid at his door. Abu Hamza goes way beyond that. In his mind the extermination of six million Jews by the Nazis was a punishment ordained by God because of the treachery and blasphemy of the Jewish people.

The Jews are not just a threat in Israel or Palestine; they control the Western world by owning the media and blackmailing the politicians. The Muslims in Europe are in great danger from this creeping domination: 'We will see the influence of the Jews growing day by day in our countries. Not only in our countries, in our homes. Our houses are full of Jews. Where? Under the table? No. Under the bridge? No. In the television, in the radio, in the books of your children, in the chest of your children, and your wives and some of you. They are not far from us, as close as Shaitan [the devil] to you.'

Using his position in one of London's largest mosques, he preached again and again that the day was coming when the Muslims would have to fight and kill all the Jews. This, he claimed, was the prophecy of Mohammed, told to him by God. 'Every time they lit the fire for war God has put it out. And this is the imminent result and this is a universal result too. Hitler looked at their dealings and their treachery. They wanted to deceive him in his war. Some were dealing with the Allies against him. So he killed them and punished them and this is a sunna [Islamic rule]. And they will be inflicted with that

again when the stones and the shariah [Islamic law] start talking to
the Muslim – You the worshipper of God … This is a Jew dealing in
usury, so come and kill him. This shows that the Jews will be destroyed, the state will be destroyed and some of the Jews will be
running around hiding behind the trees and the stones and then they
get cursed by the earth until there is not one of them left.'

Darwin's theory of evolution was, Abu Hamza claims, motivated
by the desire to disprove that mankind might have been descended
from Jewish people. In an extraordinary and virulently anti-Semitic
passage from one of his sermons, he says: 'The story of evolution not
all of it wrong you know, because Darwin he was so emphasised by
Jews, he wanted to establish a link between human beings and
monkeys. Why? Because he was so afraid to find his own grandfather
was a Jew, the first monkey, the first ape. So he wanted to prove it to
the people from the other way round. The source of man is monkey.
So the source of monkey is a man, and he's a Jew.'

The final battleground, Abu Hamza told his listeners, was
Palestine. That was what God says: 'It is decreed that it will be the
biggest Jewish graveyard in the world and that is Palestine. We do not
want the Jews to pull away from Palestine but we want them to be
buried there. You will fight them until when, until every tree and
stone say "Oh you Muslim, you servant of Allah, this is a Jew behind
me, come and kill him." It means they are going to be finished up.'

When these words of hate finally brought Abu Hamza before a
judge and jury at the Old Bailey in 2006, he tried to claim that he was
only a preacher of the holy book, and that in everyday life he had
good relations with clerics of other faiths. He had signed a petition,
he said, to help keep a synagogue open in Finsbury Park, and had
met and talked politely with the local rabbi and a Church of England
minister.

The police officers who investigated Abu Hamza and brought him
to trial over his preaching, said they felt as if they were dealing with
two people. They had studied his video sermons in immense detail,

and were convinced that they had sufficient evidence to charge him with inciting murder and racial hatred. But the man they questioned in the Anti-Terrorist Branch interview suites at Paddington Green police station was polite and deferential: 'It was always "Yes madam, No madam, Yes sir, No sir, please and thank you." And it wasn't just us, he was the same way with the custody staff and everyone he encountered. You came out of an interview and thought to yourself, "Is that the same bloke?" You would have to go and watch the videos again to remind yourself who you were dealing with.'

They might also have reminded themselves that Abu Hamza preached that lying to and deceiving the unbelievers was acceptable, especially if it was done in pursuit of the great cause of jihad. Jihadis claim permission to lie to unbelievers under a theological doctrine called 'taqiyya'. Ultimately he was to be condemned and convicted by his own powerful and unequivocal words.

In one of his smaller study circles he sat cross-legged on the floor, a young man occasionally wiping the sweat from his brow as he talked, and explained how he sometimes entered into sham debate with the enemies of Islam: 'I talk to them when they ask me. They said to me Islam is this, Islam is that, Islam is spread by the sword. I say of course Islam is spread by the sword because for as long as there is pigs like you Islam will be spread by the sword.'

And he always knew, perhaps even hoped, that one day his words would bring him to a kind of martyrdom in prison. Speaking in Whitechapel, east London, in 1997, Abu Hamza told his audience that they should never shy away from preaching the Islamist creed of total world domination: 'So what if you are behind bars? What are you doing now in Whitechapel, what are you doing now? Go behind bars for one word … and that is the word of the truth we must propagate.'

5
Racketeers, Frauds and Fakes

'If he comes … with a different name in a false passport,
call himself Simon blah, blah, blah … then he can kill, he
can steal, he can everything.'

ABU HAMZA

The man who because of a court order can be known only as 'A' had
lived in Britain since 1989, with no obvious signs of wealth. He
arrived from Algeria as a tourist, did a little bit of work, enrolled as a
student for a while, prolonged his stay through a marriage of con-
venience, then settled down with a Polish Roman Catholic woman
who bore him twins. 'A' was eventually deported in 1993, tried to
claim asylum in Sweden but was bounced back to Britain, where he
now argued that if he was to be returned to his native Algeria he
would be persecuted for his opposition to the regime there. His case
was adjourned for review and he promptly disappeared. Over the
years he would use a variety of identities – among them Hakim, John
Caller, Amine and Mezguiche – and he was occasionally arrested in
possession of false documents. Yet somehow this apparently feckless
individual had been involved, between March 2000 and February
2001, in the purchase of sophisticated satellite communications
equipment to the value of £229,265.87.

Evidence presented in 2003 to Britain's secret anti-terrorist court,
the Special Immigration Appeals Commission, details the long list of
items purchased by 'A' and a number of associates – including Abu

Doha, one of the highest-ranking al-Qaeda operatives to have lived in Britain and a worshipper at the Finsbury Park mosque. The inventory of purchases read: one Nera Voyager car satellite phone, twelve Nera satellite phones, one Thrane satellite phone, twenty-six France Telecom SIM cards with airtime, ten Stratos SIM cards with airtime, five Iridium handheld satellite phones and one satellite pager.

All the goods were bought from the same telecommunications company, and every payment was made in cash. At first the money was handed over at the firm's premises, but later it was transferred by banks, having been lodged in cash at north London branches of the bank where the company's account was held. The customers, it was later discovered, conducted all correspondence and communication under false names. The telecommunications company had requested end-user certificates, which were supplied in the name of a defunct charity. According to Britain's intelligence services this expensive consignment of satellite communication equipment – bought in Britain – was supplied to the Arab mujahideen faction fighting a bloody war against Russian forces in Chechnya.

The accumulation of such six-figure sums in Britain to finance jihad around the world was not unusual. In February 2001, the same month that 'A's' involvement in the satellite phone purchases was uncovered, police raided the home in Acton, west London, of Abu Qatada – Abu Hamza's teacher, mentor and later radical rival. Under the cleric's bed in his untidy semi-detached house on Noel Road officers found a huge haul of cash in English pounds, US dollars, German deutschmarks and Spanish pesetas. When counted, it totalled almost £180,000. Abu Qatada claimed that the cash was intended for the construction of a new mosque. But at least one envelope full of notes was clearly marked 'for the Chechen mujahideen'. Jihad supporters have since confirmed that Abu Qatada was known throughout Britain as a conduit for funds destined for the Chechen fighters. Some of that money had been raised directly – and indirectly – in British mosques. There were straightforward appeals for the Chechen struggle, and rather more opaque pleas for charitable donations which were then siphoned off to the militants.

A clearer insight into how terrorist fundraising was organised in Britain was gained later in 2001 when – just days after the 11 September attacks in New York and Washington – police in the East Midlands arrested almost thirty men and women suspected of involvement in a terrorist fundraising ring. The tip-off had come from Paris, where the detention and interrogation of Djamel Beghal, a key terror suspect, had uncovered an al-Qaeda support network that extended through France and Spain and had connections with Finsbury Park mosque in London, but seemed to have its operational headquarters in the city of Leicester.

An eighteen-month police investigation, codenamed Operation Magnesium, took Leicestershire detectives to seven countries, including Afghanistan. It identified two principal organisers of the cell, both of them living in Leicester, attending a small back-street mosque and leading apparently frugal lives. They claimed social security benefits under their real names, yet used false French identity documents to obtain casual work at a sandwich-packing factory. When police searched a car belonging to one of the men they found the machinery of a logistical support cell. Along with muddy football boots and unwashed kit, there were skimming machines used for stealing confidential account details from credit cards, and boxes full of unembossed Visa cards and Mastercards ready to be imprinted with counterfeit details. As the investigation progressed it became clear that credit cards being cloned in Britain were used to purchase goods in southern Spain. Items bought were then returned for credit or resold on the black market to realise hard cash. This fundraising network – just one of many operating in the UK with Europe-wide connections – was estimated to have raised some £800,000, and it was clear from the lifestyles of those involved that they had not benefited personally from the profits. There was also evidence that the Leicester group was heavily involved in arranging forged visas and travel documents for people from all around Europe to enable travel to Pakistan and onward to the Afghan training camps. 'It was a bit like an al-Qaeda travel agency,' quipped one police officer. As a result of the investigations there were eighteen arrests, and the two key figures in the gang were jailed for eleven years each.

British counter-terrorist agencies now accept that in the years preceding the post-9/11 crackdown on militant Islamist networks in the UK, millions of pounds were raised to finance violent groups operating in Afghanistan, Algeria, Chechnya, Kashmir, Yemen and other jihad battlefields. Most of that money was raised through organised crime, ranging from sophisticated international credit card counterfeiting to benefit fraud and shoplifting gangs.

Racketeering was vital to the jihad. Estimates of Osama bin Laden's personal fortune and ability to finance holy war around the world have been hugely exaggerated. He had been a rich man but was cut off from much of that wealth when he was thrown out of Saudi Arabia for anti-government activity in 1991, and lost more when the Sudanese, under pressure from America, kicked him out of their country in 1996. As a greater understanding of al-Qaeda was reached, analysts realised that bin Laden was important as a figurehead, an inspirational figure and someone whose name could be used to aggrandise terrorist attacks. But he was not, as had been initially thought, in direct operational and financial control of a systematically organised movement. The mujahideen groups and terrorist cells around the world that allied themselves to the al-Qaeda ideology were largely autonomous and self-financing. Britain was a key source of that finance.

Unsurprisingly, the Finsbury Park mosque – under the stewardship of Abu Hamza – was at the centre of the racketeering. Countless imaginative varieties of fraudulent activity were organised there, and the tricks of the trade – as important to the jihad as the skills of firing a Kalashnikov or building a bomb – were taught.

The people who were to rob and deceive in the name of holy war required some form of religious justification for their criminal activity. It fell to Abu Hamza, the religious scholar, to reassure his congregation that stealing, the use of false identities, benefit fraud and other forms of dishonesty were permissible in his warped version of Islam. In one long lecture, entitled 'Holding Fast to Allah in the Land of Disbelief', he set forth his rationale for giving Muslims permission to steal from non-Muslims, including the British state. At the essence of his argument was the claim that 'the unbelievers cheated us and took it [Muslim wealth] away, but we come to take some of it back'.

Muslims, Abu Hamza argued, were protected by Allah. Their lives and their wealth were more valuable by virtue of their faith; non-Muslims were afforded no such protection, and therefore could be robbed. 'If you can claim it [Muslim wealth] back then do so,' he preached. 'It is theft but it is theft from non-protected persons. It is like killing a non-protected person, there is nothing in it; it is not protected blood. So if a person wants to protect his money, he must make his money protected – protected by the matters of Islamic laws. No Sheikh can forbid it or anyone. It must be permissible by Allah's order or barred by Allah's order … We have no concern; the nation has no concern with your acts in these things. The nation of Mohammed has no concern…'

In answer to direct questions from his listeners, Abu Hamza gave permission for specific types of crime. Asked about repaying a student loan, he replied: 'Any debts, you just take it; you just take them all and go.' Shoplifting was also allowed: 'You break by force and you take it, this is OK.' The only Muslims who were not allowed to steal in a land like Britain were those who owed it a debt of gratitude because they had arrived there seeking protection from religious persecution elsewhere. Any other Muslim, however, could come to the UK using a false identity and do whatever he pleased. Abu Hamza explained: 'If he comes as a secular person, if he comes with a different name in a false passport, call himself Simon blah,

blah, blah and he's Mohammad, then he can kill, he can steal, he can everything.'

All this thieving would not amount to jihad, however, unless it was done in an organised way by a recognised group committed to the struggle. 'If they take money from the kuffars, is that jihad? Not necessarily. To make a group and fight and go for jihad, then you take money from the kuffar, this is jihad.'

Such groups were hard at work inside the Finsbury Park mosque, where Abu Hamza's acolytes diverted money from the weekly collections to their causes and were busily running fraud networks. While Abu Hamza sat cross-legged in one corner of the mosque, surrounded by a circle of young men listening to his views on the Koran and world affairs, his henchmen would be teaching more base skills and conducting other business in darker corners and different rooms.

Reda Hassaine attended the mosque for five years – risking his life as a police and security services informant – and witnessed the multitude of illegal activities going on there. 'It was going on all around you in the evenings and the afternoons,' he said. 'People were selling passports, stolen credit cards and cloned credit cards. There were black boxes of the kind they used for skimming the numbers. They would recruit people who were working in petrol stations, hotels, restaurants, and give them the black boxes to collect the details from customers' cards. Then they would use these cloned cards to buy trainers, Levi's 501s, designer clothes which would be sold inside the mosque for cash. Sometimes they would take orders for stuff like televisions, hi-fis, that sort of thing, they would agree a cash price then go and buy the products with a forged card.

'If you wanted, you could buy a credit card for your own use, but it was always a gamble. You might pay £250 for a card but you didn't know what the credit limit was on it, whether it was £1,000 or £5,000, so people often bought two. And even if they were caught they were usually carrying a false identity. The police were never too bothered. The most common documents for sale were French identity cards, French driving licences and French passports. The ID cards and the driving licences you could pick up for £40 or £50. Passports varied in price according to the nationality and the length of time before they expired; the most expensive were French passports which had been stolen in France from people with Arabic names. Those were what the Algerians really prized, but they were also the ones that were most useful to the terrorists.'

Possession of a false identity document opened the door to any number of other dodgy practices, and those most involved in jihad activities were given a number of passports and ordered to perpetrate multiple identity frauds.

Hassaine explained some of the methods used by the Finsbury Park fraudsters: 'The passport was useful because they could use it as proof of identity and then they could set up electricity, gas or telephone accounts using a temporary address. British Telecom bills were the most useful. Then they would have proof of identity and proof of address, all that was needed to open a bank account. Using several identities they would open several bank accounts, manage them carefully for six months, keep maybe £1,000 in there, and the bank would offer them a credit card. So they would take the legitimate credit card and use it carefully for six months and the bank would offer them a loan. That's when they strike.

'One man might apply for loans of £10,000 in six or seven different names, and because he appeared to have a good track record the bank would give him the money. The money would never be repaid, and when the bank checked up they would find that the person the cash was loaned to had never existed at the address they had for him. They must have lost millions to people who were operating scams like that out of Finsbury Park.

'Those same people were all claiming income support and subletting rooms for which they were receiving housing benefit while living for free in the mosque itself. They had also lodged asylum

Valerie Traverso married Mostafa Kamel Mostafa, the man who became Abu Hamza, less than a year after he arrived in Britain from his home in Alexandria, Egypt. He was 'romantic, tender and softly spoken'.

When Valerie's daughter was born in September 1980 Mostafa Kamel Mostafa, then an illegal immigrant, was named in the birth certificate as her father. But Valerie has since insisted that she was pregnant before she met Mostafa, and that he is not her daughter's father.

Abu Hamza became a radical Muslim in the late 1980s and went to live in Afghanistan with his family. He was photographed (right) in 1993 talking to Pakistani journalists about engineering and reconstruction projects just months before he lost his arms in an explosion near Jalalabad.

The North London Central Mosque on St Thomas's Road, Finsbury Park. Opened in 1994, it became Abu Hamza's fiefdom after he was invited to become the khateeb (Friday preacher) in 1997.

After his injuries – he lost both arms and suffered a damaged eye – Abu Hamza was fitted with a leather-and-metal prosthetic limb. The hooked hand became an essential part of his public image.

ABOVE: Haroon Rashid Aswat (left) from Dewsbury, Yorkshire, became one of Abu Hamza's most loyal aides at Finsbury Park. He was arrested in Zambia in 2005 and deported to Britain. He was imprisoned as he fought a bid to extradite him to the United States where he is accused of trying to set up a jihad training camp.

Nizar Trabelsi was a talented Tunisian footballer who played at professional level in Germany. But he became a radical Islamist, attended Finsbury Park mosque and was jailed in Belgium after being convicted of plotting a suicide attack on a NATO base.

claims; there were guys who set themselves up as translators and would sit in the mosque coaching people in stories of how they had been persecuted in Algeria or faced torture if they returned home. Once they got the story right they would be taken along to a friendly solicitor who would take on their asylum claim.

'And don't believe for one minute that all this money went to the jihad. There are men who were into all these rackets at the mosque during the 1990s, who claimed to be mujahideen, who said they were Islamists but are now living happily back in Algiers in big houses and driving around in brand new Mercedes cars. The truth is that a lot of them had one foot in the mujahideen and one foot in the mafia.'

Abu Hamza's own financial affairs have come under increasing scrutiny, especially since the post-9/11 crackdown. He supposedly had all his assets frozen in October 2001, when his name was placed on the United Nations Security Council list of persons associated with the Taliban and al-Qaeda. This grandiose announcement meant that the Bank of England ordered a freeze on any bank accounts held in his name, and all welfare benefits he was entitled to receive were stopped.

The sanctions sounded severe, but in practical terms they made little difference to Abu Hamza. The five-bedroom house in Shepherd's Bush where he lived with his five youngest children was rented by Hammersmith and Fulham Council in the name of his wife Nagat, who obtained full British citizenship in 1997. The property was extensively renovated by council workmen – who installed a new bathroom – at public expense in 2004. Nagat collects an estimated £520 each week in benefits from the British state that her husband professes to hate so vehemently. Her rent and council tax payments are also met out of public funds. Before he was blacklisted by the UN, Abu Hamza had also received substantial welfare payments, including allowances for his disability.

In an interview conducted in 1999 with the Yemeni newspaper *al-*

Ayyam, translated by the Middle East Media Research Institute, he insisted he had every right to take money from the British government. 'I never lived off their money,' he claimed. 'I paid a lot of taxes to the infidels while I worked as an engineer. I take back from them the booty they plundered from the Muslim lands, in accordance with my needs. This is money that originally belonged to the Muslims. What they invest of this money in Muslims here [in Britain] is leftovers and crumbs of bread in comparison with the meat and honey they eat in our land.'

In September 1999, a month after he gave that interview, Abu Hamza somehow found £100,000 to buy a first-floor flat in Adie Road, Hammersmith, west London. The property was acquired at a discount from the local council under the 'right-to-buy' scheme introduced by Margaret Thatcher, which allowed tenants of local authorities to buy their own homes at reduced prices. Abu Hamza managed to retain the tenancy of the flat – in which he and his family used to live after their return from Afghanistan in the mid-1990s – despite the fact that they had moved to a substantial period house not far away. Five years later, at a time when he was in prison awaiting trial, he nevertheless managed to sell the flat at Adie Road. Documents lodged with the Land Registry show that the sale fetched £228,000; a healthy profit of £128,000. Embarrassed British authorities have been trying to find out where that money went. With his assets supposedly frozen under anti-terrorist financial controls, Abu Hamza should not have been able to dispose of the property.

Another financial investigation – with potentially more serious implications for Abu Hamza – is being conducted by the FBI. It claims to have evidence that he diverted money, probably from Finsbury Park's hijra (emigration) fund, directly to his old comrade Abu Khabbab al-Masri, who was running al-Qaeda's Darunta training facility in Afghanistan. Abu Hamza is thought to have been training under Abu Khabbab when the explosives accident in which he lost his arms occurred. The money was moved, says the FBI, in

March 1999, at a time when Abu Hamza was already under active investigation by Scotland Yard for his alleged involvement with terrorist activity in Yemen.

If the allegation is proven – and the US authorities have claimed in court that they have copies of email traffic to support it – it suggests that Abu Hamza's role in the worldwide al-Qaeda network was of huge significance. Under his stewardship Finsbury Park supplied not just funds to the Afghan camps but a steady flow of raw recruits, some of whom would prepare for 'martyrdom operations'.

6

The Recruiter

'Once the child reach ten years old, teach him some kind of thing which is scouting, sleeping rough, sleeping tough, going for training, sweating, getting couple of punches in his face, teach him the reality of life and then show him how to become a good mujahid.'

ABU HAMZA

A handful of volunteers were clearing away the remnants of the evening meal at about 9 p.m. when Abu Hamza joined his followers sprawled around the first-floor prayer room. It was rare to find the cleric still at the mosque this late. Normally one of his minders would have driven him back to his comfortable home in Shepherd's Bush, leaving it to a couple of his favoured lieutenants to keep an eye on the squatters he allowed to bed down inside Finsbury Park.

Mealtimes were chaotic. Groups took it in turns to cook, elbowing each other around to find some room to work in the cramped kitchen. The menu rarely varied from curried or spiced chicken with rice and vegetables, and those wanting to eat were supposed to throw £1.50 into a collecting tin. Abu Hamza joked that if anybody stole the cash from a mosque or dodged paying they must be desperate, so their sin should be forgiven. If the volunteer cooks needed more money to buy the night's ingredients they had to ask one of Abu Hamza's inner circle to get it from the petty-cash box kept in the cleric's locked office.

The group of about forty men gathered on a humid summer night towards the end of August 1998 stood to greet their imam. He nodded, exchanged pleasantries with some and then beckoned them all to sit down. Salman Abdullah was among the crowd. He had been living at the mosque for three weeks after leaving his home in Bradford following a row with his father over his walking out on his job at a plastics factory. Abdullah had left school at seventeen with a few undistinguished O-levels, then drifted through a number of menial jobs and picked up a couple of cautions from the police for fighting with skinhead gangs.

Two older boys from the gym he used in Bradford told Abdullah about the preacher from Finsbury Park, and took him along when they went to hear Abu Hamza, who was appearing at a community hall near their home. The cleric spoke about the frustration of Abdullah's generation, who felt no genuine affiliation to Britain, the country of their birth, nor to their ancestral land, Pakistan, which they had never visited. He spoke quickly, his voice rising as he offered his audience an alternative allegiance – Islam. Joining his Supporters of Shariah, he told them, meant more than showing up at mosque for an hour on a Friday lunchtime, or handing a few pounds to the colleagues outside collecting for 'brave mujahideen in Algeria' or 'our brothers in Bosnia'. Following Abu Hamza was a way of life. Abdullah remembered the phrases he used that night: 'You have one gift, your life. Islam needs blood today. We either have to kill or be killed, that is the only way to bring back Islam.'

In conversation afterwards with stalwarts from the north London mosque Abdullah learned that volunteers from all over came to Finsbury Park, and could stay if they wanted. They promised that there he would meet men who had fought for Allah. 'I had read the books, I had heard the preacher and now I could meet the real fighters,' he said. After the dispute with his family, Finsbury Park seemed as good a place as any to be until he decided what to do with himself.

The reason for the cleric's late appearance in the mosque that evening was that an honoured guest wanted to address them. Abu Hamza was like a ringmaster. He warmed up his young audience, drawing them into his world by teasing them about the surprises to follow. He held up both his amputated forearms and, in a trick familiar to his entourage, cast his gaze to the floor and lamented that his disability meant he could no longer fight, so his gift to Allah was to encourage those who could. He was the great facilitator. He stared into Abdullah's eyes, then slowly turned to look at each of the faces fanned out around him. The group were transfixed, and didn't notice a giant figure in a grey, loose-fitting shalwar kameez ghost into the room.

Members of Abu Hamza's entourage rushed to embrace the heavily bearded man, who greeted them warmly, then bowed and kissed both cheeks of his mentor. Abu Hamza introduced the guest only by his first name, Mohammed. The cleric explained how Mohammed had sat in this same room, and had proved himself a true Muslim by travelling to Kashmir to learn how to fire a gun, and do all the things the Koran says a young man should. Then Mohammed had taken the extra step and fought in battle with his Muslim brothers.

For the next couple of hours the young warrior, who was clearly still in his early twenties, recounted his experiences, lacing his tales of war with verses from the Koran, and censoring the bits about how truly miserable life was fighting through a winter in the dark hills of Kashmir.

Abdullah and the others were entranced, and Abu Hamza looked on contentedly. This is what he did best – open the door to jihadi groups around the world. Recruitment is a gradual process, and it begins crucially with manipulators like Abu Hamza. He takes the raw material, the gullible and the confused, and decides whether these young minds and bodies can be shaped at training camps abroad, then sent on terror missions or employed to do other chores for the cause of Islamist extremism.

The volunteers that August night were a typical mix of school dropouts, petty criminals who had had brushes with prison, the homeless, drug users, asylum seekers who had run away from their own conflicts, and enthusiastic teenagers like Abdullah at odds with their families. They came from various nationalities, but all shared a feeling of alienation and anger. These boys were almost all from immigrant backgrounds, and felt cheated that their fathers' hard work had not been amply rewarded since they came to Britain. They were ashamed that their parents had been too subservient. This generation was not going to stomach what they regarded as second-class treatment, or the racist taunts and violence from white gangs who wanted to drive them from their inner-city communities.

Abu Hamza's role at Finsbury Park was to instil self-belief among these boys, inflame them with his rhetoric and make them feel they had a purpose in life, namely to pursue the twisted course he and other militants mapped out for them. Teenagers like Abdullah who felt moved to do more than demonstrate or stand up in mosque and shout about the abuse of Muslims from Chechnya to Bradford could not look up the Yellow Pages to find a jihad recruiting bureau. They asked around and were directed to places like Islamic bookshops that were springing up in major cities, or to youth clubs in the grip of militants who steered them to academies like Finsbury Park, which was fast earning a reputation as a magnet for radicals. Abu Hamza regarded his mosque as a stepping stone to holy war. Waiting inside Finsbury Park for the new arrivals were the talent-spotters, men who had trained in Afghanistan or other war zones and whose job now was to weed out the poseurs and exhibitionists from the boys who might be of some use.

Foreign intelligence services knew this selection process was happening within months of Abu Hamza taking over in north London in March 1997. They had their own informants inside, but the cleric made light of the infiltration, recognising that no matter the accusations flung at him, the British authorities were reluctant to intrude into a place of worship.

Earlier in the evening Abdullah remembered a question being asked about an Algerian spy caught recording Abu Hamza's sermons inside Finsbury Park. Abu Hamza laughed and said: 'Not just them, but the Saudis, the Egyptians, Iraqis, the Jordanians and Yemenis all have their secret services here. We have even caught them filming in the toilets, but these people cannot defeat us.'

Britain's security services would realise too late that the redbrick mosque was a cover for a production line of 'wannabe terrorists', and that Abu Hamza's links with militant groups extended from Afghanistan to Chechnya, Kashmir, Bosnia, Yemen, Turkey and northern Iraq – even to Africa. A trusted lieutenant who served him at the time thinks it impossible to put an accurate number on how many left Britain for camps overseas. One reason is that various militant groups were active in London, openly poaching each other's recruits if they could, and squabbling over funding. There were at least half a dozen Pakistan-based factions scouting for support around the UK, and exaggerated claims made on rival websites about the numbers of Britons among their martyrs, killed abroad, were impossible to prove.

Some who ended up at Finsbury Park had previously dabbled with different groups like Hizb-ut-Tahrir, Omar Bakri's al-Muhajiroun and any one of the Pakistani organisations like Lashkar-e-Tayyaba.* Most novices were like Abdullah, possessed of a burning desire to do something, to go somewhere to fight for Allah, but with no clear idea where. Abu Hamza would sometimes steer raw recruits like him to adopt an interest in their own roots – in Abdullah's case the ugly, interminable fight between India and Pakistan for control of Kashmir. His grandfather was born on the Pakistan side of the

---

* Hizb-ut-Tahrir wants to do away with national borders and establish a single Muslim state under Shariah law. This should be achieved by political means. Al-Muhajiroun, which split from Hizb-ut-Tahrir in 1996, wants everyone to convert to Islam and accept it as a political way of life. Lashkar-e-Tayyaba (Army of the Righteous) is a Pakistan-based armed militant group which is banned in the UK.

disputed border, but once settled in Bradford the family refused to discuss the politics of Kashmir. Abdullah said, in his broad Yorkshire accent, that he learned more about the troubles blighting his ancestral homeland from watching videos at Finsbury Park and listening to that night's visitor than he had from seventeen years of living in a Kashmiri community.

Enthused by his experience at the mosque, Abdullah signed up for a stint at a training camp. He was handed an airline ticket to Islamabad by one of Abu Hamza's aides, an envelope containing £700 cash and the telephone number of somebody to contact in the city. Once there he was dressed in local garb and smuggled by pick-up truck and on foot through exquisite valleys sloping down to teeming rivers, to forests so thick he could not see the sky, and on to forbidding mountain passes so steep he had to gasp for air to fill his lungs. He had no idea where he was going. Exhausted after a week trekking, he stopped one evening at a clutch of shacks in a clearing overshadowed by tall trees. There were no road signs or maps to show him where he was, not even what country he was in, but as his guide left to go back the way he had come, the young Yorkshireman was welcomed to his new home.

This was not how it was supposed to be. The videos he had watched time and again at Finsbury Park showed lines of well-drilled, eager young fighters in identical camouflage, each with a rifle in hand, being put through their paces on an obstacle course and a firing range by day, then sharing meals and stories of jihad and the Koran in their barracks after dark. Here it was a different story. Abdullah's clothes were filthy and torn, and permanently wet from the incessant rain. But it was not the living arrangements that depressed him so much as the monotony of the daily strength-sapping runs he was sent on by comrades, most of whom he could not understand. His group of trainees ached to see some front-line action.

What he did not realise was that this month-long, introductory session was meant to be grim. The organisers wanted to find out who among these pampered British teenagers was genuinely up to the task. Most suffered fevers, mosquito bites or chronic stomach disorders and were glad to leave. If you wanted the opportunity to fire a gun you had to pay for the ammunition. The only chance the British contingent usually had to handle a Kalashnikov was if they bought one from a villager.

If you passed the initiative test, then life improved immediately. Graduates like Abdullah were moved to a comfortable guest house in Peshawar, or to a district of Islamabad – known by its grid reference on the roadmap as I10 – where they were given good food and expenses while rival groups tried to enlist them. These outfits may have had broadly the same objectives, but they were obsessively secretive about their operations, and did their best to entice foreign recruits away from other terror cells. Before leaving Finsbury Park Abdullah was warned not to hand over his identity documents to militants trying to secure his services, as they were closely monitored, and sometimes run by elements in the Pakistani intelligence service, the ISI.

Abdullah spent much of the next three months in the forests of Kashmir engaged in sporadic firefights, which he described as being as terrifying as they were chaotic. Gunmen were darting about in all directions, appearing to him to fire at anything that moved, including their own side. Casualties were high, but the medical facilities his unit carried with them consisted of a half-empty first aid kit you might stash in the back of your car, meaning that the wounded often had little chance of survival.

Abdullah's tour of duty guaranteed him a hero's welcome on his return to north London. His stature as a 'jihadi' meant that Abu Hamza could employ him in a new role, as a propagandist, inciting others to follow his path.

Finsbury Park had need of various talents for its network. Forgers, benefit cheats, computer programmers, accountants, shoplifters, orators, confidence tricksters, smugglers, film editors, clerks and drivers were required as well as front-line fighters if Abu Hamza's elaborate operation was to function successfully. His ambition was to create SoS training facilities across Britain and America.

As a man who enjoyed his home comforts, Abu Hamza was aware that dumping his recruits into a mujahideen base in the middle of nowhere might be too much of a shock to the system for a generation of British-born teenagers weaned on central heating and microwaved meals. He told the inner circle at the mosque that their priority was to accelerate plans to establish the first SoS camp. He assembled a team to examine what the laws were about firing guns on private property, as he was looking to acquire an English country retreat to accommodate his militia. America's gun laws proved to be more tolerant of this sort of activity, which is why he would spend thousands of pounds trying to establish a training centre in Oregon.

Until he found his own site Abu Hamza was forced to use the sort of venues that blue-chip companies in the City thought it fashionable to send executives to for a weekend of paintballing, white-water rafting and mountaineering. 'Team bonding', the brochures called it, though Abu Hamza had a more sinister intent for his paintballers. In 1997 he hired an old monastery in Tunbridge Wells, Kent, and a farm estate in Scotland for small groups from SoS to learn how to strip down AK-47 rifles and decommissioned handguns, and to try their hand with a mock-up of the rocket launchers used by the mujahideen in Afghanistan.

His preferred site for his training regime was the Brecon Beacons in Wales, where Britain's elite SAS regiment trained, and where he believed a gang of young men camping out for a few days would be unlikely to draw unwanted attention. In a bizarre move he hired the services of two ex-soldiers who advertised their services in the back pages of combat magazines. Both men claimed to be former Special Forces, but then, many British Army veterans make similar boasts, knowing their bluster is unlikely to be challenged by customers like Abu Hamza.

After one of these sessions in Wales in 1998 his SoS team – which included his teenage son and his adopted stepson – were stopped by police who had been following their Citroën car for some miles down the country lanes. The authorities clearly had this group on a watch-list. The SoS men appeared nervous as they were asked to open the boot of their car, then two officers searched the glove compartment and the seat pockets, making it clear from their remarks that they expected to find firearms. Nothing was found, as the two ex-soldiers had taken the weaponry in their own vehicle.

The team from Finsbury Park who travelled back from Wales that afternoon were among the ten men sent on a terror mission to Yemen later in the year. Providing money and muscle for terrorist operations abroad would help Abu Hamza establish himself as a major player in the international terror network.

His own trips to Afghanistan and Bosnia impressed on him how the extremist movement was gathering strength and spawning a new tier of leaders among the Islamic community. He saw the implications of what al-Qaeda was achieving through its chain of training camps long before British intelligence woke up to the danger, and he was determined to be involved. He yearned to run the terror network's British franchise, and confided to his inner circle at a meeting in his office in January 1998 that he was convinced it was his destiny to inspire a generation of jihadis. It did not matter how young they were; he was convinced that the sooner he had the chance to influence juvenile minds, the better.

Reda Hassaine, the spy who worked for both British and French intelligence, watched the brainwashing techniques Abu Hamza employed in his afternoon sessions with schoolboys. 'They would come to the mosque after they finished school, from eleven years old and upwards, and he would sit them down and first tell them a few funny stories. This was his little madrassa. Parents were sending their kids to learn about Islam, they didn't realise they were sending them to be brainwashed. Abu Hamza would talk very slowly to them, telling them about the teachings of the Koran, and the need for violence. He talks very, very well. When he starts speaking you want to listen to him.'

Most afternoons Abu Hamza would entertain the older novices, in groups of between ten and fifteen, in the first-floor prayer room. 'This was the heart of the action,' Hassaine said. 'It was how the recruitment began. Many of these kids were British Asian boys, and he would talk to them in English. He would talk about Kashmir. His message was always the same: "Islam is all about jihad and at the end the reward is paradise. Paradise is held by two swords and you must use one of those swords to kill in the name of Allah to get to paradise."

'When the people were Algerians he would sit with them with coffee and dates and show them the GIA videos, and he would say, "Look at your brothers, look what they are doing, they are heroes, most of them are now in paradise and if you go there with them you will have seventy-two wives. All of this will be for ever, for eternity. This life is very short, you have to think about the big journey."

'He used to talk about Yemen and Egypt, but after 1998 all the talk changed, it became all about Afghanistan. Osama bin Laden was there, the Taliban were building the Islamic state. This was the beginning of the recruitment of a second generation of people to go to Afghanistan, not to fight this time but to learn how to fight, to train and then go elsewhere to do damage. It all began in the summer of 1998.'

Finsbury Park was the ideal venue. Most of these boys had little else to do. They did not have jobs, their faith meant they could not drink, smoke or gamble, nor should they be going to nightclubs to pull Western girls. They were, admits Abdullah, 'full of testosterone, ready to burst with no outlet for our energy save keeping fit in the mosque's gymnasium set up in the basement'. After the communal meals their only evening entertainment apart from watching jihadi videos was to challenge one another to bouts of kickboxing or ju jitsu.

Finsbury Park was also an administrative headquarters for these boys. It organised benefit payments for them, provided them with fake addresses and gave them pocket money if they needed it. Hassaine, who monitored this covert operation for months, told how 'The mosque was secure. It offered money, tickets and names of people to meet in Pakistan who would escort them safely across the border to Afghanistan. It was an al-Qaeda guest house in London. The boys could come back from the jihad and find a place to stay, to talk about war, to be with their own kind of people, to make plans and to recruit other people. These people, if they thought you were willing to do the jihad they paid special attention to you. If they thought you were willing, that is when Abu Hamza would step in to do the brainwashing. Once he started, you wouldn't recover. You would become a "special guest" of the mosque until they could measure your level of commitment and they could organise your trip to Afghanistan.'

Abu Hamza was not the only person using the mosque as his recruiting ground. Hardened veterans were also exploiting the environment he had created there to find and groom soldiers for Allah. One of the most influential figures was Djamel Beghal, an Algerian who had been al-Qaeda's man in Paris before relocating to London in 1997. Beghal was frustrated by the tough anti-Islamist climate in Paris. His French wife Sylvie said he was also disenchanted with life in France – stuck in a run-down flat in an immigrant quarter south of the city, the only work he could find was in street markets. Blessed with intelligence, charisma and ambitions of leadership, he felt frustrated, and decided to re-invent himself on the other side of the Channel.

Beghal rented properties in London and Leicester, and insinuated himself into Muslim immigrant communities in both cities. He travelled extensively, telling neighbours he was involved in the clothing trade on the Continent, but going much farther afield to meet terrorist leaders, and proved adept at impressing the higher echelons of al-Qaeda when he visited Afghanistan. He embroidered his own standing among militant groups in the UK, and when he returned to Britain he exaggerated his status with bin Laden's operational commanders. He showed off a set of prayer beads that he said the al-Qaeda leader gave him as a thank-you gift for his work at training camps.

Beghal had the élan to carry this off. One who watched him at close quarters in Finsbury Park, a former teacher who gave his name only as Omar, described how impressive the Algerian was in engaging eager young followers with his soft voice and easy manner. With his floppy black hair, fringe falling over his eyes and his handsome looks, Beghal could have made a fortune as the perfect confidence trickster on the French Riviera. Instead, he chose to employ his talents delivering a steady supply of men for al-Qaeda to mould into suicide bombers.

A prodigious story-teller, Beghal would breathe life into his tales, like that of Britain's first suicide bomber, a Birmingham man known as Khalid Shahid ('martyr') who died in Afghanistan. During a battle in 1996 Khalid was wounded, but rather than try to escape he insisted his Taliban comrades leave him and hide a bundle of grenades inside his bloodstained jacket, which he detonated when the soldiers of the Northern Alliance tried to arrest him.

Neighbours regarded Beghal as the perfect husband and father, unaware of his double life as an al-Qaeda recruiting agent. He kept his first-floor apartment in a public housing project in the Paris suburb of Corbeil-Essonnes, which he let to an Algerian friend, Kamel Daoudi. Daoudi was a computer wizard, and one of the first terrorists to exploit the internet. He established a coded communication system to enable members of Beghal's network to stay in touch with each other and their leader, 'Brother Djamel'. Daoudi abandoned his university course in Paris and headed for England with the £6,000 his parents had set aside for his education. He proved to be brilliant at encrypting orders and information in email messages.

Word spread among the British Muslim community about the lure of Finsbury Park. Some nights there were up to two hundred people sleeping inside the building, laying down their bedrolls, sleeping bags and flimsy mattresses wherever they could find space in the basement. The higher-ranked figures bedded down in offices and meeting rooms on the same floor as Abu Hamza had his command centre.

The mosque residents were a mixed bunch. There was a bodybuilder, a figure of such formidable strength that he would take on two contenders at a time in wrestling matches in the mosque. While most of the novices could best be described as social misfits, the roll-call included university students and professional men who had given up their jobs for a time to follow the jihad path. One, a doctor from Birmingham, took up brief residence in north London before travelling to Afghanistan using the mosque's funds and contacts, but fled after the US-led invasion in November 2001, and has since returned to general practice in the West Midlands. His patients are unaware of his recent exploits.

One of the more eccentric recruits was a wealthy young man, born in London of Lebanese parents, who had upset his family by dropping out of public school to pursue a career as a disc jockey. He made a fortune, spending his summers in resorts like Tenerife, where by his own admission he consumed enormous amounts of drugs and lost count of the women he had sex with. His parents were thus surprised – and appalled – when he abandoned this hedonistic lifestyle and pledged himself to Finsbury Park. He changed his appearance, covered up his body tattoos, grew his beard and hair and ended up fighting in northern Afghanistan against British troops.

The recruits were kept entertained with an endless supply of violent videos – standard martial arts fare mixed with gory mujahideen propaganda. One film they never tired of watching opened with a soundtrack of sung verses from the Koran as commands in Arabic script rolled across the screen, telling followers: 'You have to kill in the name of Allah until you are killed. Then you will win your place for ever in Paradise. Our enemies are fighting in the name of Satan. You are fighting in the name of God.' The camera then follows a group of Algerian fighters hidden behind bushes as they watch the approach of an army convoy grinding its way up a steep mountain track. As the first vehicle draws level with the insurgents there is a monstrous explosion, and the sound of prolonged automatic gunfire.

The camera jerks left and right as the gunmen rush the burning trucks, stamping over the broken bodies of Algerian conscripts lying motionless in the dirt. A corpse hangs over the tailgate of one army truck. His head is missing. The screen then fills with the image of another soldier whose brain has spilled out of his shattered skull. A fighter empties a clip full of bullets into the already lifeless corpse. Worse still is to follow. The mujahideen realise that one soldier is alive, though only barely. One of the militants kneels in the dirt and, grinning at the camera, gently picks up the soldier as though offering his help, then slowly draws a knife across the young man's throat and spits in his face. The image of the blood pumping out of the severed artery is shown five times during the forty-minute film.

The young insurgents, gorged on their bloodlust, are seen dividing the rifles and ammunition looted from the conscripts, and some of them hold up the metal dog-tags and bloodstained identity documents of their victims as the commentary intones, 'God loves people who kill in His name.' The film ends with a grotesque ritual of fighters lining up to be blessed by a comrade dressed entirely in black, who represents the 'angel of death'.

A recurrent theme of Djamel Beghal's nightly lectures was to tell the young men sitting at his feet that there was no higher duty than to offer themselves for suicide missions. Many in Finsbury Park heeded his call. Salman Abdullah tells how, from the autumn of 1998, up to a dozen men were staying at the mosque and being groomed as suicide bombers. This corps of volunteers knew not to discuss their mission, but Abdullah says: 'You could tell from the way they were treated by Abu Hamza and his aides that they were marked for something special, but we didn't know it was for suicide attacks.' They would disappear periodically, but Adbullah and the rest of the commune knew better than to ask questions on their return.

Among these chosen men were Richard Reid and Saajid Badat, both British-born, who al-Qaeda ordered to blow up two trans-atlantic planes in mid-air in December 2001. Abdullah says that others were stunned when they learned the identities of the so-called suicide shoe-bombers squad, describing them as 'the last people you would have picked. Badat was so timid and Reid so stupid and dis-organised.'

Another of the quieter figures at the mosque was twenty-one-year-old Asif Hanif, an airport worker who lived with his parents in Hounslow, west London. In late 2000, after leaving Cranford Community College at eighteen and working part-time in duty-free shops at Heathrow airport, he told his family he was going to Damascus to further his study of the Koran. A few years later, in April 2003, he walked into a Tel Aviv bar called Mike's Place and detonated his explosive belt, killing himself and three others. His co-conspirator, Omar Khan Sharif, had been another visitor to Finsbury Park during his years as a student at King's College, London. The twenty-seven-year-old Sharif, a father of two, had once been a pupil at Foremarke Hall, the prep school for Repton, Derbyshire, one of Britain's finest private schools. He ran away from the seafront bar when his device failed to explode. His body was found in the sea a week after the attack.

The attack was sponsored by Hamas, and both men – who were also in touch with other radical groups – had crossed into Israel using their British passports and posing as peace activists. A police raid on the Finsbury Park mosque four months earlier had uncovered a letter written to Abu Hamza by Sharif seeking advice on the proper conduct of jihad. The letter, giving Sharif's address in Derby, was not followed up as an investigative lead.

Many of Abu Hamza's followers remained in touch with him, and what is clear from their letters is the adulation they have for the man who set them on the road to jihad and the possibility of martyrdom. One of the more notorious alumni of Finsbury Park, Zacarias Moussaoui, shared his Brixton flat with a number of the Finsbury suicide recruits. Moussaoui remains the only person in America to be convicted as part of the 9/11 conspiracy, although his precise role remains in doubt. The FBI at first believed he was to be the 'twentieth hijacker', but the subsequent capture of senior al-Qaeda terrorists who masterminded the plot forced US authorities to alter their view.

In an attempt to confuse and mock his interrogators, Moussaoui has given differing accounts of why al-Qaeda paid for him to take flying lessons in America. His appearances in court in Alexandria, Virginia, in early 2006 were watched by a fascinated public, still trying to grasp why al-Qaeda had inflicted such suffering on them. Moussaoui did little to enlighten them. He used these occasions to proclaim his allegiance to Osama bin Laden, and to perplex those trying to judge him. Prosecutors wanted him to face the death penalty, arguing that had he told police all he knew about why al-Qaeda was paying for its followers to learn how to pilot passenger jets in the West then 9/11 could have been prevented.

All Moussaoui wanted was to grab the headlines. He did so by telling the jury who would decide whether he should be executed by lethal injection or spend the rest of his life in prison that he had been intended to hijack a fifth plane on 9/11 and crash it into the White House. He claimed he was to be helped by his old friend from Finsbury Park, Richard Reid. His own court-appointed defence lawyers dismissed this as fantasy, as did the American intelligence authorities and some high-profile al-Qaeda figures in US custody – but Moussaoui had achieved the desired effect. His testimony reignited the debate in America over how the country's feuding security agencies had missed this threat.

The publicity given to his spurious boast meant that prosecutors paid little attention to other aspects of his testimony, particularly his measured account of how his time at Finsbury Park had shaped his beliefs and steered him and his 'brothers' towards al-Qaeda. Nobody asked who these 'brothers' were. Nor did they enquire who was their leader in London, and what role he played in introducing them to al-Qaeda and its emerging network of training camps.

There was a strong foreign contingent among those who adopted the mosque as their British retreat. One of them was Nizar Trabelsi, a lanky Tunisian and once a professional footballer in Germany, who was picked to be the first al-Qaeda suicide bomber to strike in Europe. He was arrested in September 2001, just days before he was supposed to drive a truck filled with explosives into a NATO base in Belgium.

Abdullah well remembers two brothers from the medieval village of St Pierre-en-Faucigny in the foothills of the French Alps, David and Jerome Courtailler. They were the sons of a well-off butcher, but the boys tumbled into the world of drugs and petty crime after their parents' acrimonious divorce. Brought up as Catholics, the pair drifted through drug hangouts in Brighton, where they converted to Islam and moved to London to find a welcome at Finsbury Park.

Abdullah says: 'This was like that generation of West Indies cricketers who made up their unbeatable team of the 1980s. It was a one-off to have that many talented men all coming together at the same time. It was extraordinary how many of these people were ready to die in suicide attacks.'

Regulars like Abdullah did not know the real identities of some of the men in the suicide squad. Foreign visitors were only ever addressed by their kunyas, or nicknames, and had often been dispatched to Finsbury Park from other militant centres around Britain and Europe. They stuck together, and enjoyed special attention from the imam. Abdullah remembers that they received better food than the rest of the gang.

It was in north London that the suicide bombers were provided with money, documents and the names of the contacts who would steer them to their intended targets in the Middle East, Afghanistan, Chechnya, Kashmir and cities in Europe. Many died, although most did not make the headlines in British newspapers. Among them was Xavier Djaffo, a French former Catholic and a close friend of Zacarias Moussaoui since childhood, who was killed in Chechnya in April 2000. He surprised his parents in Perpignan by suddenly announcing that he was leaving his young child to go to London to link up with Moussaoui and find work. The next they heard from him he had converted to Islam and adopted a Muslim name, Massoud al-Benin. His despairing parents had no idea he had then travelled to the Caucasus to fight alongside a Muslim group calling itself 'The Martyrs Battalion' against Russian troops. All they were told of the circumstances of his death was that he was wounded when a mortar round tore off his leg, and then shot by Russian soldiers.

Abdullah estimates that there may have been as many as fifty men from Finsbury Park who died in terror operations and insurgent attacks in a dozen or more conflicts abroad. But most of the elite team of suicide bombers did not get a chance to fulfil their missions because of the folly of their favourite instructor, Djamel Beghal. In July 2001 he was travelling back from Afghanistan after receiving his orders from the al-Qaeda commander who ran the day-to-day operations when an immigration officer at Dubai airport asked to see his passport. Beghal forgot his training. He looked anxious and began to argue. The officer studied his travel documents a lot more closely, ignoring Beghal's protestations at the delay. He discovered that the Algerian was travelling on a forged French passport. In custody in the United Arab Emirates, Beghal confessed, and revealed the details of a series of plots. He later retracted the confession, claiming that he was tortured. But the information he gave led to a string of successful anti-terrorist investigations across Europe – including the winding up of his fundraising and recruitment operations in London and Leicester. Despite Beghal's clear links to Finsbury Park, however, there was no search of the building and no attempt to arrest the chief recruiter who led the prayers there. The mosque continued to be at the centre of jihad recruitment.

7
Training Camps

'It's time for you and me and everybody to sacrifice, it's a time to prove that we are not here in the West just for the honey pot.'

ABU HAMZA

In the early summer of 2001, just three months before the 11 September atrocities, a new instruction appeared on the noticeboard in the entrance hall of the Finsbury Park mosque. Worshippers were urged to take an oath of allegiance to Osama bin Laden. The pledge, known as bayat, was mandatory for members of Abu Hamza's own militia, the Supporters of Shariah. Others were 'encouraged' to comply.

Few voices were raised in opposition, but one was that of Abdul Kadir Barkatullah, still a trustee of Finsbury Park, though with little say in how it was being run. Moderate Muslims like Barkatullah had long been sounding the alarm over the rise of militant Islam and the poisonous effect it was having on their community. He tried once more to reason with Abu Hamza, telling the preacher that a mosque was no place to praise a terrorist. But before he could make his argument two thugs grabbed the bespectacled imam and manhandled him into the street.

Once more Barkatullah turned to the local police for help. He knew there was little point in reporting the assault on him, but he patiently tried to explain why the police should do something to prevent Abu Hamza demanding that young men swear allegiance to the leader of a terrorist organisation.

Barkatullah's concern had been growing since ten young men from the mosque were tried for terrorism in Yemen in 1999. 'We had no doubts that Abu Hamza was dealing with extremist groups and was supplying recruits to these dangerous people,' said Barkatullah. 'Now here he was openly touting for al-Qaeda in the mosque.' The police listened politely, but Barkatullah said they did not regard Abu Hamza's brazen support for al-Qaeda as an offence. Seven times prominent Muslims from the local community lodged complaints with the police about the extremist antics of the Finsbury Park 'Sheikh'. On no occasion, said Barkatullah, did the complaints result in any formal action being taken against Abu Hamza.

Whether the message was ever passed on to the intelligence agencies, the local elders never knew. In any case, those bodies were still preoccupied with the threat of terrorism from Northern Ireland. A dozen friendly governments, including those of France, Spain, Italy, Belgium, Pakistan, India, Germany, Russia, Turkey and the United States, also had reason to register protests with Whitehall over what was happening at Finsbury Park. They too were overlooked.

Abu Hamza confidently told his sycophantic aides that he was beyond the reach of British law. He didn't bother to pay electricity and water bills for the mosque, so those living there had to make their own arrangements for lighting, heating and hot water. A few skilled electricians among his supporters rigged up ways to furnish the building with some power by rerouting supplies from other buildings.

Increasingly Abu Hamza acted as if Finsbury Park had divorced itself from Britain and was operating as an independent Muslim state. He contacted extremist groups, offering his services as an ambassador for them in the UK and presenting the mosque as a place of guaranteed asylum. Many took advantage of his invitation.

In the CIA's headquarters in Langley, Virginia, there is a computerised print-out of the names of thousands of men from many nations who passed through al-Qaeda's chain of training camps in Afghanistan. When agents trawled through this list what surprised them was the sizeable number who had also passed through north London's infamous Finsbury Park mosque.

For some visitors the mosque was a secure retreat for rest and recreation after a tour of duty in the holy war. Such was Finsbury Park's reputation that an international brigade of Islamic militants used it as a safe haven for a spot of leave before they returned to the jihad front line or undertook terror operations. But for a group of young Britons this was their testing ground to prove themselves worthy of a place at one of bin Laden's camps. US investigators claim it was Abu Hamza's job to ensure that the conveyor belt kept delivering a steady supply of apprentices for the cause.

FBI Special Agent Fred Humphries told how after the invasion of Afghanistan in 2001, a search was made of al-Qaeda safe houses in Kabul and Kandahar. Agents found dossiers on men who applied for jihad training. These candidates of many tongues had been asked a series of questions on their application forms. One of the first was who had referred them to the camps. Some had answered 'Abu Hamza'. Asked to state their ambitions after training, these men replied with one word: 'jihad'.

Nominees sent from Finsbury Park were given plane tickets, spending money and, most importantly, a letter of introduction from Abu Hamza. One of these cadets, a French convert to Islam, David Courtailler, confessed at his trial in France how the mosque facilitated his trip to Afghanistan with $2,000 cash and the name of a contact who would smuggle him over the Pakistan border to the notorious Khalden camp in eastern Afghanistan. This facility had been turning out terrorists since the early 1990s, including some of the al-Qaeda bombers who first tried to demolish the World Trade Centre in 1993.

Such was Abu Hamza's stature that having his name as a reference would guarantee his nominees acceptance at Khalden, which was run by al-Qaeda's operational commander, a young Palestinian known as Abu Zubaydah. He was only twenty-five, but bin Laden had installed him as gatekeeper and director of Khalden and half a dozen other camps. Abu Zubaydah would meet his new intake at a guest house in Peshawar, a dusty, steamy, chaotic Pakistani frontier town crawling with arms dealers, spies, drug barons and mujahideen veterans of the war against the Soviets. After a lecture on their religious duty, he would hand out traditional Afghani robes to the novices and give them a metal trunk in which to store their designer jeans, expensive trainers and any personal items they had brought with them. This locker could be retrieved when they returned from Afghanistan. Many of them remain unclaimed, the fate of their owners unknown.

The newcomers were instructed to grow beards to blend in with the locals, and spent their days in conversation with their fellow raw recruits, studying the Koran and praying. All were given new names, and there was no advance warning when it was a cadet's turn to be shoved into a car full of strangers and driven over the Khyber Pass to his assigned camp. Many of these al-Qaeda facilities had been used by the CIA in the early 1980s for training Afghan rebels fighting the Red Army. Now they were the places where bin Laden's strategists devised plans for attacks on American targets.

Surrounded by high mud walls and dug into the mountains of Paktia, Khalden was a natural hiding place for outlaws. Accommodation was spartan: candidates slept on the hard desert floor in a ring of stone buildings and tents. Khalden had its own firing ranges, tunnels and bunkers to store weapons and explosives, and a hospitality section where the stunned British novices were given a brutal introduction to life as a jihadi.

At first light the recruits were called to formation, almost like cadets on a British military parade ground. After a meagre breakfast of black tea and bread, sometimes sweetened with honey or dates, the men went through hours of strength and endurance training. To break the monotony mujahideen veterans tutored the exhausted novices in self-defence, using knives and garrottes.

Afternoons were devoted to the firing range, where they practised with small-arms, assault rifles and rocket launchers. Next door was a demolition site where explosives experts taught the students how to lay landmines and rig up booby trap devices. Local tribesmen disturbed by the deafening racket from the test ranges knew better than to enquire what was going on. The students' day would end with lectures from visitors from various terror groups, then the obligatory hours of prayer and Koranic lectures.

This punishing regime, coupled with the inedible diet and the miserable hardship of the living conditions, drove many to beg to go home after their two-week induction. Those who remained were screened for 'leadership training'. Among the Britons who graduated to the next stage was Liverpool-born Mohammed Rashed Daoud al-Owhali, who told the FBI of taking courses in intelligence gathering, codes and communications, hijacking buses and planes, how to seize and occupy multi-storey buildings, kidnapping and how to stop yourself from divulging al-Qaeda's secrets if captured, a lesson he clearly failed to learn. Such comprehensive training seems to have been wasted on candidates like Owhali, whose one mission was simply to drive a truck, packed with tons of explosive, into a US embassy in east Africa. Owhali failed at this as well, as he jumped clear of the driver's cab as the truck careered through the security gates.

The CIA had long been aware of the training camps from satellite photographs, but it was not until after the synchronised attacks on two US embassies in east Africa in August 1998 that killed 224 people that President Clinton ordered the US Navy to fire seventy Tomahawk Cruise missiles at two camps near the eastern city of Khost. He had been told that bin Laden was staying there, as he often visited his string of camps, but the al-Qaeda leader had fled and the damaged training centres were quickly rebuilt.

Bin Laden set up a couple of camps – Siddiq and Farooq – for terror tourists who paid for the privilege of attending them. These were wealthy young men from the Gulf and Middle Eastern countries who could afford to make their own way to Afghanistan. These places had bunks and showers, which appealed to pampered Saudis who just wanted bragging rights when they got home, where they would boast of having trained with mujahideen.

Khalden was for the hardcore. Their trips to Afghanistan were sponsored by the likes of Finsbury Park mosque, and from this crop al-Qaeda would find recruits to fight alongside mujahideen, or to undertake terror missions. The brightest of the new intake were shifted on to another of bin Laden's camps, at Darunta, close to the eastern city of Jalalabad. The name was taken from the nearby dam on the Kabul River, and the camp sat only a few metres away from the one main road that runs from the Pakistan border to Kabul. It had formerly been used as a base for the 1st Corps of the Taliban army, but was converted into al-Qaeda's prized academy for testing poisons and explosives.

The most heavily protected facility behind the red gates of Darunta was a dark, cramped laboratory which was run by Abu Hamza's old friend Abu Khabbab al-Masri, al-Qaeda's chief chemist. Abu Hamza is accused of sending money to Darunta and of playing a part in the recruitment of some of the camp's best-known students, such as the shoe bomber Richard Reid and the would-be hijacker Zacarias Moussaoui.

When the camp was overrun by US-led forces in late 2001 they uncovered evidence of the experimental work which Abu Khabbab had been undertaking. His laboratory was lit by a single bulb, and the one small window looked over a vegetable garden and a well. There were brown glass jars of chemicals stacked on dusty shelves, and in one corner lay a batch of dangerous toxins packed tightly together in a rectangular metal box lined with wood shavings. Antiquated gasmasks hung from the wall, and there were sets of protective clothing, goggles, earplugs and other equipment made by British manufacturers. Thick piles of instruction manuals in English and Arabic lay scattered around the room, including a number downloaded from the internet on how to make detonators and use household materials to make explosives. One worksheet told students, 'explosives have a way of making governments change their opinion'. Outside were cages which the fifty-two-year-old Abu Khabbab used to test his poisons on dogs. The Americans had offered a $5 million reward for the capture of Abu Khabbab, but he is thought to have been killed in January 2006 in a US missile strike on a remote Pakistani village where he was reportedly arranging his wedding to the young widow of a Taliban fighter. The attack killed a total of eighteen people.

Security services concede that they have no idea how many young Britons passed through these camps and others in combat zones in different parts of the world. Investigations around the globe have linked hundreds and hundreds of suspects – ranging from fighters to fraudsters to operational terrorists – to Finsbury Park. The former Scotland Yard Police Commissioner, Sir John Stevens, estimated that more than two thousand had undergone terror training. His successor, Sir Ian Blair, who saw the same intelligence reports as Sir John, put the number closer to two hundred. MI5 has never revealed its tally. However many it was, not a single recruit who attended these camps was ever arrested when he got home. Many never returned.

Those closest to Abu Hamza would occasionally learn of the deaths of some of those sent from Finsbury Park, though Abu Hamza ordered them to keep their mouths shut. He was not worried about deterring others at mosque from following in their footsteps so much as that changes in the law, and the different atmosphere following 9/11, meant he might face arrest. Many bereaved families have no hope of discovering what happened to missing fathers, sons and brothers, or where they are buried, because the men were using false names. Relatives argue that this was not to protect others in their terror cell, but was a cynical ploy by the likes of Abu Hamza to insulate themselves from prosecution.

The result of Abu Hamza's recruitment regime – and that pursued by the other fundamentalist groups which had made London the world capital of political Islam – was that more young men from Britain embarked on suicide missions than from all the other countries of Europe combined.

8
Londonistan

'MI5 said it wasn't Londonistan just because of me.'

ABU HAMZA

When it came to Abu Hamza's turn to take the stage at a London rally in February 1999, he was determined to eclipse his rivals. The previous speakers had churned up the young audience with the usual repertoire of insults aimed at the British government, while Abu Hamza sat motionless with his arms folded under a capacious blue cloak, a thin smile playing on his lips.

Those in the draughty Friends' House meeting hall in Euston Road who had heard him speak before nudged the newcomers with anticipation as Abu Hamza rose slowly to his feet with the help of one of his ever-present minders. As he walked to the lectern, a huge white sheet dropped from the ceiling with a curious-looking diagram printed on it. Across the top in black lettering it said: 'MUSLIM ANTI-AIRCRAFT NET'. The lights dimmed a shade as the cleric studied the bewildered look on the faces in the front few rows.

He was fed up with listening to all the usual rhetoric. Now it was the time to come up with some practical ideas on how to engage the enemy. Pointing with his hook to the diagram behind him, he announced that this was his plan to bring down aircraft over London. Even by Abu Hamza's theatrical standards this was a scene-stealer. He let the thought sink in for a few moments, watching as his audience craned their necks forward to get a closer look at the bizarre drawing.

Abu Hamza picks his style to suit the moment, and at this gathering he was not hollering and whipping his audience into a frenzy. Instead he behaved more like a benign college professor, delivering his lecture in a slow, deliberate voice so his students could follow the logic of what seemed like a crazy invention. 'This is to make the skies very high-risk for anybody who flies,' he said.

A dozen rows back, an olive-skinned man in loose-fitting Arab clothes fidgeted in his seat and felt sweat run down the back of his neck. Algerian-born, looking to be in his early twenties, he told those alongside him that he was a student at a college in east London. In fact he was a French secret service agent. He had been operating in London for three months, monitoring men like those onstage whose activities had led irate French intelligence chiefs to rename the British capital 'Londonistan'.

Undercover agents from France's DGSE – the General Directorate for External Security – had been shadowing a number of fugitives who had sought asylum in Britain. They were mostly North Africans, and some were key suspects in a series of terror attacks, including the bombings on the Paris Metro in the summer of 1995 which killed eight people. These new arrivals in London had been given sanctuary and a base to continue their operations by preachers like Abu Hamza.

The agent knew he could not take notes, so he summoned all his concentration to follow what Abu Hamza was saying, intrigued whether this was just another display of bravado, or a serious plot to cripple air traffic over the capital.

Abu Hamza described how a series of wire nets, held aloft by gas-filled balloons, would have small mines attached to them so that when an aircraft snagged itself, it would explode. To make the point there was a drawing of a US fighter jet diving nose-first into one of the traps, which he said proudly were invented by men from his Supporters of Shariah group.

'Now when a plane goes down is it a Lockerbie or a Supporters of Shariah net?' he said, making a cheap jibe about the bomb which exploded in mid-air aboard a Pan Am Jumbo jet over a small Scottish town in December 1988, killing 270 people.

Abu Hamza smirked about the havoc his nets would cause above Heathrow. The agent could not believe what he was hearing, and wondered if Scotland Yard had someone at this meeting. If so, he would surely report to his superiors that Abu Hamza had gone too far this time.

The extravagant preacher ended with a challenge to his audience, saying, 'This is not very clever, but it will work. Now invent your own idea and never give up.' As he returned to his seat, ecstatic applause rang around Friends' House. The British headquarters of the pacifist Quaker movement seems an unlikely setting for a gathering of violent Islamist revolutionaries. But the Quakers were almost certainly unaware of what would be discussed and debated under their roof when they accepted a booking for the Conference of Islamic Revival Movements.

Sitting one place away from Abu Hamza at the table set up on the stage for the guest speakers was another cleric the French regarded with suspicion. He was Omar Bakri Mohammed, who ran a group called al-Muhajiroun (the emigrants). Bakri Mohammed clapped and smiled appreciatively as his fellow preacher was helped back to his seat, but in truth there was no love lost between them. The two were rivals in trying to enlist young followers. Bakri Mohammed argued that, having escaped religious persecution, he had a better pedigree than Abu Hamza, a rich boy who came to the West to enjoy its fleshpots.

Born in Syria in 1958, Bakri Mohammed fled his homeland after joining the Muslim Brotherhood in a failed revolt against the government of President Assad in February 1982. He slipped across the Lebanese border to Beirut, but within a year he had moved on to the Saudi Arabian city of Jeddah. In 1985 he was one of a number of

Islamist dissidents expelled by the Saudis. He came to Britain, where he claimed asylum and was granted indefinite leave to remain because of the risk that he would face political persecution if deported back to Saudi Arabia. He became a leader of the first British branch of Hizb ut Tahrir (the Islamic Liberation Party) and preached firebrand sermons – mostly on an anti-Israel theme – across Britain. Hizb ut Tahrir, which advocates non-violent revolution to establish an Islamic state, has been labelled by Tony Blair as an extremist movement. Bakri Mohammed split with the international leaders of Hizb ut Tahrir in 1996, and set up his own organisation, al-Muhajiroun.

Bespectacled, heavily bearded and with a wide-eyed stare, Bakri Mohammed lacked Abu Hamza's oratorical skills, but was a more accomplished organiser. His al-Muhajiroun followers toured university campuses and shopping precincts energetically touting for recruits, while his website carried lurid accounts of young Britons martyred in overseas combat that were intended to encourage others to follow in their footsteps. Bakri Mohammed had tried to get the job at Finsbury Park before Abu Hamza wooed the selection panel and beat him to it. The disgruntled Syrian had to settle for running his organisation from a grim industrial estate in Edmonton, north London, and sniped in one interview that Abu Hamza was just the 'caretaker' at the Finsbury Park mosque.

Known as 'the Tottenham Ayatollah', Bakri Mohammed staged marches and rallies across British cities. Abu Hamza's supporters would often tag along and use the occasion to coax protestors to drop along to Finsbury Park some time if they wanted to listen to men who didn't just talk about jihad but had actually fought it. It was pure one-upmanship, but there was money and prestige at stake.

The third member of what foreign security agencies referred to as 'Londonistan's unholy trinity' was a heavy-set Jordanian with what seemed a permanent scowl on his face. Abu Qatada would occasionally share the platform at Muslim rallies with the other two, but he regarded himself as their spiritual superior. Indeed, he had taught Abu Hamza, and never let his protégé forget it. Such was his reputation as a scholar that Abu Qatada would charge exorbitant sums of money to give advice, sending subscribers to his 'agony uncle' service long-winded written judgements on what the Koran said about their family problems.

Bakri Mohammed tried to go one better by appointing himself the head of Britain's shariah court, which of course had no legal standing. This did not stop him travelling across the country, administering justice – for a fee – to plaintiffs who appeared before him complaining about wayward teenage daughters who wore make-up or sons who preferred computer games to studying the Koran.

A lucrative sideline shared by all three men was selling cassettes and videos of their speeches, with rival salesmen hawking cheap copies of their sermons outside mosques after Friday prayers. When they did show up together, observers say they behaved like rival actors at a Hollywood Oscar ceremony. They chatted convivially, applauded one another's speeches, but were desperate to take the night's honours. Abu Qatada's clique would remind the audience that their man had written many more books than the other two put together.

Judge Baltazar Garzon, investigating Islamist terror networks in Spain, claimed that many extremists regularly travelled to London to visit Abu Qatada. Among them were some of the masterminds of the gang who blew up four trains in Madrid in March 2004 by leaving explosives packed in rucksacks on rush-hour commuter services heading into the city's main Atocha station, killing 191 people and injuring more than 1,800. The Spanish judge thought Abu Qatada was such a dangerous link for foreign terror groups that he described him as 'al-Qaeda's spiritual ambassador in Europe'. This was a view shared by intelligence agencies in half a dozen other Western countries, though it is a charge Abu Qatada has always denied.

The Jordanian authorities had sentenced him to life

imprisonment in his absence for masterminding a series of bombings in Amman in 1998 aimed at Western tourists. One device had been discovered, and disarmed, in the American School in Amman. Another, hidden in a car, exploded outside the Jerusalem Hotel, a favourite with visitors from the US. Prosecutors made great play at the trial of the bombers of the fact that they named Abu Qatada as their leader.

The clerics all claimed that Islamist radicals felt safe in London as they were protected by what they called the 'covenant of security'. This, they explained, was a deal whereby if extremist groups pledged not to stage attacks or cause disruption in the UK, the police and intelligence agencies left them alone. British government ministers were appalled at the suggestion that they had entered into such a pact. But other countries were left to wonder aloud why Whitehall continued to ignore warnings that radical organisations were using London as a safe haven, and allowing these extremists to behave as if they were immune from prosecution. There were repeated requests from foreign governments to hand over suspects – including Abu Qatada and Abu Hamza – but Britain ignored them. To European eyes, these men seemed to do as they pleased.

When Britain's laws finally changed following the 9/11 attacks to clamp down on the activities of men like Abu Qatada, he disappeared on the eve of his planned arrest in December 2001, despite his house being under police surveillance. Exasperated French secret service chiefs questioned how this was possible, and speculated that Abu Qatada must have been an informer for MI5. For more than a year he hid out in a flat in Bermondsey, a few minutes' walk from MI6's headquarters. What made his flight even more embarrassing was that his wife and children regularly visited him at his bolthole in south London, as did supporters from abroad.

Abu Qatada used his time on the run to publish an essay on the internet offering a legal justification for the 9/11 attacks. The US State Department was speechless that he was still at large, continuing to cause trouble. After his capture at his housing association flat in Bermondsey, south London, in November 2002 he boasted to followers that Britain's ponderous extradition laws meant that it was far from certain he would ever be expelled.* The same is true of scores of other terror suspects living in the UK wanted by over a dozen friendly governments. Russia claims prominent Chechens who helped organise bombings on civilian targets in Moscow are sheltering in London. The Indian, Pakistani, Sri Lankan, Israeli and Turkish authorities, together with half a dozen European allies and the US government, have all presented Whitehall with lists of suspects they want to put on trial, but all of them are still waiting. The prominent French judge Jean-Louis Brugières was so appalled by Britain's attitude that he talked of 'Londonistan' as being the city of choice as a safe haven for Islamic terrorists, and a place 'full of hatred'.

The French did not know whether their British counterparts did not understand the lurking menace in their midst, or were still too preoccupied with terrorist splinter groups in Northern Ireland to devote money and manpower to the danger of Muslim extremists. MI5 was spending twenty times more money on tracking drug barons than on watching al-Qaeda terrorists operating in London. Brugières wondered whether Britain was just being selfish, and whether because these radical groups had not struck in the UK the security agencies simply did not care what they were doing. The French investigators protested that Britain was also ignoring the systematic fraud and corruption carried out by these groups. Brugières found it galling that at security conferences British diplomats were always the first to call for increased cooperation between allies, yet they refused to practise what they preached.

Senior figures in MI5 and in Scotland Yard's counter-terrorist

---

* Qatada is currently detained in prison pending the outcome of an attempt to deport him to Jordan.

squad, SO13, now admit that they thought Brugières and his ilk were being hysterical with their allegations about al-Qaeda penetration in the UK and the numbers of dangerous Islamic extremists sheltering in mosques. One said: 'The French would periodically bombard us with warnings and get very worked up and we decided they were over-exaggerating on Islamic extremists colonising London. Fact is, they were right, we were wrong, and we have not stopped apologising since. Frankly, we were not equipped to deal with this menace. For thirty years everything was geared to combating terrorists from Republican and Loyalist paramilitaries in Ireland. That danger was still with us when the French were screaming about Islamic terror cells. We did not know how to monitor these people or how to combat the threat of suicide attacks. We did not have the techniques. We missed our chance to deal with this a lot sooner than we did, but a lot of Western countries made the same mistake.'

The drift of Muslim extremists into Britain had begun in the early 1980s, when they joined an exodus of refugees from North Africa and the Gulf escaping civil conflicts and purges by dictatorial governments. Sections of the Arab press, stifled by censorship and closure at home, moved to London to print their newspapers. Saudi dissidents soon followed, using these papers and websites to call for the overthrow of what they dismissed as their corrupt royal rulers. Before long hundreds of Muslim politicians, academics, journalists and religious scholars were running their affairs from their exile in London. One of those eager to take advantage of Britain's 'open door' policy was none other than Osama bin Laden.

Michael Howard, the Home Secretary in 1995, recalls receiving overtures from some of bin Laden's supporters in London enquiring whether their leader could claim political asylum. Howard admitted that he knew little of the man, though a swift investigation by his staff resulted in a banning order on the al-Qaeda leader.

Although he could not come in person, bin Laden was able to establish his European headquarters in an obscure suburb of north-west London, not far from Wembley football stadium. In 1994 he opened an al-Qaeda media office in a back street of Dollis Hill, in a semi-detached 1930s family home rented by a Saudi businessman, Khalid Fawwaz. From behind the net curtains Fawwaz issued seventeen communiqués on behalf of bin Laden on all sorts of matters, from slating the Saudi royal family to the need for Muslim parents to ensure that their offspring were taught Islamic law. Whitehall thought these bulletins harmless enough, but US investigators claim the press office at Dollis Hill was a front from which Fawwaz played a role in planning the bombing of two American embassies in east Africa in 1998.

The CIA thought of the pudgy, baby-faced Fawwaz as bin Laden's 'de facto ambassador' in London. From there he was free to spy on rival factions and purchase equipment that bin Laden could not get in Afghanistan. In October 1997 he arranged the purchase of a satellite telephone for bin Laden, and organised for it to be delivered from the United States to Pakistan and on to al-Qaeda's high command at their headquarters near Kandahar. Delighted with his acquisition, the first call bin Laden made was to the small upstairs bedroom Fawwaz was using as his office.

After two more operatives were sent to London, the al-Qaeda team moved to larger premises, renting two rooms in a rundown Victorian office block at Beethoven Street in Queen's Park, where they posed as the Advice and Reformation Committee offering practical help for new Arab-speaking arrivals to Britain.

The British authorities ignored the turgid bulletins Fawwaz would pump out, including the fatwa dictated by bin Laden in 1996 against the Americans for keeping troops in Saudi Arabia. In February 1998, following a barrage of calls from bin Laden's satellite telephone, Fawwaz published another fatwa, this time threatening all Americans, which he issued in the name of the International Islamic Front for Jihad on the Jews and Crusaders. Again this caused little stir in Whitehall.

To cover his tracks Fawwaz often used the fax machine at a local post office in nearby Formosa Street and a cheap calls bureau, the Grapevine, on Kilburn High Road. It was at the Grapevine at 4.45 a.m. on 7 August 1998 that a fax arrived from an al-Qaeda agent based in Baku, Azerbaijan, claiming responsibility for the bombing of the two US embassies. As the paper scrolled out of the machine in Kilburn the attacks, which killed 224 people, had not yet happened.

Al-Qaeda agents captured after these bombings revealed that Fawwaz was far more than a mere propagandist, but had trained them in Afghanistan, and was in Nairobi to scout one of the two bombed American embassies. For the past eight years he and his two accomplices have successfully blocked efforts to have them extradited from London, to the continuing bewilderment of prosecutors in the United States.

All told, the names of the terror suspects who passed through the UK on bin Laden's business, or lived here, run into the hundreds. Judge Garzon in Spain claims that if you take every major al-Qaeda attack, including 9/11 and the Bali bombings, then list all those who played a part in their planning, funding and execution, you will find a line that always draws you back to Britain. Foreign ambassadors in London continually petitioned John Major when he was Prime Minister, then Tony Blair, to act against the extremists in their own backyard, but complain that nothing happened.

The French were enraged at the latitude shown to a group of GIA Algerian militants who used Finsbury Park as their home and published a crudely printed newsletter called *al-Ansar*. This was handed out at mosques, youth clubs and restaurants popular with young Arabs. It eulogised atrocities carried out by mujahideen in Algeria, recounting graphic details of their operations, and described in deliberately provocative language an attack on a packed passenger train and the hijacking of a French airliner in December 1994 which was intended to be flown into the Eiffel Tower. The magazine's editors, at different times, included Abu Qatada and Abu Hamza.

Determined not to be left out, Bakri Mohammed helped run a magazine in which he suggested that it was time Britain became a Muslim state. In one article it was claimed that John Major was 'a legitimate target' for attack. Fearing that he may have pushed his luck too far, a flustered Bakri Mohammed explained that this only meant that assassins could kill the then Prime Minister when he was in a Muslim country. He was interviewed by police but not charged – one of almost a dozen incidents when British legal authorities studied his offensive outbursts but decided he had not broken the law.

Another Bakri Mohammed gem came during the wars in the former Yugoslavia, when he argued that Bosnian Muslims should 'eat Serbs' rather than accept food aid from the West. Britain's lawmakers cringed, but succumbed to the temptation to treat these outbursts as the harmless antics of loud-mouthed exhibitionists, and to argue that free speech was sacrosanct.

Paris had argued that the GIA's *al-Ansar* newsletter be outlawed. Whitehall replied that it could not do that. French agents complained that the past editors of *al-Ansar* read like a who's who of Islamist extremists. Apart from Abu Hamza and Abu Qatada, there were a couple of militants working on the newsletter who are blamed for two of the most devastating terror attacks witnessed in Europe. One was Rachid Ramda. Now thirty-six, he came to Britain in 1992 following his escape from his home in Algeria after police there linked him to terror attacks. In the summer of 1995 a GIA gang under his leadership assembled devices including cooking gas canisters packed with nails and bolts and left them in Paris's underground trains. Eight passengers died and more than 140 were injured, many of them maimed for life.

In raids in 1994 on suspected safe houses of GIA activists in Paris, French detectives had uncovered the telephone and fax numbers of London addresses that were passed to the British authorities, along with the names of suspects – including Ramda. The French claim that had MI5 and others acted on their information the Paris bombings would have been averted. Even after the atrocity on the Metro it would take Britain eleven years to send Ramda back to France to face trial. He was finally extradited in December 2005, and in March 2006 he was sentenced in Paris to ten years' imprisonment for assisting the metro bombers and acting as their banker.

One of his successors as editor of *al-Ansar* was a tall, red-haired Syrian who used a host of aliases. In London he used the name Mustafa Setmarian Nasar. Staff on the newspaper always thought he was built more like a weightlifter than a newspaper reporter. A skilled explosives expert, nurtured at a training camp in eastern Afghanistan, he was first sent to Spain, where investigators claim he helped establish the terror cell that carried out the Madrid train bombings in March 2004.

Al-Qaeda always made sure its prized assets left the scene long before the crime, so in 1995 Setmarian moved to London to assist Abu Hamza on *al-Ansar*. He was a product of bin Laden's finishing schools, where the training is far more thorough and sophisticated than some Western security agencies believed. A stint at an al-Qaeda camp does not just provide candidates with the facility to fire a Kalashnikov, rig a booby trap and recite the Koran. Bin Laden's agents were schooled in the tradecraft of a spy as much as any Oxbridge graduate joining MI6. The indoctrination was so thorough that it governed every aspect of a recruit's life. There were lectures on how to behave so that they could blend comfortably into their new surroundings. They learned the language and embraced local customs, even if by going to pubs and nightclubs it meant disobeying the Koran. Chosen men, such as Setmarian, obeyed their instructions to find a local wife, which helped them fit in with the neighbours, and also made obtaining citizenship much easier.

In the late 1990s many of these trained and dangerous fighters arrived in London to rest, recuperate or hide out. Shortly before 9/11 many were sent to the West to prepare for a planned wave of attacks across Europe. They arrived in London equipped with nothing other than the address of Finsbury Park mosque and the telephone number of a capable lawyer. The former would provide accommodation, money and fake identities; the latter was essential if they were caught. Abu Hamza was happy to shelter and assist these al-Qaeda envoys. He was busily cultivating a relationship with bin Laden's associates, and was anxious to provide funds and recruits for the camps. He could also learn news, tips and techniques from the camp veterans.

Bin Laden's men would also help Abu Hamza sift through the hundreds of young applicants at Finsbury Park who had ambitions to sign up for the camps in Afghanistan. Londonistan was the terrorists' preferred financial centre, and a safe and convenient logistical base. Bogus charities were set up to fund terror groups abroad, and leading banks were used to launder cash from the extremists' criminal enterprises. It would take the trauma of 9/11 to shake the City of London's secretive financial institutions into examining their books to track the terrorists' money trail. The Bank of England began freezing accounts, but al-Qaeda and others were a step ahead of them and had already shifted their assets elsewhere. They avoided the major banks and used high street money-changers to send huge amounts of cash to agents abroad. Pakistani terror groups raised around £10 million a year from British donors who thought they were giving to humanitarian causes in Kashmir, but some of their cash was being funnelled to armed fighters who included young Britons.

Communications networks were a gift for terror groups, who recruited computer experts to teach agents how to use code and disguise their electronic messages. Cheap internet cafés and international call centres were a new fad on the high street, making it difficult for intelligence agencies to eavesdrop on conversations or coded electronic messages. Even if they did, the law says this material cannot be used in British courts.

What foreign agencies did discover was telephone numbers

linking their suspects to well-known names back in London. Prominent among them were Abu Hamza and his mosque. His response was to argue that as a world-famous scholar and cleric, it was not surprising that any Muslim passing through London would want to hear him preach. He asked if the Archbishop of Canterbury knew the name of everyone who turned up to hear him deliver his sermon on a Sunday.

Judge Stephano Dambruoso, a leading Italian investigator, was astounded at how often Abu Hamza cropped up in his enquiries into the activities of radical mosques in Milan, but his repeated requests to interview him were politely declined by Scotland Yard, who explained that they could not force the ruler of Finsbury Park to talk to anybody, even them.

Scotland Yard received persistent requests from abroad to detain suspected terrorists or to investigate alleged plots. One from the Italian Secret Service (SISDE) concerned a plan to attack President George W. Bush during his visit to the G8 Summit in Genoa in July 2001, using hijacked aircraft. Italian agents claim this outlandish scheme was hatched at Finsbury Park mosque on 29 June 2001. The planners were closely linked to Abu Doha, an Algerian al-Qaeda operative better known to intelligence agencies as 'the Doctor'.

Pierre de Bousquet de Florian, the head of the French security service the Direction de la Surveillance du Territoire (DST), has called 'the Doctor' al-Qaeda's main recruiting sergeant in Europe. 'It is not possible to over-emphasise his importance,' said de Florian. Abu Doha was the 'principal catalyst' in setting up a network of North African Islamist terrorists in the UK which would spread its tentacles across Europe and North America. He was one of the first of the North African jihadis to embrace bin Laden's global vision. In 1998 he sought and was granted al-Qaeda's permission to establish and run a camp for Magreb fighters inside the Khalden training complex in Afghanistan.

In May 1999, with Khalden under the command of experienced

operatives, Abu Doha moved to Finsbury Park to take command of the rival Algerian factions operating in London and to increase the flow of funds and recruits for his camp. He operated with Abu Hamza's knowledge, and exerted a major influence over the conduct of affairs at the mosque.

A British judge sitting in the secretive Special Immigration Appeals Commission (SIAC), which hears sensitive terrorist cases, described the significance of the network that Abu Doha established: 'In Afghanistan he had held a senior position in the training camps organising the passage of mujahideen volunteers to and from those camps,' said Mr Justice Ouseley. 'He had a wide range of extremist Islamic contacts inside and outside the United Kingdom including links to individuals involved in terrorist operations. He was involved in a number of extremist agendas. By being in the United Kingdom he had brought cohesion to Algerian extremists based here and he had strengthened the existing links with individuals associated with the terrorist training facilities in Afghanistan and Pakistan.'

'The Doctor' had been arrested at Heathrow airport in February 2001 as he tried to board a plane to Saudi Arabia with fake passports in his hand luggage. A series of expertly made passport photographs depicting him in various disguises were found at his London flat, together with twenty credit cards, a telescopic rifle sight and what police described as other terrorist paraphernalia. His capture was a major blow to al-Qaeda's recruiting operation in Europe, but de Florian lamented that Abu Doha had been found 'far too late'. He had already put in place a complex network of terrorist cells around the Western world. Some of his 'sleepers' lived seemingly mundane lives in quiet countries like Canada and Ireland, simply waiting to be activated. Most of his men were trusted Algerians, Tunisians and Moroccans, but they also included a number of Britons who passed through the hands of al-Qaeda instructors abroad. The evidence given to SIAC listed some of the many terrorist plots 'the Doctor' is said to have conceived.

America was first in the queue of countries asking for his extradition, claiming that he choreographed the plan to bomb Los Angeles
airport on 31 December 1999 – Millennium eve. One of his team was
in custody in Belmarsh high-security prison in London, and United
States prosecutors said they had arrested another, Ahmed Ressam,
who freely testified about 'the Doctor's' activities in Finsbury Park.

Abu Doha's recruits planned to carry out synchronised bombings
on British, American and Australian embassies in Singapore in
December 2001. So many plots were scheduled for that one month,
investigators say, that had they succeeded the death toll would have
been far heavier than that on 9/11. He had also shown an apparent
fascination for targeting sporting events, and is accused of plotting
an attack on the Paris–Dakar Rally in January 2000, and before that
on the football World Cup in France in 1998. Schemes to attack the
Christmas market in Strasbourg were also considered. Later,
members of his group would attempt to make poisons and
explosives for an attack on London.

'The Doctor' is among the few who might reliably estimate how
many recruits were sent to train overseas. But even after five years in
a top-security British prison fighting extradition to the United
States, he will not say. The estimate given to the judge hearing the
SIAC cases in 2003 was that 'over a thousand individuals from
the UK had attended training camps [in Afghanistan] in the last
five years'. Some senior Scotland Yard officers, including the former
Metropolitan Police Commissioner Sir John Stevens, think this is a
modest estimate.

Throughout these SIAC hearings the names of Abu Hamza and
Abu Qatada kept cropping up, described as having 'played a vitally
important role in radicalising young Muslims and recruiting them
as volunteers for the [al-Qaeda] camps'. The sudden appearance
of young men with British links in training camps, mujahideen
units and terrorist cells around the world reinforced the image of
Londonistan as a fertile breeding ground for extremists.

One infamous graduate of the revolutionary fervour in London is Ahmed Omar Saeed Sheikh, a former public schoolboy who once harboured ambitions to represent his native Britain in the Olympics. He now sits on death row in an Islamabad jail, convicted of kidnapping and murdering a journalist from the *Wall Street Journal*, Daniel Pearl, in January 2002. Intelligence officials in Islamabad believe that Sheikh abducted the American reporter, but handed him to one of bin Laden's most valued lieutenants, who hacked off his head with a ceremonial Arab dagger. Sheikh has kept his silence rather than implicate the real killer, Khalid Sheikh Mohammed, who is accused of organising the 9/11 attacks and is now among a select band of al-Qaeda prisoners kept in secret detention by the CIA.

Whatever his role in the Pearl killing, Sheikh's parents are still unable to understand how he went from being a dutiful son to a terrorist. The transformation was remarkable. Like many who attended Forest School in Snaresbrook, an affluent suburb of east London, he was the son of wealthy Asian parents. After emigrating from Pakistan in the 1960s his father, Omar Saeed Sheikh, established a successful clothing business and sent his boy to a prestigious school where the former England cricket captain Nasser Hussain was a pupil. After a couple of years at Forest School Sheikh's family decided to move back to Pakistan, believing that Britain had become too decadent a place to raise children. They were troubled that Omar was hanging around with older girls, and disciplined him after catching him drinking and vandalising cars.

They enrolled him in the prestigious Aitchison College in Lahore, a favourite with Pakistan's elite, though at a local mosque Sheikh was clearly impressed by a gang of young men who stood up to the imams and argued for them to do more to help Muslim brothers being persecuted around the world. Sheikh enjoyed being seen in this radical company.

At sixteen he returned to London and to Forest School, where contemporaries noticed a dramatic change in his appearance. One friend said: 'He was obsessed about his muscular physique. He boasted how in Pakistan he had hijacked a bus, and was a kickboxing champion, which we took to be fantasy.' Some now thought him a bully and an attention-seeker. He would lie about his age so that he could enter arm-wrestling contests with younger opponents. The sport became an obsession after he saw his idol, Sylvester Stallone, arm-wrestling in the film *Over the Top*, and Omar would tour pubs in the East End of London, winning money in local contests. He once demanded that the school's headmaster present him with a medal he had won at one tournament at morning assembly, and was outraged when some of his classmates began jeering him as he made an acceptance speech. 'He had a desperate desire to be noticed. He wanted to make a mark,' a friend said.

Classmates remember the man who now portrays himself as a holy warrior as being interested only in impressing girls with his physique. 'Omar liked to hurt people,' one said. 'He loved to use his strength to show off.' His prowess as an arm-wrestler was such that in 1991 he was a member of the British arm-wrestling squad that came fourth in the world championships in Geneva, and his coach, Stephen Brown, recalls the boy's pride at wearing his country's colours. 'He talked of carrying the Union Jack at the opening ceremony of an Olympic Games,' Mr Brown said.

Teachers at Forest regarded Sheikh as a gifted and attentive pupil. George Paynter, who taught him economics, thought him 'pleasant, communicative and [he] had a jolly good brain'. Standing in the hall of the school he said: 'I can't understand why a boy who was in the system is now fighting to destroy it. He was a success here.' As well as being the school chess champion, Sheikh passed four A-levels, with two grade As and two Bs, and went on to study mathematics and statistics at the London School of Economics. Once there he showed little appetite for his studies, and seemed far more interested in meetings of Islamic societies who prowled the university on the lookout for willing hands. Desperate to get noticed, he stood up at

ABOVE: London was a home for many Islamist radicals in the 1990s. The Palestinian Abu Qatada was described by a Danish judge as 'al-Qaeda's spiritual ambassador in Europe'.

The Syrian-born Omar Bakri Mohammed ran the al-Muhajiroun group in London before going into exile in Lebanon after the 7 July 2005 bombings. He rivalled Abu Hamza in trying to recruit young Muslims to fight jihad.

Reda Hassaine, an Algerian journalist, risked his life to gather information about Abu Hamza and his associates for the intelligence services in Algiers, Paris and London.

BELOW: Abu Hassan (left), leader of the Islamic Army of Aden, who led the kidnap of sixteen Western hostages in December 1998. He was in touch with Abu Hamza by satellite phone throughout the hostage-taking.

t a remote spot in the Yemeni desert four of the hostages died after the kidnappers
sed them as human shields when soldiers mounted an armed rescue operation.

he Yemen kidnappings were staged in retaliation for the arrest of ten young Britons
nt from Finsbury Park to train for jihad in Yemen. They stood trial accused of
rrorist offences; second left in this group is Mohsen Ghailan, Abu Hamza's stepson.

ABOVE: Grenades, explosives and a rocket-propelled grenade launcher, all allegedly found in the British men's car, were put on display in the courtroom in Yemen.

January 2002: Mohammed Mostafa Kamel, Abu Hamza's eldest son, arrives at Heathrow airport after spending three years in prison in Yemen.

one meeting and shouted that all British Muslims should 'prepare for religious conflict because it will be here soon'.

Sheikh was delighted at the invitation to join a charity called the Convoy of Mercy on their journey to Bosnia in 1993, taking food and clothes to Muslim communities driven from their homes by their Serb neighbours in the former Yugoslavia. He writes of the anger he felt at seeing the body of a thirteen-year-old Muslim girl who had been raped and mutilated by Serb soldiers. Yet organisers of the trip remember that he fell ill as soon as they arrived in the Croatian port of Split, and never reached Bosnia. Sheikh simply changed his story, saying that he had met a Pakistani veteran of the fighting in Afghanistan, Abdul Rauf, who showed him images of Serb atrocities and persuaded him that he could be more use to the Islamist cause if he had arms training in Afghanistan. He obeyed, and after a short stay at the infamous Khalden camp he was sent to India to kidnap Western backpackers.

Never modest about his exploits, Sheikh would write in his prison diary about his first terror mission, which he called 'My Big Adventure'. He flew to Delhi as instructed and was told to book into a hotel until he could make contact with an intermediary for a Kashmiri separatist group, Harakat-ul-Ansar. Sheikh found it amusing, and somewhat embarrassing, that he ran up a £210 bill for one night in the Holiday Inn, where he registered using his own name and a genuine British passport. He befriended a group of English backpackers and offered to act as a guide on their journey to Saharanpur, ninety miles north-east of Delhi. Instead he led them straight to a house where gunmen were waiting. Several weeks later Indian police rescued the hostages in an operation in which Sheikh was shot and wounded.

One of those kidnapped, Rhys Partridge, twenty-seven at the time, described how one minute Sheikh wanted to play chess and talk about cricket and London, and the next he would hold a knife to his throat and threaten to behead his hostages: 'He told us how he would only kidnap people who he considered intelligent and wanted to spend time with. I don't agree with the death penalty, but if it was ever justified, this would be the case. He showed such contempt for the lives of others it is difficult to show any different for his.'

Sheikh spent five years in Delhi's high-security Tihar prison, until Kashmiri gunmen hijacked Indian Airlines Flight IC184 on Christmas Eve 1999 and flew it to Kandahar in Afghanistan, where they demanded the release of three top terrorists, the former London public schoolboy among them. The Indian government caved in and freed Sheikh, who was handed over to the Taliban and returned to Pakistan, where he joined up with the militant group Jaish-e-Mohammed. He also visited Afghanistan. Indian officials were appalled when they learned that Whitehall officials said he would face no charges if he wanted to return to London. The sympathetic handling Sheikh received only reinforced Britain's international reputation as a soft touch for terrorists, whether foreign or home-grown.

9

The Infiltrator

'Anything that hinders jihad movement, Islam will kill it.'

ABU HAMZA

'Perhaps we could snatch him off the street, kidnap him, take him to Paris and deal with him properly there.'

The remark stopped the conversation across the lunch table just as if a waiter had dropped a glass, smashed a plate or thrown water in a customer's face. Reda Hassaine peered through the fug of his own cigarette smoke at his French paymaster, trying to gauge how serious the suggestion had been. The silence remained unbroken, the word 'kidnap' hanging in the air between them. Hassaine did not know what to say, or quite how to respond. His job was to move quietly, unobtrusively inside the mosque, to write reports, to feed information back to Jérôme, the man he was now having lunch with on a day in March 1998. No one had said anything about snatching Abu Hamza off the streets of London.

Jérôme, the immaculate 'diplomat' from the French embassy, smiled at his companion's discomfort. 'Something has to be done. Chevènement says he cannot sleep on Thursday nights wondering what threat is going to emerge from London Algerians the next morning or what Abu Hamza is going to say in his Friday sermon. Paris is very anxious that they will threaten France again.'

Jean Pierre Chevènement, France's Minister of the Interior, had one worry in particular. The 1998 football World Cup was to be held in France, and it was a huge security headache. Algerian terrorists of the GIA had bombed the Paris Metro in 1995, and the architects of that atrocity were still on the loose, still regarded France as their deadly enemy and were living untroubled lives in London. The World Cup offered them an opportunity, and there were whispers in the intelligence world that something was being planned. It might only take a word from their spiritual guide Abu Hamza, an article in his newsletter, or a line in a communiqué pinned to the noticeboard in the hallway of the Finsbury Park mosque to set the wheels in motion.

Friday was consequently the busiest day of the week for Hassaine, a former journalist turned fledgling spy. On Fridays it was imperative that he heard Abu Hamza preach, made a mental note of any proclamations on the board and picked up a copy of the newsletter. There had been panic in 1997 when *al-Ansar* carried a GIA logo in which the three letters were arranged in the shape of a triangle. Was it a signal that terrorists were going to target the Eiffel Tower? In 1994 four GIA men had hijacked an Air France jet in Algiers and threatened to fly it to Paris and smash into the tower. The plane was stormed by French commandos at Marseilles and the terrorists were killed.

France was on edge. Such was her anxiety about the World Cup that she demanded cooperation from her European neighbours. Where she deemed that collaboration was lacking, or less than enthusiastic, she was sending her own teams of agents abroad to carry out the task of gathering intelligence on Islamist militants. Hassaine was part of the team in London, recruited by the French foreign intelligence service, the DGSE, to be their spy inside Finsbury Park's Algerian community and its mosque.

Hassaine had fled Algeria after the GIA killed some of his closest friends and threatened his life. He was motivated by anger and a burning need to see justice done. Although he was married with a young son, and the entire enterprise made him feel nervous and unsafe, some sense of righteous purpose carried him on, recklessly risking his safety. He had been working for the man he knew as Jérôme for several months when the idea of kidnapping Abu Hamza was lobbed like a grenade into a long lunch at one of their regular haunts, the Bangkok Brasserie, a basement Thai restaurant. This was, the Frenchman said, 'the ideal place' for their meetings. Located in London's clubland, the traditional haunt of spies, it was below street level, hidden from view on the corner of St James's Street and Piccadilly. No one could see in from the street. Jérôme insisted that he and Hassaine always arrived for lunch at 12.30 p.m. to ensure they got the table in the far corner, from where he could see everyone who came and left.

Hassaine finally ended the silence. He leaned across the table, and spoke nervously. 'How would we do it?' he enquired, fervently hoping that there would be no 'we', that this was something he would not have to be involved in.

Jérôme sketched out some ideas; clearly the plan was not at an advanced stage yet. Essentially it required taking Abu Hamza off the street. Sending a squad into the mosque, where he was surrounded by followers and bodyguards, was not feasible. He would have to be surprised. It might be best to take him as he left his house in west London; Aldbourne Road in Shepherd's Bush was a quiet street of family homes. Abu Hamza might have his sons to protect him, but there would be the element of surprise. And the hit squad would be armed. They would need a van, or a large vehicle with darkened windows. Then there would be a drive, a mad high-speed dash to Dover – maybe another, quieter port – and a ferry across the Channel. 'It would have to be a French ferry,' said Jérôme. 'Once we got one of his feet on board that would be it. No coming back.' Hassaine might not have to take part. His role might be to give a signal, act as a lookout, or create some sort of distraction at the mosque. The kidnapping would be left to the professionals.

Unknown to Hassaine, there were a number of undercover

French agents operating in London, and a team of assassins from Draco, a DGSE unit, had been placed on standby to take out individuals regarded as senior terrorists. The extent of the French operation in London has been confirmed by Pierre Martinet, who in 2005 published a book, *La DGSE: service action, un agent sort de l'ombre*, about his adventures as an agent. In 1997 Martinet was in London spying on a man called Abu Walid, who was allied to the GIA and was wanted in connection with the Metro bombings. Abu Walid, a Palestinian, lived with his family in Wembley, north-west London, and was a frequent visitor to Finsbury Park mosque. He was highly regarded among the jihad veterans gathered in London, who spoke of him in reverent tones as 'a fighting scholar'. To the French he was a possible target for their execution squad. Another DGSE surveillance team was watching the mosque. Again, the agents had been told that the purpose of their mission was to prevent any attack on the World Cup.

The problem hampering all the plans – assassinations or kid-nappings – was the attitude of the British authorities. Over lunch, Jérôme made it clear to Hassaine that while his contacts in the undercover worlds of MI5 and MI6 might be prepared to turn a blind eye to such an operation, there was unlikely to be any such help from the regular police. 'We might get some help from the British,' he said, 'but we will not get any help from the British law.'

In short, if anything went wrong, all hell would break loose. If there was an incident, a gunshot, if Abu Hamza was injured, if a traffic policeman stopped the kidnap vehicle – if just one thing tripped up, there would be a huge diplomatic incident. What the French were proposing was to kidnap a British citizen off the streets of London and take him to face justice in France. The scandal could be bigger than the blowing up of the Greenpeace ship *Rainbow Warrior* in 1985 in New Zealand. But such was the level of French frustration – from the Minister of the Interior downwards – with the British that all options were being countenanced.

As far as the French were concerned, the British had entered into a Faustian pact with the extreme Islamist groups assembled in London. They were free to organise, propagandise and speak, as long as there was no threat and no trouble on British soil. Abu Hamza seemed to enjoy a friendly relationship with MI5 and Scotland Yard's intelligence wing, the Special Branch. They called him regularly, invited him for meetings and were generally on cordial terms. He himself had been witness to the tension between the British and the French over his activities when he attended Scotland Yard after one summons. The call from the Special Branch officer stressed that this was not a British police matter. 'They called me and said, "Would you like to come to Scotland Yard, it's not about us or anything we are doing"; they said the French police wanted to speak to me,' Abu Hamza said. 'They told me I was a British citizen and I didn't have to answer if I didn't want to.'

Abu Hamza, who was at that stage offering the pretence of cooperation with the authorities because it seemed to allow him complete freedom to carry on his activities as he pleased, decided to attend. At Scotland Yard he was taken to a room where two French detectives were waiting to speak with him. A Scotland Yard detective sat in on the meeting, acting almost as Abu Hamza's protector.

The French officers were enquiring about Christophe Caze, a medical school dropout who converted to Islam and fought in Bosnia, where, it was suggested, he had met Abu Hamza. Caze had been killed in March 1996 near the town of Roubaix after a shoot-out with French police who had thwarted a plan to attack a G7 summit. A huge cache of arms and explosives was found, and the French authorities were still hunting for Lionel Dumont, Caze's accomplice. They would not find him for years. In 1997 they wanted information from Abu Hamza, and showed him pictures of members of the Roubaix gang. He said he knew nothing. They persisted with another line of questioning about al-Ansar's pages and pages of GIA propaganda. 'I told them that al-Ansar was not against the law in Britain,' recalled Abu Hamza at his Old Bailey trial in 2006. 'The main Frenchman was really upset and angry, he showed on his face he was angry. But the Englishman was very easy about it all, he said I didn't have to answer. At the end of the meeting he walked with me back to my car, he was smiling and chatting and everything.'

To French eyes, the British were protecting Abu Hamza and many more dangerous men in the mosque. After a few glasses of wine during lunch, Jérôme would often express his anger, and refer to the British capital – as many in France did – as 'Londonistan'. Hassaine said: 'Jérôme would complain that Scotland Yard was sympathetic to Abu Hamza. They would say, "They are doing nothing wrong, we cannot arrest them for anything." But the French believed that this plot to attack the World Cup was real, that it was being drawn up in London and that Finsbury Park mosque was the capital of Londonistan. The names of many suspects were passed to the British – veteran terrorists arriving from around the world – but the British did nothing. They did not take it seriously even when the French really got angry and told them that if anything were to happen in France they would declare publicly that they held the British responsible.'

In the event France thwarted the threat to attack the tournament. The process of unravelling it began with the arrest of an Algerian terrorist in Belgium in March 1998. The man had been convicted *in absentia* by a French court in connection with the Paris Metro bombs in 1995, and was subsequently jailed by the Belgian courts for nine years for attempted murder, criminal association, sedition and forgery. In the three months before the World Cup began, more than a hundred North Africans were arrested in France, Switzerland, Italy, Belgium and Germany as suspected terrorists. In Britain ten people were detained. The extent of the World Cup plot has never been revealed. Some sources have claimed that the key operation was to have been an attempt to assassinate the members of the USA team in their hotel as they watched the game between England and Tunisia on television. Others say the fear was a bombing campaign. Ultimately the greatest problem for French police was caused, once again, by the English, in the shape of their rioting fans.

As France's team lifted the trophy and sparked nationwide celebrations, the World Cup plot was best forgotten rather than trumpeted as an anti-terrorist victory. It was a happy moment too for Hassaine, watching from his flat in north London as Zinedine Zidane, his fellow countryman who was playing for France, emerged as the star player of the tournament.

Reda Hassaine had been born in Algiers in 1961. The son of a journalist, he followed his father into the newspaper industry, starting as a copyboy in the wire rooms of an Algiers daily. He was also a political animal, and in 1990 had flirted with the rising Islamic Salvation Front (FIS), which seemed on the verge of overthrowing years of corrupt rule that had beleaguered Algeria since the end of French colonisation in 1962. But his dalliance with the FIS was short-lived. After meeting senior figures in the movement, including its leader Abassi Madani, Hassaine decided that they were militant Muslims bent on turning his homeland into an Islamic state. Hassaine was a Muslim, but one who fudged the religious rules somewhat to enjoy life. He prayed on Fridays, fasted during Ramadan, but loved a bottle of red wine, a cigarette and the nightlife of his home city.

Life in Algiers changed terribly in 1992 after the military cancelled the elections that were set to record a FIS victory and bring the Islamist movement to power. Large sections of the FIS meta-morphosed into the Armed Islamic Group (GIA) and the country was pitched into an orgy of killing that would last more than ten years and claim thousands of lives. At the beginning, recalled Hassaine, the GIA had lists of its enemies: 'The policemen first, then the journalists.' Anyone deemed to be an opponent of the cause or a servant of the state was killed. State schools were burned down and their teachers shot dead.

Hassaine lost close friends and, fearing for his own life, moved to Paris with a plan to establish a weekly newspaper, *Magreb Hebdo*, for the exiled Algerian community. On 9 June 1993, a week before publication of its first edition, he was slashed on the street by a man with a knife and received a death threat. Afraid and with a new wife who was pregnant he fled back to Algiers. In December that year a more specific death threat came from the GIA, and Hassaine was placed under police protection. He became friendly with the officers looking after his safety, and when some months later they asked him to perform an undercover operation for them, his sense of curiosity and adventure kicked in. He agreed to travel to London in the summer of 1994 posing as a supporter of the GIA, and to make contact with another Algerian intelligence agent working undercover in London. On an evening in August 1994 he found himself standing outside a pizza restaurant on Lordship Lane, north London, waiting for a red Ford estate car to pick him up.

At the rendezvous Hassaine was handed a fax machine and a quantity of cash in a variety of currencies – money collected at London mosques – to be taken back to the mujahideen in Algeria. In return he passed over a false passport, which could then be tracked and traced. He flew back to Algeria, handed over his consignment of money and equipment and went home. Hassaine was deeply uncertain about the life of a spy, and concerned for the safety of his wife and newborn son. They decided to emigrate quickly, moving to London in late 1994 and taking a flat in an area where they had friends who had also sought refuge from events in Algeria. Hassaine sought the company of his countrymen in the coffee shops of Finsbury Park, and his reporter's instincts drew him to investigate what was going on in the local mosques. Abu Hamza had not yet arrived there, but other radical preachers were delivering their message of jihad and fundamentalism. There were also more and more Algerians beating a path to London; among their number were GIA fighters and gunmen.

Early in 1995 news reached Hassaine that Mohammed Abderrahmani, a respected editor, his journalistic mentor and a dear friend, had been murdered in Algiers. Abderrahmani had just dropped his children at school and was stopped at traffic lights when gunmen shot him. More than ten years on, the memory still brings tears to Hassaine's eyes. 'The following Friday I was in Finsbury Park, it was after prayers and a man approached me in a coffee shop who I knew used to be an influential figure in the FIS. I was having coffee when he said to me, "I remember you, you were a journalist, all journalists are spies and they deserved to be killed." Then he told me that Mohammed Abderrahmani, my friend, had deserved his fate. At that moment I decided I would become a radical. Here were my enemies, they admit it to my face. I decided there and then I would work against them. They justify what they do with a verse from the Koran, but they only cite half the verse.'

On his own initiative Hassaine contacted the Algerian embassy in London, and persisted until he was put through to someone who might be interested in the information he was offering. The man who eventually took his call said he held the rank of colonel. He was very interested in meeting Hassaine. They agreed a neutral rendezvous point, outside Holland Park Underground station. The colonel arrived in a sky-blue Peugeot, picked Hassaine up and drove him to a pub in Notting Hill, then still a fashionably bohemian corner of west London. The atmosphere between the two Algerians in the British pub was strained. Hassaine was a reporter, not a natural friend of authority and certainly not of army officers; like most Algerians he distrusted the military deeply. The colonel was suspicious about the bearded man who claimed to have information, but who might just as easily be an Islamist activist.

'Can I buy you a drink?' asked the officer.

'I'd like a whisky,' replied Hassaine.

The colonel was a whisky drinker, and appreciated Hassaine's choice on a personal level. But he also knew that a puritanical

Islamist would not drink alcohol. That simple exchange broke the ice, and forged a relationship between the two men that would last until the colonel – who Hassaine refers to only as Ali – left Britain for another posting.

'I told him I wanted to help and explained why,' said Hassaine. 'Sitting there in that pub he began to explain to me the cartography of the different Islamist groups in London – so many factions and groups and leaders, all of them living here without any trouble from the police. He asked me to go to Finsbury Park, to go to the mosques and coffee shops, to be his eyes and ears and to tell him what was going on. There were specific people to keep an eye on, GIA people. We met in Notting Hill pubs many times.'

When Abu Hamza took over the mosque in 1997, the Algerians needed to find out everything they could about him. They knew he had associated with Algerian mujahideen fighting in Bosnia. Since his return to Britain he had emerged as a spiritual influence over the GIA, and had been elevated to the top of its foreign network of supporters. 'I had to go to the mosque every day,' remembered Hassaine, 'to make myself a familiar face. I knew two people who were close to Abu Hamza, so if they were going to speak with him I would go too. If he was sitting and talking to a small circle in the mosque I would go and sit there too, on the edge, not participating, just taking in what was going on. He knew my face, I would say "*a salaam alaikum*" to him and he would greet me, but otherwise I did not speak. If I found an opportunity to sit and listen then I would sit and listen, but I did not want to give them any opportunity to suspect me. If I was with people that I knew and they knew, then no one took any notice of me. The talk from Abu Hamza was always the same kind of thing – about jihad, about killing, the life after death. He claims to speak about the Prophet and the creation of the khilafah [Islamic state], but over the years there is nothing really new in his words. The important thing to watch was the people who gathered around him; the faces changed all the time. People would come and go, come and go. They came from all over the world, spent some time there and went somewhere else – Kashmir, Afghanistan, wherever. And many of them would come back again. The mosque was a place of rest for them, they would return from jihad and start telling the younger ones about it, brainwashing another lot of recruits.'

The faces of the young men around him, clad in jihad chic of Afghan blankets or with their heads swathed in Palestinian scarves, would mean nothing to Hassaine until years later, when some of them appeared on the front pages of newspapers around the world. Faces like that of Richard Reid, who tried to blow up a transatlantic airliner in December 2001 with a bomb in his shoe, and Zacarias Moussaoui, convicted of being part of the 9/11 conspiracy. Hassaine saw others too – including Abu Dahdah or Yarkas – later convicted in Spain of masterminding the Madrid train bombings in 2004. But many of the faces he did not know, and many of the names were false.

To Hassaine it is not the whereabouts of the people who have become notorious that is important, but the details of what happened to the many hundreds of others who came and went from the mosque on their way to holy war and terrorist training. 'I was concentrating mainly on the Algerians – that was what I was there to do, and that was my personal cause. But there were so many others passing through, sitting at the feet of Abu Hamza and being told how pleased Allah would be if they gave their lives for him. Where are they all now? There were dozens and dozens of them much more dangerous than Richard Reid and who are still at large – names we have never heard of because their faces have never been in the newspapers or on the TV.'

After Colonel Ali left London in 1997 he and Hassaine remained in contact. They still met occasionally in west London pubs when the officer passed through Britain. But Hassaine was now being courted by the French foreign intelligence service. The Algerians had few resources to offer him much reward beyond a glass of whisky. By comparison the French were lavish. The restaurant lunches were accompanied by regular envelopes containing £300 in cash and the promise – never fulfilled – of French citizenship.

Hassaine initiated contact with the French in early 1997, arranging a meeting with the embassy press attaché in London and telling him he had important information about the 1995 Metro bombings. Within days he was meeting the enigmatic Jérôme, a moustachioed, smart-suited, carefully-coiffured Frenchman from the Mediterranean south who held a senior diplomatic post at the embassy. 'He wanted to know the names of everyone in the mosque. They showed me hundreds and hundreds of photographs. They seemed to have taken a photograph of everyone with a beard in London – even if you were an Irishman with a red beard they took your photograph. I asked: "Is everyone with a beard a suspect?" He said: "Why not?" '

Jérôme broadened Hassaine's remit. He wanted someone on the inside at the prayer circle organised by Abu Qatada, now based in the Four Feathers community centre off Baker Street. While Abu Hamza's giant mosque operated on a mass-production scale, churning out rookie martyrs, foot soldiers and identity fraudsters, Abu Qatada concentrated his efforts on a handpicked few. His associates were an elite hardcore of activists, and while Abu Hamza was busy forging links with the al-Qaeda leadership, Abu Qatada was well respected by bin Laden.

If Hassaine was to infiltrate this group, something would have to be done to increase his profile and boost his credibility. It was the spy himself who suggested he use the fact that he was known to have been a journalist in Algeria to his advantage. He proposed writing and publishing a pro-Islamist newsletter which could be sold at Finsbury Park. Jérôme agreed, and the French stumped up £1,500.

The *Journal du francophone* appeared for the first time in 1998, with its front-page headline reading '*Djihad contre les États-unis*' (Jihad against the United States). There was a colour photograph of bin Laden on the front, and the content was anti-America, anti-Israel and full of florid praise for the mujahideen and the struggle of Muslim peoples around the world. Hassaine's aim was to obtain advance copies of the communiqués from the GIA and its splinter group the GSPC – Salafist* Group for Call and Combat – before they were read aloud or appeared on noticeboards inside the mosque. They could then be passed to Jérôme for analysis, and might reach the ears of the Interior Minister before he spent another sleepless Thursday night.

The newsletter helped Hassaine have free run of the mosque. He was able to come and go, picking up on gossip, hearing Abu Hamza preach and watching the expansion of the extracurricular activities being conducted in corridors and office rooms inside the building. He saw false documents being ordered and traded, stolen goods offered for sale, widespread benefit frauds organised and credit card cloning taking place on a cottage-industry scale. Much of the money was being passed to mujahideen groups.

Despite his unprecedented access and his detailed reports, the French were becoming wary of Hassaine. The Algerian was a maverick, beyond their official control. Frequently frustrated by the lack of action against men he knew to be killers, Hassaine had made contact with Fleet Street journalists, and would provide the material for exposés in British newspapers. Paris's obsession with Finsbury Park continued, despite the thwarting of the World Cup plot, and there was a need to have a tighter rein over its agents there. The final straw came in the autumn of 1998, when the Algerian embassy appointed a new intelligence officer about whom the French were suspicious. They could no longer risk the security of

---

* Salafism is a very doctrinaire and intolerant strain of Islam. Its adherents believe themselves to be followers of the pure religion (see page 276).

their London operation by employing an Algerian agent.

Hassaine was summoned to the Bangkok Brasserie, where Jérôme was waiting at his usual table. This was to be the longest lunch of their eighteen-month relationship as spy and spymaster. Over six and a half hours and as many bottles of French red, they talked about the mess that London had allowed to accumulate on its doorstep, the daily tragedies in Algeria and the dangers that loomed if the Islamist phenomenon was not tackled. Had they been more significant men, it might have been a prophetic and influential conversation. But to anyone observing, they were just two doom-mongers predicting the worst. It was 4 November 1998. Two US embassies had been blown up in east Africa just three months before, in al-Qaeda's biggest show of strength to date. But those in power did not seem to have the resolve to tackle the threat.

'Jérôme told me he thought his bosses were making a big mistake, that they still needed me inside the mosque,' said Hassaine. 'He had argued but he had been overruled. At the end of the meal he reached inside his jacket pocket, produced a brown envelope and handed it to me. "This is for you," he said. I took it, looked inside and it was full of £50 notes. My severance pay, about £2,000. Then he passed me a sheet of paper which he said I should sign. It was a promise that I would not talk. I said nothing but I signed. He said: "If you should see me again, if our paths cross, do not speak to me. Please, Reda, keep your mouth shut."'

They left the restaurant, climbing the steps onto St James's Street and the gloom of a late-autumn night in Piccadilly. Without another word they walked off in opposite directions.

10

A Spy Unmasked

'Anyone who is cooperating and spying on Muslims is a legitimate target.'

ABU HAMZA

Reda Hassaine stewed for a week, infuriated by the abrupt end of his relationship with French intelligence. Then, fortified by three measures of neat Scotch, he marched into New Scotland Yard and announced to the receptionist that he had vital information for the anti-terrorist branch. The eager spy was asked to wait for what seemed like an age before two plain-clothed officers came to speak with him. He was led to a windowless interview room behind the reception area.

He told the policemen that he had been working in Britain for almost two years for the DGSE, and was in possession of information about Abu Hamza and Algerian terrorists living in London that might be valuable to them. The young officers looked somewhat perplexed. It was clear to Hassaine that he was discussing a subject they knew very little about. In November 1998 the minds of London's two hundred anti-terrorist officers were still focused on Irish terrorism. The IRA was on ceasefire, the Good Friday Agreement had been signed, but the Omagh bombing three months previously, the worst atrocity of Ulster's Troubles, was fresh in the mind, and the threat from dissident Republican bombers was still real. The officers promised that someone rather better informed than them would be in touch.

This was the inauspicious beginning to an occasionally bizarre and, for Hassaine, frequently frustrating eighteen-month relationship with the Special Branch of the Metropolitan Police, and MI5, the domestic secret service. Sometimes it seemed as if he was inhabiting the world of George Smiley – all secret drops and clandestine meetings – at others the set-up was much more Austin Powers. Not once did James Bond make an appearance. His meetings with Special Branch always took place at Holiday Inn hotels in central London, but never the same one twice in succession. He would be summoned to a nondescript rendezvous, perhaps a burger restaurant at Waterloo Station, a news kiosk beside Green Park Underground or a public payphone inside a post office. From there he would take further instructions by phone or would follow a man with a tweed cap and a copy of *The Times*, to whom he must not speak, on a circuitous walk around the streets. Always the meander would end at a Holiday Inn, where his handlers would be waiting in a room or having coffee in the lounge. 'They were testing me, checking that I wasn't being followed or that I had no one else with me, but it was very frustrating and, after a while, totally insulting,' said Hassaine.

Six months into his work for Britain he was passed from the control of Special Branch into the hands of an MI5 officer whose anti-surveillance techniques were either more rigorous or more ridiculous. Hassaine could not be sure. One call required him to be at Warren Street Underground station in the West End of London at 11.10 a.m. He was to wait for his contact to arrive and enter a telephone box outside the station. When the man left the phone box Hassaine was to nip in quickly before anyone else and pretend to make a call. Once in the box he was to pick up a cigarette packet that the agent would leave behind. Inside the packet was a photograph of a man and a piece of paper with a name and brief instructions telling Hassaine that this was a terrorist suspect who was thought to be attending Finsbury Park mosque. If possible, he was to identify the man in the photograph. 'It was like something out of *Mission*

Impossible. I was expecting it to self-destruct in ten seconds,' said Hassaine. 'It was just so silly, because sometimes the same guy would meet me in a coffee shop.'

Before relinquishing control to MI5, his Special Branch handler had asked Hassaine to sign a letter: 'It said I might face jail if I told anyone about the nature of my work for them. But the same letter said that if I was arrested by the police I was not protected by any kind of immunity from prosecution. I was so angry with them. I refused to sign it.'

MI5 offered Hassaine a £300 per month retainer plus £80 expenses for a 'six-month trial', and handed him a Motorola pager which they would use to contact him. It wasn't much compared to what the French had been prepared to pay for information; but then, the French took the threat of Islamist terror more seriously. Hassaine's MI5 contact, who told him to call him 'Simon', suggested that he supplement his earnings from espionage by claiming social security benefits. 'They said they would pay me something and the taxpayer would pay me something and that was all right and proper because, after all, we were dealing with the security of the country. So I had to apply for unemployment benefit and housing benefit. They said it would be a good cover story too, because everyone in Finsbury Park was foreign and on benefits.' Such remarks tripped frequently from the lips of 'Simon'. It wasn't his real name, and he chose not to use Hassaine's true identity either. The Algerian was given the code-name 'Kevin'.

Hassaine said: 'It was not a good relationship because basically he was a racist. He hated the Scots, he didn't like the Irish, and he detested black people. I always wondered what he thought of me, an Algerian, an Arab. He certainly never cared about what I cared most about, that hundreds of people were being killed in Algeria and that many of the killers and the organisers of the massacres had escaped to London. "Oh, what can we do?" he would say. "We can't stop them, there is nothing we can do." '

Even during 1998 and 1999, as the focus of activity at the Finsbury Park mosque switched from the conflict in Algeria, to ill-fated adventures in Yemen, to supporting the Taliban and recruitment of trainees for the jihad camps being run in Afghanistan, there was still no hint of alarm from the British.

Hassaine's tentative contacts with British intelligence had begun in November 1998, and were stepped up in January of the following year. Four weeks before, Abu Hamza and the Finsbury Park mosque had made national news headlines for the first time. Sixteen Western tourists, twelve of them British, had been kidnapped in Yemen in retaliation for the arrest there of a group of young British men who were accused of being involved in terrorist activity (see next chapter). These men had been sent from Finsbury Park after attending an 'Islamic training camp'; they included Abu Hamza's son and stepson. When the story broke there was a media clamour to discover what the hell was going on in north London. Who was the one-eyed imam with the hook, and was he really sending teenagers to set off bombs in Yemen? The authorities realised that they too knew little about what Abu Hamza and his supporters were doing in the huge redbrick mosque just off the Seven Sisters Road.

In late January, Hassaine was called by his Special Branch contact and asked to come to lunch. The venue, unsurprisingly, was the Holiday Inn in Mayfair. But this time there was a distinct sense of urgency and no sign of the cloak-and-dagger meanderings before they met in a hotel bedroom. Lunch and a bottle of wine were ordered from room service, and for two hours Hassaine was quizzed on every detail he could provide about what went on at Finsbury Park. He was shown a handful of photographs, but nothing like the quantity of film that French agents had expended in their months of surveillance. There were questions about individuals, about Abu Hamza and about other Islamist groups in the capital. Could Hassaine draw a sketch plan of the mosque, indicating the prayer rooms, Abu Hamza's office, the kitchen and dormitory areas? The British were, belatedly, waking up to the realisation that there was rather more than prayer and the odd rabble-rousing sermon going on. When they asked Hassaine to provide them with regular reports from inside the mosque, he agreed. In early March he was asked to pass over copies of all the material he had gathered – his daily notes, Supporters of Shariah newsletters and any other statements or communiqués he may have picked up.

A little over a week later, on Monday, 15 March 1999, Abu Hamza was arrested in an early-morning police raid on his family home in west London. More than 750 video and audio tapes of his sermons were seized in a search of his house, as were the eleven volumes of the *Encyclopaedia of the Afghani Jihad*. More immediately, however, the officers who arrested Abu Hamza wanted to question him about his connections with events in Yemen, specifically the sending of young men for terrorist training and his links with the Islamic Army of Aden. Telephone tap evidence showed that Abu Hamza had been in direct contact with the leader of the kidnappers of the Western tourists, four of whom had died in a botched military rescue attempt.

Abu Hamza and his inner circle had been expecting some reaction from the British authorities over the bloodshed in Yemen. Nevertheless, there was consternation at Finsbury Park. The actual arrest of their emir had not been anticipated. Hassaine's notes from the time record that the core group had gathered in the café area. One disciple claimed to Hassaine that Abu Hamza had always known he would be arrested 'because he must tell the truth'. Among many ordinary Muslims outside the Abu Hamza clique and gathered in the Algerian coffee shops along Blackstock Road there was cautious optimism that the police would now move in and clean things up in Finsbury Park. 'But someone told me we must wait forty-eight hours to see if he will be charged, wait and see.'

Without their leader, Abu Hamza's group became fragile and

fractious. Hassaine recalled: 'The mosque was their base, they thought they were secure, that the police would not interfere with them. They were jumpy.' The mosque's housekeeper, named by Hassaine in his notes as Toufiq, had also been the subject of police attention. He had been detained and questioned by police as he tried to board a flight to Italy. He missed the flight and returned to Finsbury Park. Another influential figure at the mosque was becoming suspicious; he told Hassaine that he had been shown Toufiq's photograph by police and asked questions. An Algerian whose real name is Rabah Kadre, Toufiq has since been named in secret British court hearings as having played a major part in establishing Abu Doha's Europe-wide network of north African terrorists. He would be re-arrested alongside Abu Doha in February 2001, but was released and disappeared from Britain for eighteen months.

Abu Hamza was detained in Charing Cross police station, central London. His rival cleric, the Syrian-born Omar Bakri Mohammed, organised a demonstration outside the police station which was attended by, among others, Hassaine. The spy put the crowd at just sixty people. He recorded that Toufiq and the group closest to Abu Hamza were present, but spent only a short time at the protest before returning to the mosque to discuss the crisis. Hassaine's contemporaneous notes state that after the last prayer of the evening, the group 'held a meeting with a man called Abdul Raheem, known as an adviser for Supporters of Shariah from the Balkans. It was very, very private.'

Friday, 19 March dawned with Hassaine hoping for news that criminal charges would be brought against Abu Hamza. Instead, around noon the cleric, reunited with his entourage of young bodyguards, swaggered into the mosque a free man. Far from being cowed, the imam delivered the Friday khutbah, concentrating on the need for parents to teach their children the principles of Islam so they might triumph in the forthcoming battle, which would be the biggest of all time. After finishing his preaching, Hassaine's notes record, Abu Hamza spoke about his brief period in police custody. 'He said thanks to all the people who supported him during his arrest. He told us that "they" [the police] have been very respectful of him, "they" know about Islam, "they" gave him the Holy Book in a respectful way, "they" gave him a mat to say his prayers and "they" told him to teach Islam ... "They" didn't want to hurt him or make him a hero. He told them that he said nothing wrong and he is just saying what the Holy Book, the Koran, said to the nation of Islam.' As he finished speaking a handful of people came forward to hug Abu Hamza and congratulate him on his release. But privately they were told that he feared the inquiry into him was not over.

Hassaine was disappointed, and noted cynically that the British might consider the arrest operation successful, believing that it would ward off the danger of Abu Hamza or his followers carrying out any operations too close to home.

Hassaine's assessment was not far off the mark. But what neither he nor many of Abu Hamza's followers knew at the time was that the cleric had been in close and regular contact with British police and intelligence for a number of years.

Special Branch, the intelligence-gathering arm of Scotland Yard, had been talking to Abu Hamza since early 1997, when he was still preaching in Luton. In the classified records of the meetings he is referred to by the codename 'damson berry'. Unknown to the police, MI5 had also begun meeting Abu Hamza at the behest of French intelligence; he was given the MI5 code number 910. Neither intelligence service shared its information with the other, each hoping and partly believing that it had persuaded Abu Hamza to become its secret informant. Both were mistaken. As he had duped the mosque trustees and the immigration authorities before, Abu Hamza was happily pulling the wool over the eyes of the spies with a sham show of cooperation.

Confidential memos of meetings between the imam of Finsbury

Park and his MI5 and Special Branch contacts reveal a respectful, polite and often cooperative relationship. There were at least seven meetings between Abu Hamza and MI5 officers between 1997 and 2000. In the official notes of those meetings, his handlers repeatedly make it clear to 910 that they don't want any trouble, and try and persuade him to tone down some of his more inflammatory comments. Abu Hamza listens respectfully and politely, but adamantly tells the officials that he is committed to jihad. But he helps them out with information, discusses the ideology of particular factions, divulges the odd name or salacious titbit about other Islamist groups. It was a successful tactic, diverting attention from himself onto other radicals, posing as a peaceful preacher while labelling others – his competitors in extremism – as dangerous. Occasionally he is also seen to ask favours – including the release of some associates who, he promises his interviewer, pose no threat in the UK.

The meetings with his Special Branch contacts usually took place in Abu Hamza's family home, where the police officers would be welcomed warmly into a room lined with books and countless pictures of the cleric. Abu Hamza liked to talk – couldn't stop talking – and these chats, always convivial and polite, could drag on for up to two hours. Abu Hamza's children, some of them still very young, tore in and out of the room, playing, squealing and asking their father who his visitors were. He treated them with kindly tolerance, and showed his guests hospitality and politeness. Sometimes one of his henchmen would be present when the meeting began, but he would be sent away – perhaps to buy pastries for the guests – before the serious talking began. There was an element of mischievousness in Abu Hamza's warnings about the activities of other extremist groups; he particularly liked to tell tales about Omar Bakri Mohammed's al-Muhajiroun organisation. But 'damson berry' is also said to have given concrete information to police which led to the detention of two terrorist suspects.

If a meeting with the police took place at Finsbury Park mosque the atmosphere was quite different. There was always a theatrical display of welcoming the officers. Abu Hamza liked to poke fun at his visitors as a way of reassuring and entertaining his followers. But any important talking was done behind closed doors in the imam's first-floor office. Some meetings took place at Abu Hamza's own instigation, including one at which he enquired about his personal security.

Quietly, Abu Hamza also took on board the message from the intelligence agencies, and began to use a little more cunning and restraint in his public speeches. The verbal assault on 'the Jews' was to be replaced over time by vitriol for 'the Zionists'. He would later say: 'I asked them, "My sermon, is it a problem?" They said, "No, freedom of speech, you don't have to worry unless we see blood on the streets." '

The files on Abu Hamza's meetings with his handlers make curious reading. The record of one conversation, on 1 October 1997, begins with a note that 'pleasantries were exchanged' between Abu Hamza and his MI5 contact. Whitehall had sought the meeting after learning of Abu Hamza's public breach with the leadership of the GIA and his condemnation of massacres of civilians by terrorists in Algeria. The author of the memo writes: 'Hamza is bowed but certainly not broken. For him the jihad goes on, if not in Algeria then somewhere else.' Crucially, the agent receives a reassurance that Britain is not regarded as a target. He records: 'The UK is seen as a place to fundraise and to propagate Islam.' The admission that Abu Hamza and his followers were using the UK to raise funds to finance terrorism overseas did not seem to cause a blip on the MI5 agent's radar.

On 20 November 1997, MI5 were back with Abu Hamza. Just three days earlier sixty people had died when Islamist radicals opened fire on a bus carrying tourists to the ancient temples at Luxor, Egypt. Abu Hamza's handler reminded him of his 'heroic condemnation' of the GIA the previous month, and wondered if he might use his position as an Egyptian and a man of influence among

Islamist radicals to denounce the murders at Luxor. MI5 were keen that he should speak out; it might help to calm tensions in Britain and further afield. But this time Abu Hamza was less than helpful. He told his MI5 contact bluntly that Egypt was under the control of a corrupt, Satanic tyranny, and repeated warnings that British tourists should not travel there.

In his sermons and lectures at the same period he went further, condemning the tourist industry and condoning the killing of children at Luxor. He told one audience: 'The tourist becomes like the Shaitan [devil] of all our countries now and it is not the tourists who are being targeted really by the Islamic groups, it's tourism itself. The industry is haram, it should be Islamicised.'

In September 1998, classified records show that 910 was once again in one-to-one discussion with MI5. They were concerned about reports of 'training camps' being organised by the mosque; but they clearly had no inkling of the scheme, then being finalised, to despatch a group to Yemen, or of the involvement of London-based Algerians in the establishment of a camp in Afghanistan with the blessing of Osama bin Laden. The author of the notes stated that once more he reminded Abu Hamza that in some of his preaching he was 'walking a dangerous tightrope'. Another agent noted: 'I informed him that incitement even to commit terrorism and violence overseas was fraught with peril.'

But if there had been thoughts of a prosecution against Abu Hamza over his words or actions, they faded quickly. Nine months after his arrest in March 1999, the video and audio tapes that had been seized from him – packed with the usual messages of intolerance and hatred, and culminating in exhortations to kill the enemies of Islam – were returned to his home. Also given back to him was his Afghan encyclopaedia. A decision had been taken that its hundreds of pages of instructions and diagrams on making bombs, organising ambushes, laying landmines and selecting targets – among them Big Ben, the Eiffel Tower and the Statue of Liberty –

were a legitimate thing for an advocate of eternal Holy War to have in his library. Scotland Yard did, however, retain Abu Hamza's passports and travel documents. The British policy would continue to be one of keeping him in Britain and keeping an eye on him. The authorities did not seem to grasp that he was far beyond their control.

Reda Hassaine continued to be one of those entrusted with keeping his eyes and ears open around Finsbury Park. But his sense of frustration with the lack of action against the jihadis had by now turned to one of betrayal. He was still writing his reports on Abu Hamza's sermons, the very documents which MI5 and others would draw upon to judge whether the cleric was still on, or had tumbled off, his 'dangerous tightrope'. Hassaine was also being used to try to turn a senior GIA figure who had been identified as a potential informant. He was ordered to befriend the man, help him with his benefit claims and find him a flat to get him away from the group sleeping inside the mosque. The association provided new information for Hassaine, which he dutifully passed on to his contacts. In August 1999 he told Special Branch that three figures in the GSPC – an Algerian terrorist splinter group which was now allying itself with bin Laden's ideas of global jihad – had arrived in Britain and were living in the outer London suburb of Edmonton.

That November he had further information that a group of Afghan Arabs, veterans of the jihad against the Red Army, had slipped into Britain on a flight that arrived at Gatwick airport from Yemen. Hassaine passed over names and passport numbers, and told his handlers that the men had settled in the Birmingham area. He was eager to travel to the Midlands to gather more information, but was told to stay in London.

Hassaine's anger was now close to boiling over. 'Are any of you interested in actually catching these terrorists?' he shouted at one rendezvous. Part of his deal had been that he would be granted the immigration status of 'indefinite leave to remain' in return for his work. Instead, in February 2000 he was handed papers in a hotel near Scotland Yard which gave him leave to remain in the UK for four years.

The journalist in Hassaine began to reassert itself. If the authorities wouldn't take action, he would. He went to Birmingham on behalf of the *Sunday Times* and supplied the paper with information on the jihad group assembling there. In early April 2000 the *Daily Mirror* splashed the story of a terrorist warlord who was collecting thousands of pounds monthly in British welfare payments.

Hassaine also began to renew his interest in the Four Feathers centre, where he had heard that Abu Qatada was preparing to hold special prayers and blessings for an emissary who was travelling from London to meet al-Qaeda leaders in Afghanistan. Hassaine informed MI5 about the gathering, and was told to attend the prayers at the Four Feathers on the morning of 21 April.

The passage of time has dimmed Hassaine's certainty about what brought him to the Four Feathers community centre, a squat little building off Baker Street, that Friday morning. Was it a reporter's instinct, or an informant's sense of duty? He is no longer sure. But he cannot forget what happened to him there.

Shortly after 11 a.m. Hassaine walked into the community centre, took off his shoes in the hallway and slipped into the room where Abu Qatada hosted his prayer meetings. It was two hours before Abu Qatada was due to preach, but the cleric was already there – a portly figure with a long, wiry black beard, sitting at the far end of the room surrounded by about a dozen men. They were murmuring in prayer. Hassaine stayed back, trying to look as if he wasn't intruding, yet straining to hear what was being said. He recognised the prayers and verses as incantations for a martyr or a warrior, someone preparing to lay down their life for Allah. It fitted. There had been rumours that Abu Walid, the same man the French had spied on and talked of assassinating in 1998, was going to meet bin Laden and would not be returning to London or to his family. Abu Qatada was quite unlike Abu Hamza. While the Egyptian raged and raved and poured fury into his subject, the Palestinian spoke with slow deliberation, as if placing each carefully chosen word inside the mind of his listener. Abu Hamza sought to stoke the fires of the weak and the wavering; Abu Qatada preached quietly to those who were already committed and firm.

As the prayers drew to a close, Hassaine became aware that one of the men in the group was looking at him. He recognised the watcher as a man was friendly with a Finsbury Park fixer, an arranger of passports, documents and benefits who had become suspicious of Hassaine. There was a nudge, a whispered word, then another head turned to look at him. Hassaine knew he was in trouble. If he ran now, they would get him. He continued to pretend he was completely wrapped up in prayer. Rising from the floor, he moved quietly into the hallway and quickly pulled on his right shoe. He was bent over, wriggling his heel into his left shoe, when a foot slammed into the side of his face. Off balance, Hassaine toppled sideways to the floor. There were three or four men around him, kicking and punching at him. He took a blow to the ribs and felt punches hammer into his back and onto the top of his head. Another foot connected with his mouth. His tongue tasted blood, and felt a loose tooth. He heard shouts of 'Get him, kill him, kill him, he's a spy, kill him.' Fear and adrenaline propelled him to his feet. He thrashed out with his arms, throwing one assailant off his back, and ran for the doors, bursting out onto the street and pounding down the pavement. 'They were behind me, running, shouting, but this was the middle of the city, there were people around, I was going to get away. I think if I'd not got out of the building they might have killed me. As I ran I pulled out my mobile phone and called "Simon". I was shouting, "I'm being attacked, I'm being attacked." He told me to go home. "Go home and whatever you do don't involve the police." '

Only when he reached home did Hassaine realise the significance of the attack. His cover was completely blown. Some of those at the Four Feathers were powerful men at Finsbury Park. Hassaine could not go back there. He had been exposed, and if he returned to the mosque, the coffee shops or just the streets of Finsbury Park his life might be in danger. He had a wife, a growing son and, now, a baby daughter too. His spying days were done. Two hours after he arrived home a Special Branch officer called him and suggested they meet at a hotel in Victoria later that day.

In the hotel bar, a shaken Hassaine drank quickly to try to steady himself. His handler had brought an attractive female officer along with him. What did that mean, Hassaine wondered. They had never introduced him to a woman before. Why was she there? In case he broke down? Or to soften him with a hint of seduction?

'They told me to keep a low profile for a while,' Hassaine remembers, laughing and shaking his head. 'Low profile. They seemed to have no idea. These men were killers, but that still had not sunk into their heads. For me it was the end. I had had the scare of my life. I thought that day that if I had been killed they would have put out a false story, said that I was a terrorist suspect or that I had been killed in a feud between immigrant gangs. Nobody would have known what I had been doing, what risks I had taken or why.

'These guys I was risking my life for – they hadn't arrested anybody, they didn't do a proper job. All the work I had done, all the risks I took didn't seem to amount to anything. All this killing was taking place abroad, but the British didn't give a shit that the killers were here in London. As long as nothing happened in Britain, then everything was all right. Abu Hamza was left to do whatever he liked, to brainwash, and recruit, and send people off to the training camps. I was telling the British this all the time. "This group is going to Afghanistan," I would say. "They're leaving on Friday, they have tickets to fly to Pakistan." And the only reply I got was, "There's nothing we can do about it."

'I wasn't surprised. When I began to work with MI5 I already knew from the French that they would do nothing, that they weren't interested in what was happening in London, the threat didn't register. They told me that they thought Abu Hamza was a "harmless clown", but I felt obliged to carry on with the work. I had started this thing, I wanted to pursue it. I later learned that Abu Hamza and Abu Qatada were both talking to MI5 and Special Branch too. The British must have thought they had these guys under control, that they were collaborating with them. Nothing could have been farther from the truth. Abu Hamza was busily recruiting hundreds of people, sending them off to Afghanistan, from where they were returning unnoticed and undetected to do whatever they like. Abu Hamza had this great big mosque where these people could hide, pick up a new identity, get money and support and receive the blessing of the imam for their actions. Seven days a week that place was producing recruits for the jihad. It was a factory for making terrorists.'

For a long time after he was unmasked, Hassaine stayed away from Finsbury Park. Occasionally on a north London street he would recognise a face from the mosque. The man might stare at him, then draw a finger slowly, in a slicing action, across his throat. In 2001 Abu Hamza was asked about Hassaine in an interview with the Canadian broadcaster CBC. Anyone spying on Muslims, he replied, was a legitimate target, and added: 'It's OK to kill them by slitting their throats or by shooting them. Any way you can deter them or others from doing such a thing.'

Fear changed Reda Hassaine. He lost his confidence and his determination. He split from his wife and went to live apart from his children. He says he thought they would be safer if they did not live with him. He now lives alone in a rented one-bedroom flat in north London. He sleeps too long in the morning, fights a losing battle against his tobacco craving and is quick to anger when he recalls the betrayals and failures of the intelligence services. In a cluttered kitchen cupboard he hoards the evidence of his years as a spy:

tattered copies of GIA communiqués and Supporters of Shariah newsletters, pages of original notes marked with coffee-cup rings, and endless documents piled into ripped envelopes and battered folders. The MI5 pager, never returned, is in a kitchen drawer. They make up a ramshackle collection of mementoes of dangerous days, the impact of which is never far below the surface. The mention of Abu Hamza's name arouses fury; the memory of the attack at the Four Feathers leaves him silent and withdrawn. Hassaine feels that perhaps he wasted many years of his life, years that he should have devoted to a successful career in journalism rather than a wasted one in espionage.

Seventeen months after he was beaten up by Abu Qatada's henchmen off Baker Street, Hassaine watched horrified along with the rest of the world as hijackers flew airliners into the World Trade Centre in New York. There was no doubt in his mind as to who might have done this, or what was happening. He knew the type of people who were responsible – young men brainwashed by fanatics like Abu Hamza and Abu Qatada. Somewhere in the back of his mind he knew he had been right to be angry, hysterical and emotional. At least, Hassaine thought, the threat would now be taken seriously.

PART II

His Chosen Ones

11
Kidnapping in the Desert

'The intifada started in Yemen when the people revolted, and do you know why it started in Yemen? Because the Prophet predicted a rise of the Aden army from Yemen.'

ABU HAMZA

To pass the time on their journey the tour guide was amusing a group of Western holidaymakers with violent tales from years past which had scarred this strange and remote corner of southern Yemen. It was 11 a.m. on 28 December 1998, and the desert highway stretching ahead of them shimmered in the haze of a pulverising heat. The party were eight days into their sightseeing tour of Yemen, and the driver leading the convoy of five minibuses shouted over his shoulder to his passengers that they were still 180 miles from the old British colonial port city of Aden.

A white pick-up truck with what looked like an old-fashioned anti-aircraft gun bolted on the back overtook the convoy, then veered sharply across the road into their path. Brian Smith, one of the sixteen holidaymakers, thought it must be a Yemeni security patrol. Peering through the window into the bright sunshine, he saw fifteen armed and masked figures emerge from behind a clump of trees beside the highway and begin firing in the air.

The fifty-two-year-old postal worker remembered that their tour guide had warned them at the beginning of their adventure trek that kidnapping was a risk of travelling in Yemen. Seeing the look of unease on his guests' faces during his introductory chat, he had grinned and quickly assured them that Western hostages were never harmed, and only held for a few hours while their captors sorted out some local grievance with government officials. The usual practice was that the hostages would be sent safely on their way with armfuls of gifts from their captors by way of an apology for any inconvenience they had suffered.

But events that morning took an ominous turn. The gunman leading the ambush, a small, wiry figure, his face hidden by a black scarf, wrenched open the door of the first minibus, dragged the startled driver out by his hair, then cracked him across the forehead with the butt of his Kalashnikov rifle. The rest of the drivers and their injured colleague were herded into the last of the buses while some of the kidnappers took their places at the wheels and the rest of the gang clambered onto the roofs of the vehicles. While all this was happening Smith noticed that a steady stream of traffic was trundling past without stopping. This was the one main road which slices through the mountain ranges on Yemen's southern tip. Locals knew it was not advisable to interfere in the tribal badlands of Abyan province.

The kidnappers had only driven for a couple of miles when their leader, Zain al-Abdin Abu Bakr al-Mihdar, ordered them to pull off the road and park within sight of a petrol station. The hostages were ordered to hand over their passports, and the gang's leader, who preferred to be known by his *nom du guerre*, Abu Hassan, seemed disappointed that there were only two Americans in the party. He carefully unpacked a portable satellite telephone, set it up on the bonnet of his pick-up truck and dialled the number of Abu Hamza's west London home. One of the tour drivers eavesdropped on the ensuing conversation in Arabic, and was struck by Abu Hassan's ebullient mood. He boasted, 'We've got the goods that were ordered, sixteen cartons marked Britain and America.'

At that stage nobody else in Britain or Yemen knew about the abductions. Nor did they know that Abu Hamza had received at least two calls the previous day from the veteran mujahideen fighter he first met in Afghanistan in the early 1990s. These early-morning calls to the cleric's home had not brought good news. Six members of his Supporters of Shariah group, sent to Yemen from Finsbury Park mosque, had been arrested by police on their way to carry out bomb attacks on a number of British targets in Aden. Abu Hamza's eighteen-year-old stepson was among those being held, as was Shahid Butt, his six-foot-four-inch enforcer from the mosque. His teenage son, Mohammed Mostafa Kamel, had evaded the round-up and was on the run; he was being sheltered at a mountaintop camp run by the kidnappers, who called themselves the Islamic Army of Aden and Abyan. Yemeni investigators discovered that Abu Hamza had sent the £2,000 satellite telephone to the kidnappers along with a bundle of cash, in return for the Army of Aden giving his hand-picked recruits weapons training.

By chance the Finsbury Park mosque was running one of Abu Hamza's £20-a-head 'training weekends' at which participants would learn about martial arts, fitness training and weapons – though the advertisements didn't say whether his potential recruits would get to fire a gun. There would be paintballing and parachuting, as well as seminars on escape and evasion techniques, map reading, surveillance and scuba diving. Abu Hamza would hector his young followers about their religious duty to train as 'warriors', and send some off to the wilds of the Brecon Beacons in Wales. But he realised he needed a more challenging environment than a glorified boy scout course, and Yemen provided an ideal setting. The high mountain passes were as forbidding as those of Afghanistan, and could surely hide a crowd of north London wannabe jihadis. The six who were being held in Aden's central security headquarters had gone to Yemen with the intention, say Yemeni intelligence chiefs, of becoming the first British terror cell.

Most of the SoS recruits hated their time at the training camp in

Yemen. The climate was brutal, the food inedible, and most of them complained that they missed their computer games and creature comforts. They got to ride horses, fire off several rounds of ammunition from an automatic rifle, and were instructed how to rig up explosive devices by men who had fought in Afghanistan. They were also taught what else they would need to do to kill hundreds of innocents in an attack planned for Christmas Day.

Abu Hassan was furious that after all the time he had spent in preparation, his plot to attack the British consulate and five other targets in Aden was thwarted by the clumsy stupidity of the men from Finsbury Park. The only way he could think of to get them out of prison was to snatch some Westerners and, with Abu Hamza's help, try to arrange a hostage swap. The first thing the cleric did after their conversation was to buy another £500 worth of airtime for the satellite telephone. Abu Hamza had bought the state-of-the-art phone six months earlier, about the time the first of his SoS team made their initial trips to Yemen. He has never explained why he purchased such an expensive gift for the Army of Aden.

Abu Hamza immediately realised that the abduction of a group of Western holidaymakers during Christmas week would grab the headlines at home, but he ignored the advice of his closest lieutenants to stay silent about his role in the unfolding affair.

At that time few British people had ever heard of Abu Hamza. Most imams in Britain spoke little or no English, and were not in the habit of appearing before the cameras. Abu Hamza was different. He turned out to be a publicity junkie. Some of his rivals, including his one-time mentor Abu Qatada, were appalled by his antics. They felt he was drawing unwanted attention to them and their own schemes to send impressionable young Muslims to fight in Afghanistan, Kashmir and Chechnya.

Abu Hamza refused to listen to their advice. Instead he tried to defend the indefensible by appearing on television and supporting the gunmen holding innocent Western hostages in the desert. Much of what he had to say in his strangled English about 'jihad' and martyrdom baffled his armchair British audience, most of whom at the time had never heard of al-Qaeda. Some of those watching his performance thought him eccentric. Most dismissed his violent posturing as an act to get himself noticed; but his television audience was not used to a preacher behaving this way. He would stab his hook at the camera lens as he issued bloodcurdling threats against politicians who did not heed his advice. His language was provocative, his demeanour threatening, but he had achieved one ambition – people in Britain suddenly knew the name of Abu Hamza.

The problem for him was that as events tumbled out of control in Yemen, his name became linked to international terrorists, and he was soon accused of masterminding the Christmas Day bomb plot in Aden. He railed against these charges, but his foray into Yemen turned out to be a public relations disaster. The British press vilified him after he admitted that he was the press officer for the kidnappers from the pompously named Islamic Army of Aden and Abyan.

Abu Hamza did not mention his own family connection when he gave interviews about the kidnappers' motives, nor did he admit that throughout this crisis he was in telephone contact with the kidnap leader.

As British diplomats and Scotland Yard officers headed for Aden to try to help resolve the situation, the authorities in Yemen did not tell them about the half-dozen men from Finsbury Park they were holding in custody, or about their search for Abu Hamza's son.

The plot might have succeeded, but for a stupid traffic offence. Shortly before midnight on 23 December, a white Daewoo hire car was spotted driving on the wrong side of the road as it approached a police checkpoint on the outskirts of Aden. Lieutenant Ibrahim Fitini Salem flagged down the vehicle and asked the driver for his licence. None of the three figures inside the car said a word. Lieutenant Salem then asked to see their identity documents. The occupants exchanged anxious glances. The driver snatched back the crumpled licence, slipped the car into gear and shot off into the darkness. The lieutenant ran back to his patrol car to give chase, but the Daewoo was already disappearing into the distance.

As the young, scruffily-dressed driver tried to negotiate a sharp corner he panicked as he suddenly found himself steering straight into a cluttered street market. The car collided with a parked truck, forcing the three men to abandon their vehicle, leaving the engine running, and escape on foot. Four hours later they and three other men were picked up in room 111 of the Al Wafa, one of the city's less salubrious back-street hotels. They seemed an unlikely band of international terrorists – a part-time shop assistant, a couple of security guards from Luton and Kingston, two students and a father of four who used to sell insurance in Sparkbrook in Birmingham.

Police claim that they found a list of targets rolled up in a metal container and hidden behind a dusty curtain in the hotel room. The plan had been to slaughter Western tourists in their beds with an attack on the Movenpick Hotel, fire rockets into a clinic in the grounds of Aden's only Christian church, murder British diplomats at their consulate building and party-goers inside the Al Shadhrawan nightclub, and attack the UN office in the city and a hotel used by American troops. Three of the Britons, including Abu Hamza's stepson, had a rendezvous with Abu Hassan in the car park of a petrol station to collect the materials needed for the attacks. Security chiefs produced for the television cameras the cache of explosives and weaponry they had retrieved from the boot of the abandoned car.

The SoS men denied all this, telling their interrogators that they had gone to Yemen to improve their Arabic, study the Koran and have some fun. The most vocal of them was the driver of the hire car, Malik Nasser. Then twenty-six, and unemployed, he explained how his mother had brought him to Yemen in July 1998, hoping to find a suitable wife for her feckless son. Friends remember Nasser as being fastidious about his looks, with a greater passion for football than the Koran. Though he was born in Yemen and had dual nationality, he had spent all but the first two months of his life in Birmingham. After five years studying information systems engineering at Westminster University, the best he could manage was a succession of part-time jobs as a shop assistant. His exasperated parents persuaded him to visit his ancestral homeland to keep him away from hanging around in pubs and amusement arcades.

The most intriguing figure was Mohsen Ghailan, a cocky Londoner with dyed red hair. Even his prison guards had to concede that he hardly fitted the description of a hardened zealot. When they invited him to pray, he told them he didn't know how many times a day a Muslim should say his prayers. Nor did he ask which wall of his cell faced Mecca. He just shrugged his shoulders and said religion did not interest him. What really fascinated the authorities was Ghailan's curious family set-up in west London, and his relationship with his stepfather, Abu Hamza. The cleric had adopted the boy, who was from his second wife's first marriage, but regarded him as a disappointment who spent more time playing computer games than studying the Koran. The trial of Ghailan and his fellow conspirators at the beginning of 1999 would reveal more about Abu Hamza's SoS network in north London, as well as his bizarre relationship with the kidnap leader, Abu Hassan.

What was apparent from the first hours of the hostage crisis was that the short-tempered Abu Hassan needed the advice and reassurance of his spokesman in London. After their roadside chat, the kidnap leader ordered his men to leave the main road and head north into the desert, bumping over a wasteland of boulders and jagged black rock that looked like the surface of the moon. Forty-five minutes later the procession of minibuses stopped again, and the bewildered tourists were forced to march for half a mile across the desolate landscape until they reached a hump of rock fringed by sand dunes that at least offered some shade from the remorseless sun. Drenched in sweat, the party sat huddled together on blankets spread out in a volcanic crater on the hard desert floor.

The kidnappers forced each of the men in turn to shin up the cliff face, where they were asked their names, their jobs and why they had come to Yemen. The only English-speaker among the kidnappers explained as best he could that they were mujahideen, then stunned his captive audience by insisting that they were nothing to do with the IRA, and forcing them to listen to his views on the Troubles in Ireland. Brian Smith said they did not know whether to laugh or cry. After the lecture on the IRA the entire party was marched back to the vehicles to collect sleeping bags and anything else they needed, though Smith said they were too nervous to sleep.

As darkness wrapped itself around the makeshift camp some of the gunmen brought the holidaymakers a meal of boiled mutton and bread, while their tour guide was told to explain to them that they were to be exchanged for some of their own countrymen. The bemused hostages had no idea what the kidnappers were talking about. They watched Abu Hassan pacing around, kicking up clouds of dust as he barked out his demands for a prisoner swap over the telephone to a half-brother of Yemen's President Salah, among others. He called Abu Hamza again, imploring him to alert the British government to what was going on.

Abu Hamza has changed his story several times about how he first befriended the wild-eyed Abu Hassan, but he was a master at attaching himself to foreign militant groups which he believed could advance his own reputation. He says both he and Abu Hassan were in Afghanistan in the early 1990s, when they were part of an international brigade of Muslims originally formed to resist the Soviet occupation of 1979. Impressed by Abu Hassan's energy and his ambition to turn Yemen into an Islamic state modelled on the Taliban, Abu Hamza offered his services as his fundraiser and mouthpiece in the West. He clearly had not been too successful in that job, as virtually nobody in Britain had ever heard of this Army of Aden outfit until the hostage crisis erupted.

Their thirty-two-year-old commander possessed a monstrous

ego, and saw himself as the only man capable of forging together the two halves of Yemen, which were united in name only after the country's most recent civil war, in 1994. He boasted to anyone who would listen how he had fought side by side with bin Laden against the Red Army in Afghanistan – but thousands of Muslims have made the same exaggerated claims, knowing that they are impossible to disprove. After the Soviet retreat from Kabul Abu Hassan believed his mission there was done, and he drifted home in the mid-nineties to set up his own band of holy warriors, which became a convenient magnet for fellow veterans returning from Afghanistan who had nothing else to do.

Yemen's suffocating security apparatus claims to have known all about Abu Hassan's antics at his hilltop headquarters in the remote Shabwa province, but to have dismissed him as an irrelevance. When in the spring of 1998 his group began issuing provocative political statements, the authorities asked members of Abu Hassan's own tribe to muzzle him. After that approach failed, the Yemenis offered a substantial reward for his capture – dead or alive. His name came to the attention of the CIA when his website praised suicide bombers who rammed trucks packed with explosives into the US embassies in the Kenyan capital, Nairobi, and at Dar-es-Salaam in Tanzania on 7 August 1998, killing 224 people and injuring more than four thousand. With relatively few US diplomats among the dead, President Clinton, embroiled at the time in the scandal of his sexual affair with a White House intern, Monica Lewinsky, offered only a muted response to the bombings. The CIA spotted that four Yemenis were among the suicide bombers, and decided to take a closer look at militants operating in that corner of the Middle East. The Yemeni government was happy to cooperate, particularly as it was keen to encourage the US military to use Aden as a refuelling base for its navy.

Before the kidnapping of the holidaymakers, intelligence officials in the Yemeni capital, Sana'a, had been compiling a dossier on Abu

Hassan's links in the West, including his fundraisers and supporters in Britain. They identified Finsbury Park mosque as 'crucial' to his operation, and allege that an emissary from the Army of Aden had been in north London addressing Abu Hamza's followers in September 1998, handing out recruiting leaflets and passing round the collecting tins. The emissary was greeted like a hero by his host.

Abu Hamza was happy to use his group's newsletter to support the Army of Aden, and in October 1998 the Supporters of Shariah issued a blustering communiqué warning the US military and other 'unbelievers' to leave Yemen or suffer. The language was juvenile and insulting, but Abu Hamza's SoS followers lapped it up. The next month's edition followed up with a 'revelation' that Marines from what he called 'the United Snakes of America' had been invited to Yemen on 'a secret operation to target Muslim fundamentalists in the region'. In a rabid commentary, he argued that the US force wanted to take over the Yemeni peninsula, but predicted that they would suffer heavy casualties if they tried: 'We see this as a powerful detonator for Muslims to explode in the faces of the Snakes of America. This will hopefully trigger a domino effect in the Peninsula. As observers have seen the more frequent explosions in the land of Yemen in the last four months, especially in the crude oil pipeline which is the blood for the American vampires.'

Infuriated by this rhetoric, Yemen's president, Ali Abdullah Salah, forwarded his dossier of allegations about Abu Hamza's interference in his country to Downing Street, claiming that the cleric had been 'planning and financing sabotage and bombings in Yemen'. The dossier cited a bomb attack in October 1998, when two soldiers were injured by an explosive device hidden beneath a donkey's saddle. Abu Hamza seized on this, and used his next newsletter to mock his accusers under the headline 'Yemeni mujahids send donkey to kill donkey officer'. The article derided the authorities' claims that they had arrested a suspect, saying that 'the mujahideen's donkey was too clever for them'. The dossier also detailed how Abu Hamza paid

£1,200 to the Army of Aden for each of the dozen or so groups of followers he sent to be trained in the hills of southern Yemen.

As the hostage drama slipped into a second day, the increasingly frenetic Abu Hassan was back on the telephone, screeching at Abu Hamza to make it known that the Yemeni authorities were not interested in a safe handover of the holidaymakers, but wanted to use this crisis as an excuse to kill him.

Military commanders had already discovered where Abu Hassan was holding the sixteen frightened Westerners, their guide and drivers.

The tourists were offered a breakfast of dates and tea at 5.30 a.m., while most of the gunmen lay around chewing mouthfuls of qat, a mildly narcotic leaf which looks as if it has been clipped from a privet hedge. Just after dawn the hostages spotted a solitary figure in traditional Arab dress walking towards them. Haythmi Ashal, a local elder, had offered himself as a go-between, and as sign of good faith brought with him tins of soft drinks and packets of biscuits.

Abu Hassan strode forward to meet his visitor, who towered above him. With little ceremony he sent him away, boasting, 'We don't need you. We have contacts at the highest level and we are expecting a response from them at noon.' The baffled sheikh bowed and left, barely glancing at the hostages as he passed.

Whoever Abu Hassan was negotiating with never had time to give their answer. Shortly before 11 a.m. Eric Firkins, a fifty-five-year-old chemistry lecturer from a Croydon college, heard the first gunshots, but peering into the blinding sunlight he couldn't make out where the firing was coming from. The kidnappers panicked. They were shouting hysterically and running around, without the first idea how to defend themselves and their captives.

In the distance some figures could be seen moving across open ground towards them. Firkins said Abu Hassan split the hostages into two groups to use as human shields. Firkins' group of eleven were told to stand up. 'I felt sure we were going to be executed, but we were made to put our hands in the air while the kidnappers fired over our heads at the troops. It was deafening.'

Suddenly one of the gang grabbed the youngest of the tour party, Ruth Williamson, a thirty-four-year-old health worker from Edinburgh, around the neck and stuck a gun in her back. She gently pleaded with her fellow hostages to stay calm. 'She looked scared, but she was so dignified, so courageous,' Firkins said. 'She was talking softly to the gunman as he made her walk slowly forward into the hail of fire coming from the army, but with this gun pointing at her. Then he just shot her in the back and ran. She was such a sweet, gentle, companionable girl. She was just laying there in the dirt on her back. Her face was as white as a sheet. She was executed in cold blood and shown no mercy.'

Firkins described how the rest of the group hurled themselves behind a narrow parapet of sand to escape the increasing ferocity of the crossfire. Without thinking they all grabbed onto each other, holding hands and praying. 'I was sure we were going to die. You couldn't tell who was firing or from where,' he said.

Lying alongside him, Brian Smith saw two more of the hostages shot. Barely five yards in front of him, Peter Rowe was trying to hold onto his wife's hand. Claire Marston was looking up at her husband's face as both were hit. Rowe, a sixty-year-old maths lecturer from Durham University, was killed instantly. His wife was bleeding from wounds in the shoulder and arm, but she ignored the pain of her own injuries and just kept talking to her husband, who was lying motionless. Close by, an American tourist, Margaret Thompson, had been wounded in the leg and was trying to crawl for cover.

From somewhere Mary Quin found the strength to wrestle with the gunman who was frogmarching her towards the advancing troops. Quin, a forty-five-year-old business executive from New York who born in New Zealand but had American citizenship, described how her captor was shot as the pair struggled on the ground. Although he was injured she feared he might still shoot her, so she grabbed for his gun. 'I must say I did with some relish kick him in the face and then stamp on his head,' she told her rescuers.

Laurence Whitehouse, a fifty-four-year-old sixth-form teacher from Hook in Hampshire, who was in the second group of hostages, told how the kidnappers screamed at them to stand still, and he felt the barrel of a gun digging into his neck. He couldn't reach his wife Margaret, and was trying to call out to her. Moments later Andrew Thirsk was shot in the thigh. The thirty-five-year-old backpacker from Sydney fell to the ground screaming in pain, and Margaret Whitehouse immediately dropped to her knees to try to staunch his gaping wound with her handkerchief, despite one of the kidnappers attempting to pull her back to her feet. Ignoring her captor's orders for her to stand up and shield him, she stayed beside the young Australian, who would later die of his wounds. Laurence Whitehouse recalls, 'She was talking to Andrew when she was hit in the leg. She gasped and she said "Bless me," which is the pet phrase she uses when she is cross, like when she misses a tennis shot. I tried to move to her, but another kidnapper clung onto me and kept the machine gun dug into my neck. Then I saw a bullet hit Margaret in the head. She was dead the instant it hit her. She never stood a chance. They wouldn't let me go to her and she just lay there, bleeding in the dirt.'

As the Yemeni soldiers edged ever closer, the surviving kidnappers ran towards a ridge of sand for cover, forcing Whitehouse and the remaining hostages to act as human shields and to carry their heavy machine guns. He was speechless at the kidnappers' incompetence. One tried unsuccessfully to load a mortar, then in desperation threw the launcher at the advancing troops. All the kidnapper had left to defend himself with was a small pistol. Whitehouse threw himself at him. He remembers twisting the hand that held the revolver, which went off, the bullet grazing his cheek and leaving a hole in the front of his shirt. He gripped onto his captor until the first Yemeni soldiers to reach them could pin him to the ground.

There was no medical team with the rescue force, and

Whitehouse, covered in blood and dirt, had to help troops lift his wife's body and the fatally wounded Australian tourist onto a van for the gruelling drive to Aden. Three kidnappers lay dead and seven were arrested, including their leader Abu Hassan, but at least as many more had somehow escaped across the open landscape.

The army denied that they had opened fire first, and Yemeni ministers insisted the assault on the kidnappers had only begun after they had started executing their hostages. This account would later be challenged by some of the captives, who were also upset that when they finally reached the safety of Aden, officials would pressure them to change their testimony.

Four of the tourists were dead. The injured, including Claire Marston, were taken to the al-Jamhouriya hospital, where British diplomats had been waiting for hours as a stream of confusing reports seeped back to Aden, leaving them unsure how many had survived the shoot-out. As David Pearce, the British Consul, waited for the wounded to arrive, he learned for the first time from Aden's security chief, General Mohammed Turaik, that he was holding six young Britons on terrorism offences. The details Pearce was given were patchy, but he recognised that his priority that December night was to comfort the bereaved and help the shocked survivors. The fate of the Aden Six would, within a few weeks, cause a diplomatic rupture between Britain and Yemen.

Laurence Whitehouse has long argued that Abu Hamza should stand trial in Yemen for his part in the kidnapping: 'We were almost certainly taken hostage to secure the release of his stepson.' He was appalled at public statements made by Abu Hamza justifying hostage-taking, and concerned about what he described as 'many young British Muslims unduly influenced by him'.

After Abu Hamza's Old Bailey trial, American prosecutors immediately announced their willingness to wait until he had served his jail sentence in Britain before they resumed their efforts to put him on trial for the bloody events in the Yemen. Whitehouse supports Abu Hamza's extradition, saying it would be justice for his wife and the others who died in the desert.

In his SoS newsletter number 7 in January 1999, Abu Hamza gave his rambling account of the slaughter, predictably blaming the Yemeni government for the hostages' deaths. He said that the army had not launched a rescue operation, but 'an assassination plot' to kill Abu Hassan, and claimed that after his telephone call with the kidnappers' leader the Supporters of Sharia offered to send a team of negotiators to arrange the safe release of all the holidaymakers, but were ignored by the authorities in Yemen and the UK.

Curiously, his next newsletter carried only a brief mention of the British detainees, and he still didn't mention his own relationships with the imprisoned men, all of them graduates of Finsbury Park mosque. The story of what these young Britons were up to, and the journey that took them from a north London suburb to a terrorist hideout in the back of beyond, would be exposed in two chaotic trials in southern Yemen that would dominate the headlines in the first weeks of 1999.

12
The Missing Man

'Look at the strength of the Muslim, why did it start in Yemen? Yemen is from the best of people and the Yemeni people do not neglect their arms.'

ABU HAMZA

In his palatial office, the size of a tennis court, the dapper figure of General Mohammad Turaik, who ran Aden's security regime, had no doubt who was really to blame for the deaths of the four tourists in the desert and the plan to kill hundreds more innocents in bomb attacks on Christmas Day. Splashing a pungent cologne on his cheeks, the General, as he liked to be called, could barely bring himself to mouth the name of Abu Hamza. Jabbing his finger at the thick dossier propped up on his desk, he was almost incoherent with rage that the man he held responsible for the bloodshed was giving television interviews in London, and not standing in the dock of an Aden court to face his accusers. Every few minutes his lecture was interrupted by the appearance of a timid official, bearing another document to add to the mounting pile of evidence that was threatening to spill onto the carpeted floor.

General Turaik kept bouncing from his chair to his feet and then back again as he emphasised that malevolent forces outside Yemen were responsible for the kidnappings. Most of those he was holding in custody for the murder of the three British holidaymakers and the Australian backpacker were Yemenis, but he insisted that their minds had been poisoned in training camps in the Afghan mountains by followers of Osama bin Laden. Ironically, outside the windows of his office were huge billboards advertising how a construction company owned by bin Laden's family was responsible for some prestigious new projects in what is Osama's father's homeland. While the world was still largely ignorant of al-Qaeda's menace, the group had already spilled blood in Aden. Six years earlier, on 29 December 1992, an al-Qaeda cell blew up a hotel being used by US servicemen, though the only casualties were two Austrian tourists killed by flying debris.

The General snatched a sheet of paper and began to scribble a map showing how al-Qaeda's tentacles were spreading across the globe. His line ran through the US and on to Britain and Finsbury Park. This was three years before the destruction of the Twin Towers forced the British authorities to change their minds about Abu Hamza and his ilk.

FBI agents and Scotland Yard detectives went to Yemen to investigate the murders in the desert. The General smiled and said he couldn't see the point of them showing up as his officers had virtually wrapped up the inquiry, but if they wanted to visit the murder scene and talk to the members of the Army of Aden he had in his detention cells, he was happy to oblige. That promise was never honoured. Over the next days and weeks, the visiting officers would find themselves restricted to hanging around their hotels. Requests to travel to Abyan to see where the hostages died were left in an in-tray. Suggestions that the Yard detectives might question the six men the General claimed had been sent from Finsbury Park to blow up British targets in Aden were ignored.

British diplomats found themselves dragged into the row. Ambassadors in both Sana'a and London exchanged harsh words over the tactics employed to free the holidaymakers, with Whitehall envoys making it clear to the survivors that they had not been consulted about the decision to end the hostage crisis by force barely twenty-four hours after they had been captured.

The first fall-out from this row was that Yemen's application to join the British Commonwealth – submitted in 1997 – was turned down. The then junior Foreign Office minister, Tony Lloyd, said on 3 January 1999 that Yemen had been rejected because it 'does not meet the entry criteria on good governance'. Yemeni ministers responded by arguing that they didn't care about this rebuff as they were withdrawing the application anyway, adding that they thought it was more of a priority for Britain to explain why it wasn't cooperating with their request to put Abu Hamza on the first plane to Aden. The facts that the cleric had not been charged with anything, and that there was no extradition treaty between the two countries, didn't matter to General Turaik and his colleagues. But the man they wanted, they couldn't touch.

Abu Hamza revelled in his ability to escape justice. By then he had sent followers to Albania, Bosnia and Pakistan for military training, his thugs had beaten up rival imams to seize control of their mosques, loyalists were running criminal rackets inside Finsbury Park, and he was behaving more like a Mafia godfather than a preacher.

His only genuine interest in Yemen was that he could use its forbidding mountain passes as a private training centre for some of his followers who were fed up with running around the hills of mid-Wales and camping in parks around Slough. Yemen was a place for him to advance his own reputation among a generation of eager young volunteers.

Prosecutors made sure that the first name the court in Aden heard when the British bomb plotters appeared for trial was that of Abu Hamza. They blamed him for everything, and he in return insulted them in his interviews with the British press. He could have easily ducked a media brawl, but that was not his style. Abu Hamza is combative by instinct, and revelled in his sudden notoriety. He invited cameras to the Finsbury Park mosque, and often disarmed his audience by chuckling and making jokes about some of the charges laid against him by the Yemenis, while insisting that despite his sinister appearance he was a peace-loving man. Moments later his anger would spill over and he would loudly curse his enemies, who ranged from the Saudi royal family to anyone who disagreed with him.

He ignored the advice of allies in London not to rise to the bait. Years later he conceded that the Yemen affair was his biggest mistake. He lost friends and credibility, and became a marked man by the security authorities in Britain. But his standing with young British extremists was boosted. Here was a man not just willing to talk about waging war on their many enemies, but taking direct action.

The spectre of Abu Hamza hung over the two terror trials that would run for the next ten months in southern Yemen. His name would crop up at every session, with prosecutors labouring the point that the real villain was not in the dock, only his footsoldiers.

First up was Abu Hassan. Hundreds of armed police cordoned off every road leading to the ornate cluster of court buildings in Zinjibar, the regional capital of Abyan, on 14 January 1999 for the start of his murder trial. The authorities had predicted that the evidence was so overwhelming that he would be convicted and sentenced within forty-eight hours. But the flamboyant Abu Hassan was not to be denied his chance to perform for the cameras. As he arrived in a prison van, crowded together with two fellow accused, the crowd which had been gathering since early morning surged towards the white-painted walls surrounding the court precinct. They climbed onto railings, roofs and telegraph poles, anywhere they could catch a glimpse of the man responsible for Yemen's biggest ever kidnapping, and the only one in recent memory to end in the death of Western hostages.

Manacled hand and foot, Abu Hassan shouted defiant slogans as the police tried to force him inside the court precincts with the butts of their highly polished rifles. A few in the crowd applauded him. Most just gawped. Breaking free for a moment, he screamed out, 'I did everything in the name of God so I am sorry for nothing. I am very famous now, but let everyone know I only gave orders to kill the men not the women.' He had yet to face a judge, but here he was publicly proclaiming his guilt and insulting those who were trying to bring him to justice.

Worse was to follow once the police managed to manhandle him into the first-floor courtroom. Abu Hassan shrugged off his escort and swaggered into the wooden dock like a prize fighter entering the ring. He stopped, looked slowly around the room at the judge, the public gallery and all the officials, then tilted his head in a carefully choreographed act of defiance and contempt.

On a raised dais Judge Najab al Khadari glanced nervously at the three armed guards standing behind him, then carefully adjusted the green sash that lay across his black robe embroidered with the scales of justice. Abu Hassan immediately set the tone for the proceedings by turning his back on the judge, and began joking with the elder of the two brothers who were the only other defendants with him in the dock that morning. Another eleven would be tried in their absence.

As the judge repeatedly banged his gavel and called for order, Abu Hassan swivelled around to face those sitting in the first rows of the public gallery, inviting them to ask him questions. Told by journalists that while he was having his day in court, thousands of miles away in Hook in Hampshire, the family and friends of Margaret Whitehouse were preparing for the funeral of the popular primary school teacher, he shrugged petulantly and said, 'That's not my problem. Why should I care?' Asked if he felt any remorse for her husband Laurence, who survived the hostage ordeal, he screwed up his mouth, spat on the floor and shouted, 'He means nothing to me. If my pistol had not jammed he would be dead as well.' Whitehouse had pleaded for the courts not to execute the terror leader, describing the death penalty as 'barbaric', but Abu Hassan pointed his finger at the judge, telling him: 'I am ready to die for my beliefs. If I live I will kill some more.'

Every time the troops surrounding the dock made a move towards the belligerent defendant, the judge wearily raised his hand, imploring Abu Hassan to listen to the charges he was facing. The accused's response was to fix him with a penetrating stare and shout: 'If you want to finish this quickly, then take me outside and shoot me now.'

The charges included training and arming the five Britons and an Algerian living in London to carry out the Aden bombings. At first Abu Hassan shook his head vigorously and said he had never heard of these men. Moments later he grimaced at the public gallery and told them how angry he was that these fellows had failed in their mission. He winked and said, 'Don't worry, others will come behind them. I have more to call on.'

Asked if he knew Abu Hamza and had spoken to him by satellite telephone during the hostage ordeal, he leaned on the rail of the dock, nodded slowly and said, 'He knows me, because I am very famous. Hamza takes orders from me. I don't take them from him.' The authorities would seize on this declaration as evidence of the link between Abu Hamza and this self-confessed killer.

Only once did Abu Hassan pay any attention to the judge, and that was when he was asked his profession. He stood up straight and declared: 'I am a mujahideen warrior working in the cause of God.' For the next forty-five minutes he harangued the court, extolling his own prowess as a guerrilla leader and lecturing everyone present on his interpretation of the Koran. He reviled his Western victims, calling them 'the grandchildren of pigs and monkeys': 'God sent them to us, so we took them.' By now in full flow, he recounted how he had only planned the kidnap the night before it took place. He had decided to lie in wait on the main highway and seize the first car that came along 'carrying Christians'. When a fleet of minibuses appeared carrying sixteen Western holidaymakers, he regarded this as a sign that God was with him.

His five-month trial was punctuated by moments of high farce. At one hearing he handed money to a policeman and told him to go and buy mineral water for everyone in the court. The judge sat open-mouthed as the officer did as he was told, and did not ask how a high-security prisoner turned up in the dock with cash in his pocket. The officer served Abu Hassan first with the bottled water, and while the police and public gratefully drank their fill, only the judge and prosecutors refused to share in this bizarre show of generosity by the terror leader.

The most illuminating testimony would come from outside the court, with the release of confessions by others in the Army of Aden. Some told how they had been arrested six days before the kid-nappings, which suggests that Yemeni intelligence services had prior warning of the bomb plot. They did not, though, alert any of the intended targets, including Roger Bruggink, the Anglican priest at Christ Church in Aden, or British diplomats occupying their consulate in the city, which was also on the list to be attacked. The other damning revelation from the detainees was that they had met some of the young Britons who had brought cash with them to pay Abu Hassan to train them. The first of those they allegedly identified from photographs was Abu Hamza's eighteen-year-old stepson Mohsen Ghailan, he of the dyed red hair.

From his cluttered first-floor office in Finsbury Park mosque, Abu Hamza laughed off suggestions from reporters that he had sent Ghailan to Yemen, together with his highly-strung seventeen-year-old son Mohammed Mostafa Kamel, on a terror operation. 'If I had sent them, I would have made sure they changed their names by deed poll. After all, it only costs £25,' he said as two acolytes sitting along-side him grinned. 'And I would have made sure they didn't check into cheap hotels. That's a very crude thing. It shows they didn't have any experience, no boss to tell them what to do. If I wanted to train them, I would have sent them to Afghanistan, it's much better there. My son didn't ask me if he could go. He knew I would have said no. There are enough people there to do any kind of job Abu Hassan might have been planning.' Asked how the pair had turned up there, he replied, 'They're hot-blooded brothers, they've their own gangs. Some of them are new to the Islamic path. They put down the bottle not long ago.' He even suggested that his young son might have gone to Yemen to get married.

Back in Aden, General Turaik was incensed that Abu Hamza's son still hadn't been caught. Tribal chiefs let it be known that emissaries from London had offered them generous amounts of money to get the teenager across the Gulf of Aden to neighbouring Djibouti by boat, using a notoriously busy smuggling route. Another apparently accepted cash to arrange for Mohammed to escape north to Saudi Arabia, but then changed his mind, and was amply rewarded by the Yemeni authorities for betraying the boy's hiding place. Abu Hamza Junior, as prosecutors took to calling him, was picked up during an armed raid on an Army of Aden camp on 27 January 1999. His capture came on the eve of the trial of the Britons accused of the Aden bomb plot.

A couple of days earlier the Yemeni president had written a personal letter to Tony Blair imploring him to send Abu Hamza to Aden. For all the public bluster about staging a show trial that would 'prove' the British involvement in recent horrors, the Yemenis were ready to do a deal to avoid a tiresome and costly prosecution. The kidnappings had seen tourists flee the country. Hotel bookings were cancelled, airlines flew empty into Aden. Far more serious to the economy was the damage the headlines were doing to an ambitious plan by Western investors to refurbish Yemen's creaking oil industry and develop the country into 'the new Dubai'. Jittery figures in the US Defense Department were already having second thoughts about using Aden's deep-water port as a stopover for its warships in the Red Sea.

One idea was for the five Britons and their friends held in Aden's main prison to plead guilty to charges of planning terror attacks, and ask for mercy. They would be sent straight home, so long as they testified in open court that Abu Hamza had orchestrated and financed the entire affair. The Britons refused, insisting that they would prove their innocence.

You could hear the defendants before you caught sight of them on the first day of their trial in Court One, which had been built during Britain's 128-year colonial rule in the image of the Old Bailey. From below the narrow staircase which led to the dock, the anguished cries of the defendants and sounds of scuffling echoed around the courtroom. Soldiers searched everyone, lawyers included, who was trying to elbow their way into the stifling room. The entourage sent over from Finsbury Park to assist with translation and living arrangements included one who three years later would be jailed by the US authorities at Guantánamo Bay.

The first of the accused to come into view was the enormous figure of Shahid Butt, hauled up the stairs in handcuffs. A soldier was kicking at his ankles. As the thirty-three-year-old former insurance assessor was shoved into the dock he called across to his brother in the public gallery, 'They are going to beat us and kill us for denying their ridiculous charges, so help us.'

Two of the other defendants wrestled with their jailers long enough for them to detail, in their broad Birmingham accents, the sexual abuse they claimed to have suffered during five weeks of interrogation. A soldier tried to clamp his hand over Ghailan's mouth as he shouted that every time he tried to sleep on the concrete floor he was kicked awake to face more questioning. He alleged that he had had bottles stuck into his rectum, and had been given electric shocks to force him to sign a confession. Malik Nasser, twenty-six, was slapped as he waved to his father who sat fifteen feet away. Sarwad Ahmed, twenty-one, a computer student from Birmingham, was hauled off his feet and bundled back down the stairs as he pointed to dark bruises all along his arms. Ghulam Hussein, twenty-five, a security guard from Luton, lay submerged beneath four soldiers who pinned him to the floor to prevent him touching the hand of his wife, Monica Davis, who collapsed in tears. The sixth suspect was an Algerian, who the authorities claimed was travelling under a number of different names. He had allegedly told his interrogators that he had obtained a fake French passport from one of Abu Hamza's lieutenants at Finsbury Park.

At the front of the court another contingent of troops stood guard over the prosecution's prized exhibits. Piled on a desk just in front of where Judge Jamal Omar was sitting were an assortment of landmines, bazookas, a grenade, fuse wire, detonators and a sackful of fifteen blocks of TNT, wrapped in red greasepaper and sweating in the cloying heat. This haul, said local investigators, had been recovered from the group's hire car, a hotel room and a villa they had rented in an affluent suburb close to Aden airport. In front of the display a senior officer propped up three audiocassettes plastered with the logo of the Supporters of Sharia.

The prosecutor's opening sentence was: 'This offence started in London in the offices of SoS which is owned by Abu Hamza and who exports terrorism to other countries.' All six men, still in the same soiled and torn clothes they were wearing when they were arrested on Christmas Eve, sat bewildered, unable to follow the early chaotic exchanges in Arabic. When an elderly translator appeared after twenty-five minutes he too struggled to keep pace with what was going on, and then caused pandemonium by telling the defendants that the prosecutor was seeking the death sentence. He wasn't. The worst they could expect was ten years in prison, but the mis-understanding brought more troops piling into the dock to lash out at the six accused. Defence lawyers threatened to walk out. Butt, a father of four, was screaming at the top of his voice, 'This is a kangaroo court,' as the judge threatened to expel family members who had come from Britain. Pleas to allow a doctor the relatives had brought with them from the UK to examine the six were refused.

This was not going the way Yemen's security chiefs had envisaged. Their attempt to prove to the world how a London cleric had masterminded their recent troubles was lost amidst the repeated fighting in court. After just fifty minutes of mayhem the judge adjourned the opening day and swept off the bench in disgust. It would set the pattern for the trial. Constant interruptions, endless adjournments, inexplicable delays and time-wasting meant the judge would not reach his verdict until the middle of August. Security chiefs in Aden resorted to a drip feed of incriminating information taken from the men's confessions. No matter that the defendants claimed their testimony was beaten out of them, their accounts supported the Yemeni allegation that Abu Hamza funded their operation.

The Yemenis lacked the sophisticated methods of the British government's GCHQ, the electronic eavesdropping operation which from its base in Cyprus could listen in on Abu Hamza's conversations with the kidnap leader. This wiretap material was useful to the intelligence services, who were trying to figure out what the cleric was up to, but it was inadmissible evidence in a British criminal court. The transcripts were shared with America's National Security Agency, and would be seized on by FBI agents, who argued that they had the right to pursue Abu Hamza as two Americans had been among the hostages. US prosecutors have made it clear that the bugged conversations from the Yemeni desert will be used in their prosecution of the cleric if they succeed in extraditing him once he has served his jail sentence in Britain. But Laurence Whitehouse and others among the bereaved do not want to wait for years to learn what Abu Hamza said in those calls, and are pressing for the British authorities to make the transcripts public.

The Yemenis also handed on to the FBI their 137-page dossier on Abu Hamza, which Britain ignored in the early weeks of 1999, though it contained illuminating details of what his SoS followers were up to in Aden.

Abu Hamza's team staggered their flights to Yemen, all of which were paid for by him. The men were asked why, if they had hotel rooms, the cleric's stepson had paid £1,250 in cash to rent a three-bedroom suburban villa, which used to house RAF officers in colonial days, and had then asked the landlord to erect a ten-foot-high breeze-block wall around the property. They claimed that more friends were planning to visit them, and they needed privacy in order 'to have some fun'. Mohsen Ghailan was driven around Aden by his captors until he identified this villa, close to the city's airport, which he claimed was for the group to study Arabic together. Among the material found there were videos of Abu Hamza's two boys brandishing Kalashnikov rifles during a trip to Albania. Yemeni prosecutors said they had gone there for military training. The pair claimed they were larking about in Rambo poses for their own amusement while on a charity convoy.

The further arrests made in January, including the teenage Mohammed, brought the numbers in the SoS gang to ten by the time the next session of the trial opened in August 1998. The Yemenis gleefully seized on supposed confessions from the two Algerians in the group, who were both travelling on fake passports allegedly acquired at the north London mosque.

Although Abu Hamza was fighting a legal action with his rivals for control of Finsbury Park, he chose to publicly rebuff the allegations seeping out of Aden rather than concentrate on his battles closer to home. He railed against President Salah's regime, and in a press conference on 20 January he called for the overthrow of Yemen's government. He also issued another communiqué on behalf of Abu Hassan's group, warning all Westerners to leave the country. In March 1999 his SoS newsletter published extensive details from lawyers of the abuse 'the Brothers' were subjected to by the interrogators, though he was still coy about revealing his family links among the accused. The detainees told of being roused from sleep and made to watch their friends being tortured, and to listen to them begging for mercy.

Ghailan claimed he was repeatedly sexually abused, had a gun held to his head until he agreed to confess, suffered electric shock treatment, and his legs, wrists and ankles were scarred and bruised. The others told similar stories, and described being 'trussed up like chickens' and suspended from a pole of wood for hours at a time. Shahid Butt said the men had been starved of food and sleep. He told of being given electric shocks by cattle prods, and relatives say he lost over three stone. Some of the young men who were squatting at the mosque at this time remember the imposing figure of Butt. Barrel-chested, with a long brown beard, he was seen as Abu Hamza's chief enforcer and one of his most trusted advisers. The pair could often be seen huddled together in the cleric's office on the first floor of the mosque, to which he was one of the few allowed entry. When Butt issued orders, few dared contradict him.

In his sermons to impressionable young recruits in the main prayer room, Abu Hamza would lionise the heroism of the so-called 'Aden Ten', and urge others to follow them. Some of the people in this crowd would later become even more infamous than the Aden Ten by volunteering themselves as suicide bombers. Abu Hamza was disappointed that despite his efforts to turn the Aden Ten's suffering into a popular campaign, there was little enthusiasm. There were no mass protest marches, no candle-lit vigils outside Downing Street. In the first weeks fundraisers did tour the mosques, and Amnesty International put its name to a petition seeking an investigation into the torture claims. But the fighting fund didn't reach £30,000, charities turned their backs, and lawyers fighting the case in Yemen had to be let go because there wasn't the money to pay them. Some relatives who took time off from work to attend the sporadic hear-ings in Aden claimed that they were threatened with dismissal by their employers, who had little compassion for the plight of their sons.

Yemen felt it was winning the propaganda battle against Abu Hamza. The authorities in Aden began to leak disparaging remarks made about him by his offspring. Mohammed was quoted as having described his father as a 'loud-mouthed windbag', which hardly fitted the accusation that the Aden Ten were impressionable young men brainwashed and manipulated by the cleric into doing what they were told, including murder.

Abu Hamza was finally arrested in the early-morning raid at his west London home in March 1999, and with his customary show-manship he complained about Scotland Yard calling so early, when the detectives watching his house must have known he was still in bed. Police took away files, computer disks, books and videos, but much to the disappointment of the Yemeni government he was released on bail four days later. The evidence relating to the kid-nappings was deemed inadmissible.

Undaunted by Britain's reluctance to deal with the cleric, the authorities in Sana'a kept up their verbal assault, indiscreetly letting slip that a squad of Scotland Yard detectives had shown up in Yemen to gather evidence against him. Abu Hamza goaded his enemies in return by continuing to release statements on his website on behalf of the Army of Aden and the crazed Abu Hassan.

When the long-suffering judge in Abu Hassan's trial delivered a death sentence on 5 May 1999, the curly-haired commander just laughed. Abu Hamza immediately fired off another press release warning of chilling reprisals if the sentence was carried out. It was, but not until five months later, when President Salah signed the execution warrant and Abu Hassan reportedly faced a firing squad an hour later. Strangely, the authorities have never confirmed how he was executed, and refused his family's requests for the return of the body for burial.

By then Abu Hamza was more exercised about the fate of his boys in Aden. On the SoS website he threatened to unleash his supporters if the Aden Ten were convicted, though he must have had little doubt what the outcome would be. The defendants knew what was coming when they were herded back into court on 9 August to hear the verdicts. They rained insults down on the judge before he could begin reading his judgement. Ghailan and Nasser faced the heaviest sentences, of seven years apiece. The pair simply grinned at one another. Nasser stuck up a thumb and said, 'That will do me.' Ghailan shouted, 'This has been a fix from start to finish.' Shahid Butt shook with laughter as the judge told him he couldn't prove he was planning to plant a bomb, so was only going to jail him for five years for being part of a terror gang.

While the rest reacted with similar contempt, Abu Hamza's son Mohammed looked the most distressed when he was jailed for three years. His mother, Valerie Fleming (who as Valerie Traverso was Abu Hamza's first wife), sobbed, 'This is not a court, it is a farce,' as she watched guards punch the teenager in the face. 'I didn't do anything wrong,' he screamed.

Every few minutes the judgement was punctuated by mentions of Abu Hamza, who the court was satisfied was deserving of most of the blame. That day his name, and not those of his followers, dominated the local headlines.

The cleric would continue to provoke Yemen's wrath with his regular diatribes against its rulers and his work for the Army of Aden. He claimed responsibility on their behalf for the attack on the USS *Cole* in Aden harbour in October 2000 which killed seventeen American sailors. He said the suicide bombers who sailed a dinghy packed with explosives into the US Navy destroyer as it lay at anchor wanted to mark the first anniversary of the execution of his old friend and their leader, Abu Hassan.

While the authorities in Sana'a conceded defeat in their efforts to put Abu Hamza on trial, they were willing to cooperate with others pursuing him, such as the FBI. When the US drew up its extradition claim against Abu Hamza it would call him to account for his alleged role in the kidnappings in the desert.

Richard Reid from Brixton, south London, pictured minutes after being taken off a transatlantic airliner at Boston in December 2001. Recruited to jihad at Finsbury Park, he had tried to blow up the plane with a bomb hidden in his shoe.

Zacarias Moussaoui went to Finsbury Park with Richard Reid. He is the only person to have been convicted in the United States of involvement in the 9/11 conspiracy.

James Ujaama (right), a civil rights activist who left the United States to become Abu Hamza webmaster in London. Ujaama wa involved in plans to set up a jihad camp at an Oregon ranch, and has entered a plea bargain deal to give evidence agains Abu Hamza in the American courts.

Feroz Abbasi was a computer science student from Croydon before discovering extreme Islamism. He was sent from Finsbury Park to train in Afghanistan, where he was captured in December 2001. He spent three years hel without trial in the US internment cam at Guantánamo Bay.

Kamel Bourgass, an Algerian who lived at the Finsbury Park mosque, plotted to make ricin, cyanide and explosives to carry out terror attacks in London. He murdered a police officer while being arrested in January 2003, and is now serving life imprisonment.

Detective Constable Stephen Oake was the first victim of the 'war on terror' to be killed in Britain. Kamel Bourgass stabbed him to death as he tried to escape arrest after being discovered in a Manchester bedsit.

Following the discovery of the ricin plot and the connections to Abu Hamza's headquarters, police staged a dramatic raid on the Finsbury Park mosque, seizing documents, computers and a cache of military material.

BELOW: Police search officers pushed up ceiling tiles in the mosque and discovered dozens of false and stolen passports, including these five Portuguese documents.

13
The Oregon Trail

'The first thing to do, number one, to be trained, to be trained of what you can do. There's no real need to go and train for tanks and aeroplanes, where are you going to find these, you can't buy these in a market, you can't make them yourselves. To be trained of what is available to you, this is number one.'

Abu Hamza

Pulling over Semi Osman's little white car had become a regular occurrence for the traffic officers of Klamath County in the American state of Oregon. The brake light was stuck. It glowed red permanently, and the newcomer, who was living on an isolated sheep ranch just outside the tiny settlement of Bly, had been stopped three times in three weeks since he arrived in this corner of the state.

This time, just before 6 a.m. on 13 December 1999 in Klamath Falls, an hour's drive from Bly, it was the turn of Officer Morrie Smith, nearing the end of his night shift, to stop Osman. The Lebanese mechanic and sometime imam was talkative and friendly – suspiciously over-polite, the policeman thought – but Officer Smith was more struck by the odd behaviour of the other two adult passengers in the vehicle.

The man in the front passenger seat had a black briefcase which he clutched tightly to his chest as Officer Smith asked questions. In the back seat another man draped his arm around a child, drawing her closer. All three men were wearing long woollen trenchcoats over combat fatigues, and 'ethnic headgear'. They had long black beards and brown skins, and when the traffic cop tried to engage the front passenger in conversation he responded in awkward, accented English. The thin-faced young man in the back seat did not speak.

Chattily, Osman explained that although his visitors were from London, England, they did not speak any English. They had been visiting Osman's family in Bly, and this morning he was taking them to the Greyhound bus depot in Klamath Falls. 'He said they were going to San Francisco, to do some sightseeing – but they sure weren't dressed for sightseeing or travelling,' said Officer Smith, now a detective in the Klamath Falls Police Department.

As another policeman drew up, Officer Smith walked back to his patrol car and radioed Osman's name through to the police operator to check against national criminal record databases for arrest warrants. None showed up. He cited Osman, not for the brake light, which had been noted before by colleagues, but for having an expired Maryland driving licence. Then Osman was sent on his way. The officer noted that he did indeed turn in to the Greyhound station.

Later that day, as he slept off the rigours of the night shift at his home, Officer Smith was woken by an urgent phone call. An FBI agent needed to speak to him. In person. Immediately. Smith's database check on Osman had triggered an alert. The Lebanese was on a Bureau watchlist, but had gone missing from his usual base in Seattle. That same day Smith had a long conversation with the FBI man at his police station. The agent showed him some surveillance photographs, including one of a group of men engaged in conversation as they walked down a street. Smith identified two of the men in the photograph as the passengers in Osman's car that morning. The FBI agent told him he had made the right call in not challenging the men in the car: 'He said, and I won't forget it, "They would probably have shot you dead." '

It was two weeks short of Christmas 1999, twenty-one months

before the attacks on New York and Washington on 9/11, and America was not on high alert for Islamist terrorists. Few people had heard of al-Qaeda or Osama bin Laden, and even fewer had heard of Abu Hamza al-Masri. But intelligence channels had been buzzing. British security services wondered why a man whose activities they monitored continually was making telephone calls from his office in the Finsbury Park mosque to a number in a little place called Bly in Oregon. A British official had called the Klamath County sheriff's department in November 1999, asking for information about the ranch where the telephone number was registered. Their curiosity pricked, the local police flew over the ranch and sent a detective to take photographs; but nothing of significance was sighted.

Had Klamath County's finest probed a little further, they might have begun to unravel the story of one of the more curious schemes to be hatched at Finsbury Park mosque. The brains behind the plan – which was to establish an Afghan-style guerrilla training camp in the United States – was perhaps the most unlikely holy warrior to emerge from north London's terrorist base.

James Ujaama was a young black American civil rights activist who had been born James Earnest Thompson in Denver, Colorado, but changed his name when he converted to Islam in the early 1990s. His work as a community activist brought him local fame and much praise. Seattle awarded him the key to the city, and 10 June 1994 was declared James Ujaama Day by the Washington state authorities. Ujaama liked to describe himself as an entrepreneur, and had written and published several self-help manuals, including one entitled *The Young People's Guide to Starting a Business Without Selling Drugs*.

But Ujaama was never contented; his restless search for solutions to the problems of the underdog somehow led him to the revolutionary Islam preached by extremists like Abu Hamza. He told acquaintances in London that he moved there after seeing a television news report of fighting between members of Supporters of Shariah and Russian journalists at a press conference on Chechnya.

He arrived in England in early 1999, headed straight for Finsbury Park and quickly became a part of Abu Hamza's inner circle. During his years in London he married a Somali refugee, had a daughter and took a number of aliases, or kunyas, including Abu Samayya and Bilal Ahmed. He is remembered as being arrogant but bursting with ideas and energy. Some at the mosque were deeply suspicious of the loud American. But he pledged bayat to Abu Hamza, and the imam warmed to him.

Ujaama was unlikely ever to be much use as a warrior, although he did go to Afghanistan a number of times and may have had training in the camps. But he had other uses. He had an American passport, and could travel widely without hindrance; during a three-year period when he had no identifiable source of income he travelled between the United States and London on eleven occasions. The purpose of one trip, it is alleged, was to raise money for Finsbury Park from US mosques. But the journey that most concerned the American authorities was the one Ujaama made in the autumn of 1999, when he flew from Heathrow to inspect the 160 acres of land in the Oregon back country where his old friend Semi Osman had set up home.

Osman, the imam of a back-street mosque in Seattle, had moved to the remote ranch after a friend of his wife started a relationship with the sheep farmer who owned the land. The ranch was on the edge of the snowline, and Osman's little saloon car was forever getting stuck in mud. Nevertheless he was enjoying the rugged life, and invited his friends from Seattle to visit. Ujaama arrived in October 1999, and became almost childishly excited at the possibilities offered by the ranch. From a Kinko's copy bureau in Tukwila, Seattle, he hurriedly sent a fax to Abu Hamza in London, proposing that the ranch be used to establish a training camp. Ujaama said that he and his associates were stockpiling weapons and ammunition. According to his description the terrain and surroundings at Bly looked 'just like Afghanistan'. Oregon was also the ideal place for a camp because it was 'a pro-militia and firearms state'. The camp would offer training in 'archery, combat, and martial arts, and rifle and handgun handling'. Ujaama appealed to Abu Hamza to come and live in Bly, where he could command the camp and would be safe from the kuffar, who would not be able to remove him 'without a serious armed fight'.

Ujaama enthused: 'We can build a big following and practise our deen [religion] to the fullest, even taking some of the external pressure off the backs of our brothers abroad.' He asked Abu Hamza to send 'two brothers' to inspect the camp, quoting a price of £616 for their air fares. 'We would hope that they can help us in raising money and preparing a program for Muslims that is consistent with our ultimate aim and objective or number one duty today in Islam on these lands.'

The idea appealed to Abu Hamza and the 'brothers' at Finsbury Park, who were desperate to find somewhere to train British recruits, legally, in the use of firearms. Following the debacle in Yemen, and given the inadequacy and the cost of survivalist weekends in Wales, Oregon seemed to offer a relaxed approach to firearms, and would present no language barriers. Not long after the fax arrived at the mosque, a London-based website began advertising a two-week training camp in the United States. The website stated: 'The Ultimate Jihad Challenge is a two-week course in our 1,000-acre state of the art shooting range in the United States. Due to the firearms law of the UK all serious firearms training must be done overseas. The course emphasis is on practical live fire training.' It stated that instructors would offer instruction in tactical ambush, cover and concealment, and night and dim-light shooting.

When Osman was arrested in 2002 on a firearms charge, his home and car were thoroughly searched. Among his possessions police found an Abu Hamza video entitled *The Importance of Training*, a range of military books and pamphlets, and three weapons – including a Chinese-made assault rifle and a Smith & Wesson semi-automatic handgun. Equally interesting was a clumsily-worded document which amounted to a syllabus for the training camp. It began: 'This training program is intended to train and prepare soldiers for combat situations in both wooded and built-up areas. The training will last 15 weeks, three days per week and occasional weekend when specified by instructor.' A programme of physical training, navigation, survival skills, marksmanship and reconnaissance courses was outlined. Much of the training would take place at night. The paper concluded: 'It is my firm belief that soldiers that is trained to use his senses and skills at night can be more effective and efficient at his missions. This is the basics of readiness, there are more training available but will require more time and effort.'

With such a programme apparently prepared, expectations were high in London. On 26 November 1999 Abu Hamza despatched two emissaries from Finsbury Park mosque to check out Ujaama's plan. Carrying £4,000 from mosque funds, they flew from London to John F. Kennedy airport, New York, on an Air India flight, then travelled west by Greyhound bus, stopping overnight at a mosque in Chicago, to Seattle, where they were met by Ujaama, who took them by car to the Oregon ranch.

The FBI has since identified the two men as Oussama Abdullah Kassir (aka Abu Khadijah), a Swedish citizen of Lebanese origin and a dedicated disciple of Abu Hamza, and Haroon Rashid Aswat, from Dewsbury, Yorkshire. They were the two passengers in Osman's car when it was stopped by Officer Morrie Smith in Klamath Falls.

Kassir, who boasted of being an al-Qaeda assassin, was to be arrested in December 2005 at Prague airport, in the Czech Republic, when a flight from Stockholm to Beirut made a scheduled stop. Czech police detained him on the basis of an international arrest warrant, and the US has lodged a request for his extradition, although he maintains his innocence of any wrongdoing.

Aswat is an altogether more curious character. His presence in Oregon indicates just how seriously Abu Hamza took the plan to build a jihad camp in the United States. Aswat was the favoured son among Abu Hamza's aides. He was intelligent, energetic and dedicated, and had shown promise as a Koranic scholar. His fervent interest in radical Islam took him from Dewsbury in Yorkshire to London, where he took up residence in the Finsbury Park mosque. He quickly became a trusted aide to Abu Hamza, acting as his spokesman and running the day-to-day affairs of the mosque, and was regularly seen at his side. His movements in the years after his American adventure are uncertain. His family in Yorkshire lost contact with him, and in 2004 the US authorities reported in legal documents that he was believed to have been killed in fighting in Afghanistan in late 2001.

But Aswat was alive. In the immediate aftermath of the 7 July 2005 suicide bombings in London his name cropped up again, and was circulated to authorities around the world. He hailed from the same town where Mohammed Sidique Khan, ringleader of the 7/7 bombers, lived. Khan is known to have arrived at Finsbury Park mosque in late 2002, carrying a letter of introduction addressed to Aswat. There was widespread speculation that Aswat had masterminded the London bombings. His name was the first one given by the British authorities to Pakistan as they searched for the brains behind the attacks. But when he was finally found and arrested in the southern African state of Zambia at the end of July 2005 and deported to Britain, he was not charged with any role in the bombings. Instead, a day after he landed at the RAF airfield at Northolt, west of London, in a private jet, accompanied by two Scotland Yard officers, the United States requested his extradition to America to answer charges concerning his activities in Klamath County, Oregon, back in 1999. He now features as Abu Hamza's co-defendant on an eleven-count US federal indictment.

A criminal complaint against Kassir, accusing him of involvement in the Bly conspiracy, was unsealed following his arrest in Prague. The case papers detail some of the activities of Aswat and Kassir at the Bly ranch in the fortnight before their car was stopped in Klamath Falls.

It had not been a good trip. From the very start things began to go wrong. On the night the party arrived at Bly, Ujaama did not have a key to unlock the gate of the ranch. In an affidavit, FBI Special Agent Fernando Gutierrez stated: 'According to an individual who was present, Ujaama personally drove two of Abu Hamza's representatives, Oussama Abdullah Kassir and Aswat Haroon Rashid, to the Bly training camp. This individual stated that Kassir was visibly angry because the camp was less than he expected. In particular Kassir noted the lack of barracks for prospective trainees and pointed to a piece of paper detailing what was promised, clearly discerning what was not readily in place.' The official US criminal complaint states further that Kassir grumbled to a witness that 'there were only a few men available to train at the jihad training camp, and that he was not going to waste his time with such a small number of men, and that the facilities and supplies were inadequate'.

Things were worse than inadequate. Osman and his wife Angelica were living in a trailer on the ranch, and the other accommodation consisted of a ramshackle collection of battered old trailers. Meals were to be eaten in another rat-infested trailer. There were no other facilities. The arrivals from London disliked the idea of shopping at Bly's one and only store, so the aspiring mujahideen eked out the meagre food supplies by shooting quail, rabbits and even robins for the pot.

In lengthy interviews with the FBI, Angelica Osman has given details of the activities that went on at Bly. There were some fifteen men from the Seattle mosque where her husband preached his brand of radical Islam, all of them equipped with automatic weapons. The talk was of jihad and 'hatred of the Jews'. The two arrivals from London were looked up to as leaders and instructors. A witness has testified that Kassir described himself as 'a hit man' for Abu Hamza and Osama bin Laden and boasted of having had jihad training in

Afghanistan, Kashmir and Lebanon. Mrs Osman said that while at the ranch Kassir 'carried a rifle slung over his shoulder. Later, while staying at Semi Osman's mosque in Seattle he was observed carrying a pistol.'

Aswat and Kassir are said to have instituted a strict regime at the ranch. They interviewed potential recruits, established a security detail with a rota for guard patrols and the use of passwords. A hand-painted sign erected at the entrance to the land said in red letters: 'What U say or do is recorded'. Firearms training and target practice were the main activities. A lot of trees and rocks were shot up, and FBI agents who later visited the site were surprised at the quantity of empty cartridge shells. Recruits were shown jihadi videos, and a computer disk detailing how to improvise poisons was allegedly displayed. Other witnesses have stated that poisoning the water supply, which has been attempted by al-Qaeda cells in Europe, was one of the favourite schemes discussed. This was not quite what some of the visitors from Seattle had envisaged. They had driven south intrigued by talk of a self-sufficient Islamic commune, and were not at all keen on becoming some sort of cowboy mujahideen.

Ujaama was alleged to have led discussions at Bly that ranged from organising further training in Afghanistan to carrying out armed robberies, building underground bunkers to hide weaponry, making poisons and firebombing vehicles. He has said his vision was to build a community of American Muslims, trained in jihad, who could then emigrate to the Islamic Emirate of Afghanistan to live, continue their training and fight.

But Ujaama was not hitting it off with the visitors from London, who suspected he saw the camp as a moneymaking venture. There were several heated rows, none of which surprised anyone who knew Ujaama and his explosive temper. Earlier in 1999 he had pleaded guilty to disorderly conduct charges following an altercation in a fax bureau in Seattle, and been ordered to undertake anger therapy. The case file in the municipal court in Tukwila contains an extraordinary letter stating that Ujaama had had treatment to control his temper. It reads:

> This letter is to confirm that Mr. Earnest James Ujaama has successfully completed 16 hours of anger management classes and counselling ... Mr. Ujaama was extremely patient, and showed kindness and courtesy to our staff and clients [at] all times. He was particularly energetic, outgoing, and willing to help. In short, Mr. Ujaama was outstanding to have work with us and will be missed sorely by all of us.

The letter, signed by one Abu Hamza, Finsbury Park mosque, London, satisfied the court's requirements.

After just two weeks on the ranch, Aswat pulled the plug on the venture – thwarting FBI plans to raid it. The group made their way back to Seattle, where Aswat and Kassir continued their work of training, lecturing and indoctrinating Osman's congregation. In February 2000 Ujaama – having completely fallen out with Aswat and Kassir – returned to London. The visitors remained in America, but the idea of establishing a jihad camp there was fading fast. Back in London Abu Hamza and his American aide were launching a new venture.

Ujaama returned to Finsbury Park to begin the task of running Abu Hamza's website under the banner of the Supporters of Shariah. He told people at the mosque that while he respected 'the Sheikh', Abu Hamza was an 'old schooler' while he was a 'new schooler'. Abu Hamza was still churning out newsletters and pamphlets, and recording endless poor-quality audio cassettes and videotapes, that were distributed by hand or sold out of cardboard boxes. Ujaama was about to make his rabid rhetoric available to the world at the click of a computer mouse.

The internet is one of the most powerful propaganda and instruction tools in al-Qaeda's armoury, offering the online mujahid everything from religious justifications for mass murder, to videos of the beheading of Western hostages in Iraq, to detailed instructions on how to make, store and use high explosives. Ujaama was one of the first to exploit the web for the Islamist cause. Before taking over Abu Hamza's website he had set up his own, stopamerica.org, which was fiercely critical of US foreign policy. In his founder's message on the site he said: 'We the people of the United States charge this government and their coalition with conspiracy to commit genocide and crimes of terrorism against Muslim people in our names.'

Ujaama now turned his attention to making Abu Hamza's rambling books, lengthy fatwas on everything from beards to food additives, and sermons available online. The SoS site also had news bulletins from the jihad battlefields and appeals for help, support and money. Still following his model, it remains online (one of the most recent incarnations was hosted from a platform in Canada), offering the writings and speeches of Abu Hamza in English, Arabic and, for his band of followers in Bosnia, Serbo-Croat.

The first version of the website credited Abu Samayya, one of Ujaama's nicknames, as the webmaster. But he was also heavily involved in other aspects of his emir's work.

Ujaama, known to most at Finsbury Park as Bilal, travelled frequently and, according to the FBI, attended a training camp in Afghanistan, to which he was admitted because he bore a letter of referral from Abu Hamza. Although he would boast about his jihadi activities, it seems the Afghan experience was not one that the boy from Seattle really enjoyed. On a later trip to the Islamist utopia, he told a British recruit that he was going home: 'I've had enough of Afghanistan. Kabul is for every Muslim but not every Muslim is for Kabul.' US prosecutors say that during one visit Ujaama fell ill and was treated by Dr Ayman al Zawahiri, second-in-command of al-Qaeda, leader of Egyptian Islamic Jihad and constant companion of Osama bin Laden.

In London he felt more at home, more comfortable and more

useful to the cause. One videotape of a public meeting, discovered by the writer Neil Doyle, reveals that Ujaama had been elevated to the status of support act for his leader. Dressed in a prayer cap and a burgundy tank top, he sits beside Abu Hamza and addresses the meeting. Speaking about the 'persecution' of the leaders of the jihad movement, Ujaama becomes more and more angry and excitable. He rants: 'It was not long ago that the evil Christians launched a crusade against the Muslims, the Jews and even other Christians. Today they are back in Egypt and Turkey and Algeria and Sudan, Somalia, Iraq and even in Islamic lands: the holy lands of Mecca and Medina. Today the crusade is against Islam and they are led by the Jews.'

It is solid al-Qaeda propaganda, filtered through the mind of Abu Hamza to his American disciple. Once he finished, Ujaama adjusted the microphone so his leader could speak. But later events would show that Ujaama was not as enamoured of the ideology as he might pretend to be.

In December 2000 he was asked by Abu Hamza to make a trip to Afghanistan to deliver money and laptop computers to the Taliban. The US district court in Seattle has heard that one of the computers was for the personal use of the Taliban foreign minister. FBI Special Agent Fred Humphries, who has travelled to Britain, Germany, Algeria, France and Canada to investigate Abu Hamza, testified to the US District Court in Seattle that British intelligence told him that Ujaama had been sent to try to 'curry favour' with the Taliban leadership. Travelling with him was Feroz Abbasi, a young Briton from south London who was on his way to undergo training in one of the Afghan camps (see next chapter). Ujaama's tasks on the trip included delivering Abbasi safely into the hands of one of Abu Hamza's contacts.

The night before they left for Afghanistan Ujaama did not sleep, staying up late to load languages software onto his computer hard drive. He had one other task: to deliver a quantity of cash, purportedly to a school for girls in the Khost area of Afghanistan. He would later state that the school did not exist. What happened to the money is unclear.

Abbasi recalled that as they set off on their journey Ujaama was 'dressed like a Westerner and doing his 007 act again … looking around him all suspicious'. Yet when they reached Heathrow to board a flight to Dubai and from there to Karachi, Ujaama's temper reappeared and he created a fuss about trying, unsuccessfully, for an upgrade to a first-class seat. His behaviour caused further trouble when they reached Pakistan and he argued ferociously with a taxi driver over the fare to take him and Abbasi from Islamabad to Peshawar, the frontier town where al-Qaeda had been founded.

Ujaama and Abbasi separated as the American went about delivering his consignments of cash and computers to Abu Hamza's contacts in Afghanistan. His task completed, he left the country as quickly as possible and returned to London. Abu Hamza was enraged to learn that he had abandoned Abbasi before ensuring that he was delivered to the right person in Afghanistan.

In 2001 Abu Hamza hatched a new scheme to increase his influence in Afghanistan: the establishment of a computer lab in Kandahar which could be used by Taliban officials and ordinary Afghanis. On 5 September 2001 – just a few days before the 9/11 attacks – Ujaama departed from London for Pakistan once more. In his luggage was £6,000 given to him by Abu Hamza, supposedly to locate and lease a building and begin the work of setting up the computer lab. He was stopped and questioned at Heathrow airport by security agents, suspicious of his travel patterns and the amount of money he was carrying. Ujaama answered their questions with the characteristic bombast that made him a second-rate operative. He told his questioners bluntly that he was delivering computer equipment and money to people in Afghanistan for use in establishing a Taliban school, and announced that he would go to the American embassy to seek a visa to cross into Afghanistan, and if he was refused he would go there anyway, because it was easy to do so. The officials were suspicious, but decided Ujaama was not committing any offence. They allowed him to travel, and requested that he make contact with them upon his return.

Despite his boasts at Heathrow, Ujaama did not cross into Afghanistan. In the aftermath of 11 September the Pakistani army was ordered to seal the border. Ujaama returned to London, where he faced the wrath of Abu Hamza, who was furious that the money had not been delivered. Ujaama was firmly out of favour. When he tried to impress an American friend visiting London in November 2001 by arranging dinner with Abu Hamza, the atmosphere was said to be dreadful. The cleric later told friends he suspected that in the course of his travels Ujaama had pocketed some of the money meant for the mujahideen.

Returning to Seattle in the early summer of 2002, Ujaama found his native country to be a different place. In the aftermath of 9/11 and the passing of the Patriot Act, large numbers of Muslims had been arrested, and the activities of many more were being monitored. One of the groups under almost constant surveillance was the collection of black American converts to Islam who had frequented Osman's mosque. Ujaama found that he and his brother – another convert, who had taken the name Mustafa and had attended the Bly ranch – were being watched by the FBI. The brothers issued a press release denying any links with terrorism, and were lauded by community groups, who accused the US authorities of instituting the McCarthy-style persecution of two respected black activists. In an email to a Seattle newspaper, Ujaama said the investigation was 'a fascist witch-hunt'.

The investigators from Seattle's joint anti-terrorism task force were undeterred. In July 2002 Ujaama was arrested at his brother's home in Denver and imprisoned. Bail was refused because of the risk that he might flee back to London; he had a return airline ticket in his possession when he was detained. By now young Feroz Abbasi was incarcerated in the US military internment camp at Guantánamo Bay, Cuba. FBI agents confirmed in court that information about Ujaama's trips to Afghanistan had been gathered in interviews with 'witnesses' in Afghanistan and Guantánamo Bay. His old friend Osman had taken on the status of 'cooperating witness'.

Ujaama was subsequently charged under a two-count indictment. The principal charge was that he had conspired with Abu Hamza 'to provide material support and resources' to the Taliban regime in Afghanistan. The charge sheet contained details of his involvement with the Finsbury Park mosque, the plan to set up a training camp at Bly and his trips to Kabul and Kandahar. After months of legal wrangling, and with the very real threat of a spell at Guantánamo Bay and/or a ten-year jail sentence looming over him, Ujaama abandoned his allegiance to Abu Hamza. In April 2003 he pleaded guilty to conspiring to supply goods and services to the Taliban, a lesser offence for which he was given a two-year sentence.

Ujaama's admission of guilt was accompanied by a detailed plea bargain under which he agreed to cooperate with future anti-terrorist investigations. He admitted being Abu Hamza's webmaster, assisting Abbasi to undertake 'violent jihad training' in Afghanistan, and supplying 'goods, software, technology or services' to the Taliban. Under the plea agreement he would serve two years in custody, then be released under supervision for three years. The requirement for him to cooperate with the authorities extended for ten years.

Ujaama is forbidden from talking publicly about the case, but according to the US website TalkLeft he maintained at the time of his sentencing that the Bly ranch was not intended as a terrorist facility. The site reported that he insisted that the ranch was intended for 'legitimate and legal religious training'. He was quoted as saying: 'I have come to accept it was illegal in the US. I don't agree with that law, and that's my right.'

The then US Attorney General, John Ashcroft, took a rather different view of Ujaama's conviction: 'An important part of our war against terrorism is to obtain the cooperation of insiders who have direct knowledge of the activities of dangerous terrorists,' he said. 'We are pleased that Mr Ujaama has agreed to plead guilty, accept responsibility for his criminal conduct and cooperate fully regarding others engaged in criminal and terrorist activity both here and abroad. We expect his cooperation to lead to the arrest of additional terrorists and the disruption of future terrorist activity.'

Ujaama's case was small beer for the US authorities. The real prize was his cooperation. What Attorney General Ashcroft was saying, with uncharacteristic subtlety, was that Abu Hamza was now firmly in America's sights.

14
Croydon to Kandahar

'We have very nice speaking leaders but when it comes to shooting you see his eyes going round and round and he goes yellow and he doesn't speak. While others you don't even think they have got the courage to go and they call the prayers in the middle of the battlefield.'

ABU HAMZA

One night in December 2001 Feroz Abbasi walked nervously across an unlit, dusty street in Kandahar, his heart banging against his ribs, nerves jangling as he contemplated the end of his own personal jihad. Suicide or surrender? Would he pull the pin on the 'big old Russian grenade' dangling by his balls and blow himself and the two Northern Alliance fighters to pieces? Would that be the martyrdom he had dreamed of, the path to paradise and the fulfilment of what he believed was his duty as a Muslim? Or would he meekly give in? Somehow it didn't seem right to Abbasi that his one and only act of war should result in the deaths of two fellow Muslims. Yes, they were on the other side, but they seemed to want to help him escape rather than hand him over to the British or the Americans. They were his Muslim brothers.

'This was it,' Abbasi would later write. 'The test. Whether I really wanted to die or not. I tried reaching down my trousers. My Afghan blanket covering my groin area. The stocky guy had his back to me as he led the way to a gate. I pulled my arm out when he turned to guide me. Another Afghan came up behind me as we entered. The stocky guy was going to lead me into the buildings when the fat Afghan said something about a body search. The stocky guy said, "He has nothing." Phew! Then he turned around – maybe he remembered what happened to his buddies when the Arab martyr bombed them. The stocky Afghan made a good search this time. They found it. His hand went right up my leg and there it was. The Russian grenade hanging by my testicles. They held my arms. He reached in and pulled it out. One young Afghan with a PK pointed it at me from his hips and said, "This guy's a nutter." My heart sank. The fight was over.'

In truth, it had not been much of a fight. Feroz Abbasi was aged twenty-one. He was a long way from his home in the south London suburb of Croydon, a long way from the Surrey college where he studied computer science, and a very long way from the Finsbury Park mosque where he had imbibed Abu Hamza's myths of martyrdom, death and glory. Confronted with the realities of the battlefield, Abbasi had found little stomach for killing and dying. In one training exercise in al-Qaeda's Farooq mountain camp he had been ordered to slaughter a camel, but shirked the task.

Now he was captured. His hands were tied with his Taliban turban and his feet bound so he could not move. The next people he saw were two American soldiers. Then two other Americans in jeans and civilian clothes, armed with handguns and knives, stood guard over him. 'I was blindfolded and taken to the Afghan prison in Kandahar for about two nights. Then the Afghans came back and I was taken to a house which I only saw briefly and served as a place of transfer from the Afghans to the Americans, who put me in the back of a van and drove me to Kandahar airport which had now become the American base. The airport was the last thing I saw before Cuba.'

For the next three years, until his release in January 2005, Feroz Ali Abbasi was held by the United States as an 'enemy combatant' in the cages of the Guantánamo Bay internment camp, although he denies any wrongdoing. He had virtually no contact with the outside world, and did not receive the letters sent to him by his anxious mother, Zumrati Juma, a hospital nurse, and his younger brother and sister. During his confinement he was one of a handful of the seven hundred detainees to be charged under US military law and ordered to face a military tribunal. He was freed, under a deal negotiated by the British government, before that trial could take place.

But as he prepared to defend himself before President George W. Bush's *ad hoc* court, Abbasi wrote one of the most remarkable documents to emerge from the 'war on terror'. His 154-page Guantánamo Bay journal, titled 'Statement of Feroz Abbasi', was submitted to the US authorities and labelled 'exhibit D'. It is a long, rambling, handwritten account of his life as a would-be mujahideen, penned whilst in confinement in the heat and brutality of Camp X-Ray. Every so often the neat, dense writing is broken up by childish illustrations. There is a picture of the Finsbury Park mosque, another of the Egyptian Islamic Jihad house where he stayed in Kabul, and elaborately decorated chapter titles.

Human rights lawyers have challenged the validity of this document, alleging that Abbasi wrote it under duress. But throughout its pages he is angrily critical of the USA, and stoutly defends the rights of Muslim fighters to carry out suicide bombings as acts of defence. There is an embarrassing honesty about the experience, and none of the florid propaganda that pours from the pages of other jihadi journals. Instead, what shines through Abbasi's jail diary is the vulnerability of a young man who regards Abu Hamza as the replacement for the father who abandoned him when he was a twelve-year-old boy. So naïve is Abbasi that he never seems to grasp just how he has been manipulated and used, and just how close he came to becoming another sacrifice in al-Qaeda's war.

Feroz Abbasi was born in Uganda in 1980, the first child of an African mother and a Pakistani father. The family arrived in London when he was aged eight, and settled in Croydon. Feroz was bright

academically and did well at school; he took A-levels and went on to
study at the North East Surrey College of Technology. But he was a
troubled teenager – beset by adolescent angst, angry at the absence of
his father, perturbed by just about all the ills of the world and frustrated by a crippling shyness. His desperate search for answers to his
and the planet's problems saw him embrace Buddhism, study the
Bible, drop out of college and embark on a series of bizarre walking
trips. On one adventure he took himself off to Scotland and hitch-
hiked the several hundred miles back to London. On another, he flew
to Paris and began walking and taking lifts across France, Germany
and Switzerland. He spent a week pretending to be an asylum seeker,
and was admitted to a Swiss refugee camp. There he met 'the
Kashmiri gentleman' who transformed his life.

The Kashmiri was a veteran of the conflict in his homeland, and
spoke movingly to Abbasi of the suffering of the Muslim people
there and the power of Islam. When he left the camp, the wanderer
had a new cause. He wrote: 'I knew that I believed in God and his
name was Allah. Also that His religion was Islam.'

Abbasi could not wait to retrace his steps back across Europe to
London to find out more about Islam and jihad. Ironically for a
young man who would later be prepared to take up arms against
British soldiers, he called at the British consulate in Zürich to ask if
officials would meet his travel expenses for his return trip (they
would not). A life which he had once tried to end with a paracetamol
overdose suddenly seemed to have a purpose. Back in Croydon, the
nineteen-year-old began to attend the local mosque, read the Koran
and frequent local Islamic bookshops. 'I picked up a book in the
Croydon Central Mosque bookshop. I had been averse to picking it
up at first because it had a purplish pink cover. Overcoming this
aversion I read the title, *The Virtues of Jihad*, and the subtitle, *The
Shortest Path to Jannah* [paradise]. I bought the book.'

This tract told Abbasi that jihad, in the form of military struggle
to defend Muslims, was a religious obligation. His impressionable

mind was eager to learn more. At the mosque he saw a leaflet headed *Chechnya Emergency Appeal*, and later that week he caught a train into central London to attend the public meeting advertised on the flyer. 'I went alone. I was naïve. I had expected the appeal to be for able-bodied men to be recruited right there and then. Sheikh Abu Hamza al-Masri was present on stage. It was an appeal for funds, Chechnya did not need people. The *New Trend* newspaper gave a telephone number as a contact for Sheikh Abu Hamza. I called the number. A gentleman answered on the other end. I said, "I would like to know how I can go to jihad please." He said: "Come to Finsbury Park mosque for Friday prayer and ask for SoS." ' Abbasi was taking his first steps towards his jihad.

The following Friday he took himself to north London to hear Abu Hamza preach at the Finsbury Park mosque. Almost immediately he was bewitched. 'His sermons were different to those at Croydon mosque. I was more inclined to Sheikh Abu Hamza's sermons. He seemed to possess a deeper understanding of Islamic knowledge.'

When prayers were over, Abbasi sought out Abu Hamza's office on the first floor of the mosque, and waited for an opportunity to speak to the imam. He was given a photocopied membership form for the Supporters of Shariah and placed in a queue to see Abu Hamza, who was holding private audiences. When his turn came, the over-eager Abbasi gabbled out his request to fight. 'I told him that I wanted to go to Chechnya and wondered whether he could help me. He said, "You have to work with us and show commitment and dedication, then we will see." He then placed an arm on my shoulder and made supplication in which he briefly paused to ask my name. "Abbasi" was what caught his attention. It was from then on that I was known as Abbasi amongst the people that frequented Finsbury Park mosque.'

Buoyed up by Abu Hamza's blessing, and immediately appointed head of the one-member SoS Croydon branch, Abbasi was filled with enthusiasm. Despite warnings about Abu Hamza from the teacher who was instructing him in the Koran in Croydon, Abbasi spent more and more time at Finsbury Park, and volunteered for night-guard duty at the mosque. 'The night vigilance was necessary,' he wrote in his jail diary, 'because the mosque had been taken over by the Pakistanis by force. What I was told was that the Pakistani establishment was not allowing the Bangladeshis to teach their children in the mosque. The Bangladeshis approached Sheikh Abu Hamza for help. Sheikh Abu Hamza, seeing that neither of the two were in any position to run the mosque, took over using the Arabs. Another duty we also had to do was regulate the curfew times for the asylum seekers who used one hall downstairs as a temporary residence as they sought asylum seeker status.'

Abbasi's serious approach irritated many of the old hands at the mosque, and he became embroiled in petty disputes. Frustrated by these, and by the fact that he was still not fighting the jihad, he returned in a huff to Croydon. But just before the celebration of the Muslim feast day of Eid in January 2000, Abu Hamza sent for him. Returning to the mosque, Abbasi was greeted with hugs and good wishes which 'softened my heart', and he took up his dedication to Abu Hamza once again. He was ushered back into the activities of Abu Hamza's group, becoming involved in printing newsletters and recording and distributing taped sermons. He moved into the mosque, living there full-time and relying solely on Abu Hamza and his followers for his education in Islam.

According to one senior British anti-terrorist detective, the process employed by Abu Hamza with Abbasi and other vulnerable young men is not unlike that used by paedophiles when grooming their victims. The target must be made to feel important, liked, useful and, eventually, indispensable. The reality is that they are being prepared for a purpose. The paedophile's victim will be sexually abused. The terrorist recruiter's victim will be deployed as a weapon. Both are disposable.

Abbasi could not see this process happening. His unworldly innocence emerges starkly from one lengthy passage in his Guantánamo journal.

> Sheikh Abu Hamza had shown a little wisdom in requesting my presence at the mosque at such a time. He knew my heart would be opened by the atmosphere of Eid and that things could then be set right.
>
> Why the Sheikh made the effort to keep me going back to the mosque is a mystery to me. A greater curiosity is the fact that the first time I met Sheikh Abu Hamza I looked like a reporter (someone had commented). Yet the Sheikh accepted me into his group. Also being a brand new Muslim (only four months in Islam) my behaviour and mannerism, almost everything about me, would have been unIslamic. Some persons have painted a picture of Sheikh Abu Hamza as an evil, scheming manipulator of naïve, easily-led new Muslim converts. I do not hold this view. I think Sheikh Abu Hamza, who I normally address as The Sheikh, had acquired an understanding of people and also gave people chances.
>
> The Sheikh saw the potential grip a manipulator could have on me if I fell prey to them and from a sense of responsibility took an active but detached role in protecting me and nurturing me into the Muslim I am today. I would go so far as to say that since my father left me there has not been anybody who had taken the role of father-figure for me other than the Sheikh. He acted as the closest thing I had to a father since my real father. Were it not for his positive influence I think it would be safe to say that my fervour for Islam as a new Muslim may have culminated in my committing acts like that of September 11.

It is a strange testament, because Abu Hamza seems to have been preparing the ground for Abbasi to travel to Afghanistan and the very same al-Qaeda camps where the 9/11 hijackers received their initial training before carrying out their attacks. Abu Hamza's role in organising Abbasi's journey to Afghanistan is featured in count seven of the US indictment against him, a charge of conspiracy to provide and conceal material support and resources to terrorists.

Abbasi states in his journal that he constantly agitated with his leader to be allowed to go to the jihad. He wanted to go to Kashmir, but Abu Hamza arranged for him to go to Afghanistan and to meet a front-line commander. The decision to let him travel followed one of Abu Hamza's more sentimental sermons on the valour of the mujahideen.

Abbasi wrote: 'Upon hearing the Sheikh say in one of his khutbahs, "By Allah, I would rather be with the mujahideen, even if it meant I just talked with them and nothing else, than be here." I struck while the iron was hot. I approached the Sheikh and said, "Sheikh, I've got to go to jihad. I don't care where. I've got to go even if it meant that all I could do was peel potatoes and polish boots." The plan transpired as such. In two months I will be going to train with the Taliban. The Sheikh asked, "They only train people who are going to fight with them. Are you OK with that?" I answered in the affirmative.'

At the end of December 2000 Abbasi, accompanied by the American James Ujaama and with £100 from his emir in his pocket, flew to Karachi via Dubai. In Pakistan they were driven to Islamabad, then on to the border towns of Peshawar and finally Quetta, where they stayed in a Taliban guest house. Abbasi separated from Ujaama and was placed in the care of a group of Afghan fighters – one of whom had been receiving medical treatment in Pakistan – and was driven into the Islamic Emirate of Afghanistan.

Abbasi was billeted for several days in properties run by the Taliban foreign affairs ministry. His sense of impatience and frustration soon returned. There was talk of 'special tuition', and he was suddenly offered a flight to Kabul, where he was put up in a house run by members of Egyptian Islamic Jihad, the organisation founded by Ayman al Zawahiri, second-in-command of al-Qaeda. Abbasi felt proud to be in this company, because the Egyptian regime of Hosni Mubarak was regarded by Abu Hamza as 'his biggest enemy'. Nevertheless, the young Briton was increasingly anxious about the 'special tuition' that he was being lined up for. He hoped for a call from his leader in London – who, he wrote, had the telephone number for the Kabul property – but it did not come.

Instead, early in 2001 Abbasi boarded a bus with fifteen other recruits – some English-speaking, others from Sudan and the Philippines – and was driven to 'the middle of nowhere, the whole area was surrounded by mountains, the backdrop to the al Farooq training camp'. This remote place, run directly by Osama bin Laden's instructors, was where he underwent his basic training.

From his diary, this appears to be the time when Abbasi was at his happiest. He made friends among his fellow recruits, and relished the challenges of training to be a mujahid. 'We were called into the line-up square and our trainer showed us how to stand to attention, at ease, what to say upon their orders, where to position our weapons. We learned the emergency signal that meant line-up and also the signal that meant evacuate all buildings (probably single and automatic Kalashnikov fire respectively). We were also taught how to evacuate whatever sheltered building we were in as a precaution against airstrikes. We ran up and down Jebal Azzam [a mountain]. This was the first time Muktar [a fellow recruit] saw me. He mentioned it later, saying, "We used to be big when we first came to Afghanistan. I remember Abbas the first time I saw him, running down from Jebal Azzam. Now look at him, he is a stick man." '

Around their lessons, the recruits prayed five times every day, recited the Koran and undertook camp guard duties. Osama bin Laden visited the camp mosque while Abbasi was there, and delivered a political lecture to his new recruits.

'The syllabus entailed weapons, land navigation, battlefield manoeuvres, basic use theory of military explosive ordnance (e.g. grenades, landmines, TNT blocks, etc.) and a theory and practice of using the walkie-talkie which I missed because I was sick.' Stomach bugs which brought violent sickness and diarrhoea were something of an occupational hazard for the Western recruits, unused to the dreadful and irregular Afghan diet.

Towards the end of the two-month basic training, Abbasi and two other non-Arabs were asked to slaughter a camel. The demand made him squeamish, and doubtful about his ability to be a soldier. 'The Arabs, especially the trainers, thought this was a privilege. I thought otherwise. Islamically there is nothing wrong, in fact much good in slaughtering an animal in the prescribed way that Allah has ordained. Nonetheless I could not bring myself to slaughter the young camel. Upon my decline the cook slaughtered my camel which I promptly claimed. But this later led to me seriously questioning how it was I was going to shoot a grown man in battle if I could not slaughter a camel.'

His basic training completed, Abbasi was still denied his desire to go to the front line, where Taliban forces were fighting the Northern Alliance in Afghanistan's seemingly endless civil war. Instead, after a three-week lull he was brought back to Farooq to take a mountain training course as part of a group of thirty mujahideen from around the world. This time the exercises included guerrilla warfare, reconnaissance and techniques for mounting ambushes.

The course left Abbasi exhausted, and he was glad of a return to the Kabul guest house. But the true nature of his value to the jihad finally began to appear while he was resting there. He and two other English-speakers (one of them a white Australian who remains incarcerated at Guantánamo Bay) were invited to attend an interview in Kandahar. One of those conducting the interview was Abu Hafs, the operational commander of al-Qaeda, who would be killed in an American bombing raid in Afghanistan in late 2001. Abu Hafs asked Abbasi directly: 'Would you like to take any actions against the

Americans and the Jews?' According to Abbasi's diary, he considered attacks such as the suicide bombing of the USS *Cole* in Yemen and the intifada in Palestine before replying: 'Yes, I would like to take action against American and Israeli forces because jihad is an individual obligation on my person.' The al-Qaeda chief ended the interview by saying: 'We'll see about getting you some special training.' If the phrase still confused Abbasi, it was clear to the Australian that it meant they were being singled out for overseas missions because they spoke English and carried Western passports. Abbasi wrote: 'He would allude to the idea of us being undetectable'.

Abbasi and his group were moved again, to a camp at Kandahar airport, where they were to receive 'city tactics' training. They encountered another Briton who had been through the so-called 'special training' and spoke of courses in explosives training and being sent on missions. He wrote: 'But this Brit was disappointed with the special training and was going home.'

Starting city tactics with Abbasi was a German mujahid. The training was carried out by a former officer in the Pakistani army. The group was trained in firing a Kalashnikov and other weapons while walking, running, aiming through a car window and mounting a motorcycle. Instruction was given in using a rocket-propelled grenade launcher, targeting and destroying vehicles, clearing a building and firing a Dragonov sniper rifle. These trainees were not, however, to be mere foot soldiers. They were shown bin Laden propaganda videos and given ideological lectures on the origins of the Islamist movement and the necessity of overthrowing 'apostate leaders' in Muslim countries. Extensive exercises were carried out in the careful reconnaissance of and making detailed notes on potential targets – a hallmark of successful al-Qaeda operations around the world. In Kabul, Abbasi practised on the then disused British embassy and a hotel. He and his fellow recruits were also lectured in the role of the City Force and the importance of mujahideen being able to hide their true devotion to Islam while planning an operation. Abbasi did not know it, but he was receiving the same training that had been followed by the special recruits who were about to hijack four airliners in the United States.

He wrote: 'The City Force are regular people (Muslims) with regular jobs and lives. They fit into society. If it is necessary that they shave their beards and show a nominal practice of Islam (such as going to the mosque for Friday prayers only) they do so. But their real worth comes into play when the target which is unable to be terminated by the Guerrilla Force is reached by the City Force. An example being a general who is crucial to an enemy army and therefore protected heavily whenever he is at a military base. But not when he goes into the City for a fun night out at the opera, brothel and whatever dirty, sleazy place he visits. The theory is, in such a relaxed environment he is easily whacked off by the City Force guys who are unknown and undercover.'

There is no disguising the fact that at this time Abbasi was being trained by his al-Qaeda masters in the practices of a terrorist sleeper cell. He detailed instructions given to him which replicate characteristic al-Qaeda operations: reconnaissance cells must have no contact with active units, information collection is absolutely vital, and only through the leadership can the different departments work.

Among the trainees on this elite course there was heated debate about martyrdom operations. The crux of the argument was not, however, whether they were right or wrong, but whether they should be directed solely against military targets. Abbasi records in his diary that he was one of the few who argued that such attacks should not kill civilians, but only be directed against armed enemies. He wrote: 'Martyrdom operations are selfless sacrifices of a noble and chosen few. Martyrs save innocent civilian lives, they do not jeopardise them.'

The pressure on him and his group was intensifying. One of the trainers called him aside and told him that if anyone was interested in performing a martyrdom operation they should approach him discreetly. A few days after hearing news of the assassination by al-Qaeda suicide bombers of Ahmed Shah Masood, the famed Northern Alliance commander, Abbasi recounts how he volunteered for a suicide mission at the al-Qaeda office where he had been interviewed before: 'I was nervous but I wanted to put my request in. I said: "I heard about Masood being killed by a martyrdom operation. I would like to do something like that against a military target." He [an al-Qaeda trainer] said, "Do you like the operation against Masood?" I said "Yes." He then caught me by surprise by saying "Do you want to make bayat [pledge of allegiance]?" I got tongue-tied. I didn't say anything about bayat. He then wrote something on a piece of paper and said go to the office in the Institute of Arabic Studies and give this to so-and-so.'

Abbasi took the paper, but claims – quite believably, given the erratic nature of his jihadi adventure – that he could not find the relevant office. Within days the situation in Afghanistan descended into chaos as the news of the 9/11 attacks in New York and Washington DC spread. Abbasi was confused by events in the USA. The Americans, he says, are the 'biggest terrorists' in the world. But he could not agree with 9/11 because too many innocent people died: 'I've had enough of innocent people losing their lives. I did not leave my home except to defend innocent people.'

After the US-led invasion, Abbasi found himself billeted with 'the English-speaking brothers' in Kandahar. They were kept back from the front line until close to the end of the Taliban regime in December 2001, when he was finally allowed to line up with an active unit of foreign fighters supposedly defending the airport. Dressed in military fatigues, wearing hiking boots and a balaclava, Abbasi was given a Kalashnikov and sent to the caves near the airport. It was a terrifying experience: 'The bombing started and I spent the rest of the time at the airport running around like a madman in the middle of nowhere trying to dodge missiles which seemed to come ever closer. On the seventeenth of Ramadan, Opposition forces attempted taking over the airport area. There was a gun fight that went into the night.'

The end came in the usual haphazard fashion that characterised Abbasi's attempts to become a mujahid. The foreign fighters around him began to disappear, some obeying Taliban orders to melt away and fight as guerrillas, others simply fleeing. Abbasi found himself teamed up with some Yemeni fighters, and they agreed to take turns to do the night watch. While his comrades slept in a cave, the boy from Croydon – having seen a snake – chose to sleep in a bomb crater. 'I woke up at dawn, my partner had not woken me up for night duty. It looked as though the brothers were still sleeping so I made the call for prayer and went to wake one of them up. He wasn't in his sleeping bag. None of them were. They had all fled, literally got up and ran. Everything else (food, weapons etc.) had been left behind.'

A few days later, the hapless mujahid was caught with a grenade down his trousers and quickly despatched into the custody of the US Special Forces. His next three years would be spent in Guantánamo Bay where, it has been reported, he suffered severe depression and attempted suicide.

Abbasi is one of the few former detainees from Britain who has not sold his story to the media since his release from the US internment camp. His remarkably candid testament is his only public attempt to explain how he almost became a martyr for Abu Hamza's cause.

On the day her son was flown back to Britain, Zumrati Juma offered her brief explanation of what she believed had happened to him. With the reserve and dignity that marked her quiet campaign for his release, she said of the leaders of the Finsbury Park mosque: 'I don't have any concrete evidence, but I think they changed his attitudes.'

15
Brixton Boys

'The idea is to … make the sky very high-risk
for anyone who flies.'

ABU HAMZA

Two hours into the busy American Airlines flight from Paris to
Miami on 22 December 2001, Hermis Moutardier was clearing away
meal trays when a passenger tugged at her sleeve and said he could
smell smoke. The forty-seven-year-old flight attendant hurried along
the aisle looking for the culprit. Thirteen weeks after hijackers had
steered their planes into the World Trade Centre and the Pentagon,
the sense of anxiety among many passengers and crew on board
Flight 63 was obvious.

Moutardier spotted the hulking seated figure of Richard Reid
leaning against the cabin window and trying to strike a match. She
thought he was trying to light a cigarette. He mumbled an apology,
and began picking at his teeth with the charred matchstick. Moments
later she glanced over to seat 29J again, and saw Reid bent double,
trying to strike another match. Her temper rising, Moutardier
grabbed at his shoulder, and was about to lecture the scruffy passenger with bulging eyes when she noticed that he had one of his
black baseball boots gripped between his knees, and was trying to
ignite a fuse protruding from its tongue.

She can't remember if she yelled for help as she lunged at Reid,
who had enough strength to easily shove her toppling back into the

aisle. Ignoring the searing pain from her shoulder, she pulled herself to her feet and ran back to the galley, where her fellow flight attendant Cristina Jones was working. Moutardier tore open drawers to grab some bottles of water, but was so unnerved she forgot to explain to her colleague about the shoe bomb as she screamed, 'Get him!'

By now Reid had turned his back, but the whiff of sulphur was obvious to those sitting around him as he lit his sixth match in his frantic efforts to ignite the fuse. Jones hurled herself at him, trying to grip him by the arms, but he bit deep into her thumb and would not let go. Her screams brought a scrum of passengers to her aid, and meal trays, drinks, books and personal belongings spilled everywhere, as two men wrestled with Reid while Moutardier tipped bottles of water over him in an attempt to ensure that the fuse would not burn.

The flight crew used seatbelts to bind Reid's ankles, and his wrists were tied to the armrests with plastic restraints. Passengers joined in, taking off their belts and braces and trussing him up with the cables from headphones, or anything they could find. He was so tightly bound that when FBI agents boarded the plane in Boston they would have to cut him out of his seat.

A doctor on board took a sedative from the plane's first aid kit and jabbed a syringe into Reid's arm as he fought to escape. The pilot, Captain Hans Mantel, ordered everyone to remain in their seats for the remainder of the trip. Anyone needing to use the lavatory was frisked and had to empty out their pockets, as the crew worried that Reid may have had an accomplice among the 185 passengers on board. One of the crew sat behind Reid for the rest of the journey, holding onto his matted ponytail until the flight landed. In the panic, it was an hour before the crew realised that nobody had thought to take away Reid's shoes, which were still lying at his feet. The co-pilot collected them and locked them in a bombproof compartment next to the cockpit.

The nervousness among the crew was understandable, as

American Airlines had had two of its planes hijacked on 9/11. Moutardier knew some of the flight attendants who died, and she and the rest of the crew on Flight 63 had been instructed how to spot suspicious characters.

At six feet four inches and weighing well over two hundred pounds, Reid was hardly unobtrusive. Moutardier had been curious about him from the start after he refused to eat or drink anything, even water, on what was going to be a ten-hour transatlantic flight. She asked him jokingly in French if he was on a diet, but he tersely replied that he couldn't understand, saying he was Sri Lankan. She didn't believe him, but decided against bothering the pilot with her misgivings.

The plane had been an hour late leaving Charles de Gaulle airport that morning of 22 December 2001 because of problems loading the bags of the many Americans who were heading home for Christmas, and the flight crew had been keen to make up for lost time. Now, as Flight 63 accelerated across the Atlantic at 35,000 feet, Reid rocked back and forth, tugging at his restraints. His face was a mask of rage as he prayed loudly and cursed those around him until the sedative began to take effect. His anger was because he knew he had failed in his mission.

Two F-15 fighters had been scrambled from Otis Air Force base in Massachusetts to shadow the silver-grey passenger jet for the remainder of its journey, while in Washington the law enforcement agencies had already begun their enquiries into the background of the gawky suicide bomber. What they discovered would astound the intelligence agencies. This was no veteran of the Afghan wars, nor some embittered youth brought up in a Palestinian refugee camp. The young man who had been seconds from bringing down an aircraft with plastic explosive moulded into the soles of his shoes was a street mugger from a south London housing estate. His graduation from petty thief to terrorist had happened in the prayer rooms of Finsbury Park mosque.

His father, Robin Reid, was Jamaican, and was in jail for burglary when his son Richard was born in Bromley on 12 August 1973. He had been working on the railways in London when he met Lesley Hughes, the daughter of an accountant and a magistrate, who was studying in the city. Physically they seemed an ill-matched couple. At six feet eight inches he towered over his bride, who barely reached his midriff. By the time of Richard's arrival she had already begun divorce proceedings, fed up that her husband had spent more time in prison than with her.

Reid, who lived with his mother and her new partner in south London, saw little of his father while he was growing up, a mixed-race child brought up in a white family. The playground jibes about his colour, and his gangly appearance, started the clumsy schoolboy thinking of himself as a misfit, confused over whether he was black or white. None of the ethnic groups at Thomas Tallis School in Eltham was particularly welcoming to Reid, who contemporaries remember as hard to like. A senior teacher, Jane Green, described him as hopelessly disorganised. When he came to class he was always the one without the right textbooks or who had forgotten to bring a pen, and he seemed uninterested in whatever subject was being taught. She said of him: 'Richard wasn't good at being good, but he didn't know how to be bad either.' Staff encouraged him to use his height and strength to make a name for himself on the sports field, but that didn't work either. The best that could be said for him, recalls Green, was that he was polite.

Socially he did not mix. He was shy with girls, and whenever he did latch on to some gang or other he would be seen straggling along at the back, shoulders bent, almost as if he wanted to make himself invisible. What was glaringly apparent in those teenage days was that Richard Reid was easily led. When a gang he was associating with played truant from school to spraypaint graffiti on shopfronts and buses, it was always Reid who was caught. Street gangs recognised the value of dragging him along, as he was an intimidating sight. A classmate at the time recalls how the ringleader of one group put a knife to Reid's throat and forced him to mug two seventeen-year-olds on a train to prove his worth to them. Reid did as he was told, but as he ran away he turned and mouthed the word 'Sorry' to his victims.

He gave up school as soon as he could, at sixteen, and drifted into an aimless existence of smoking cannabis, shoplifting and hanging around street corners, underpasses and the entrance lobbies of tower blocks, looking for easy prey to rob. In early 1992 a vicious attack on a pensioner earned him his first stint in Feltham Young Offenders' Institute, close to Heathrow Airport. By now his mother had moved to the West Country with her partner and Reid's younger half-brother, leaving him to fend for himself in a hostel near Lewisham. He fancied himself as some sort of local hard man, but was dismissed by contemporaries as a 'weirdo' who was best avoided. In spring 1992 Reid was in trouble again. Undercover police targeting street crime in south London raided his hostel, and he was charged with four counts of burglary. At his trial he readily admitted to another forty-six offences.

It was during his next three years behind bars that the feckless and rootless Reid embraced Islam. Abdul Ghani Qureshi, an imam working at Feltham, said that for social inadequates like Reid, visits to the prison mosque and conversations about the Koran were an escape from the boredom, the bullying and the racial insults from fellow inmates.

Reid had been brought up a Christian by his mother, but told friends that he was not really interested in religion. In jail all that changed, as he sought out the company of young Muslims to ask questions about the Koran and talk about the problems Islamic communities were facing in Africa and the Middle East. His rising sense of anger would be seized on by unscrupulous figures in places like Finsbury Park mosque looking for impressionable young men who could be manipulated and brainwashed into doing their bidding. This is a slow process, and one that the recruiters recognise will see many of their targets drifting away to follow their own path. That did not bother the talent-spotters, who realised that they only needed a handful of gullible inadequates. In Reid they would discover a willing volunteer.

The training manuals argue that terrorist groups have a greater impact with a small cadre of suicide bombers than with an army of stone-throwing youngsters. Converts like Reid were known as 'white moors', anxious to prove their dedication to their new cause. Reid didn't just read the Koran, he wanted to memorise it. He learnt Arabic, which was no mean feat for someone with his lack of academic prowess.

On his release from prison in the summer of 1996, the twenty-three-year-old Reid made his way to a terraced house in south London. All that distinguished it from the neighbouring properties in Gresham Road was a wooden plaque on the front wall which read 'Brixton Mosque and Islamic Cultural Centre'. Abdul Haqq Baker, the chairman of the mosque, remembers how the newcomer was eager to learn more about Islam after his haphazard introduction to the religion behind bars.

Baker encouraged Reid and other ex-convicts of his age to change their lifestyle as well as their code of beliefs, which meant no more drugs, alcohol or crime. Reid obeyed. He was always looking for someone, anyone, to tell him what to do. He accepted invitations to travel to Luton, the Midlands and other mosques around London to hear what other preachers had to say. Among them was the charismatic figure of Abu Hamza, who was then making a name for himself in the Muslim community, and who encouraged younger members of his audience to stay behind after his speeches and join in seminars about what their generation should be doing to ease the suffering of their fellow Muslims.

It was not long before Baker noticed a change in Reid. He started quarrelling with others at prayer meetings, mocking the mosque's passive stance in the face of what he saw as the violent oppression of his fellow Muslims. Over his Arab dress he began wearing the sort of camouflage combat jacket you can buy from high-street army and navy surplus stores. He told everyone that he wanted to be known as Abdul Rahmin, and would lose his temper when acquaintances forgot. He began showing up at Brixton market in his military garb, selling Islamic books, ignoring the taunts of passers-by who ridiculed his appearance.

There was one thickset figure whom Reid clearly heroworshipped. Zacarias Moussaoui was a French Moroccan who lived close to the Brixton mosque and had taken a business studies course at the South Bank University, though he appeared to devote little time to his postgraduate work. It was Moussaoui who dominated discussion groups at the mosque, shouting down those who dared to criticise his stand that violent jihad was the only way to support Islamic communities around the world. When preachers at Brixton criticised his stance he transferred his allegiance to north of the Thames, and to the Finsbury Park mosque which in the summer of 1998 was acquiring a reputation as a magnet for young radicals. Moussaoui would take some acolytes with him, including Reid, who was mouthing the same radical expressions and insults about America and Tony Blair as his shaven-headed hero.

Moussaoui was brought up in Bayonne, in the Basque region of south-western France, the youngest of four children born to Moroccan immigrants. He was raised by his mother, Aicha, a postal worker, after his violent father walked out when he was two. The teenage Moussaoui showed no interest in religion or in school, save a passion for basketball. His considerable bulk was useful to immigrant gangs in their clashes with skinheads, but his older brother was troubled by the company he was keeping of young Muslims who ranted about the brutal treatment of their brothers in Bosnia and Chechnya. In 1986 he left France, not telling his family he was going to Britain, and his mother still blames malicious influences there, particularly Abu Hamza, for leading him in the direction of military training camps in Afghanistan.

He was caught by the FBI three weeks before the 9/11 attacks, but agents took too long to interrogate him and to examine his laptop computer, which would have revealed his intricate links with al-Qaeda and the hijackers. He had been handed $14,000 cash from Khalid Sheikh Mohammed, the man who was orchestrating the day-to-day running of the hijack operation, to pay for flight lessons in the United States.

Moussaoui behaved badly. After fifty hours' flying time he flunked out of the first school in Norman, Oklahoma, where two of the 9/11 hijackers were trained. He proved no more successful at his second school, the Pan-Am International Flight Academy in Eagan, Minnesota, where his instructor, Clancy Prevost, was curious why his student, who paid cash for his lessons, did not wish to learn how to take off or land an aircraft, simply how to steer a 747, and asked questions about how much fuel a Jumbo could carry and what sort of damage it could do if it hit anything.

Immediately after 9/11 the American security services were understandably desperate to find those involved in the plot. Moussaoui was the only man they had in custody to question, and consequently the FBI made exaggerated claims about his role with al-Qaeda, while he delighted in the attention he received.

It reassured Americans to think that they had one of the conspirators behind bars. When he finally stood trial in Alexandria, Virginia, in early 2006, Moussaoui pleaded guilty to six charges of conspiring with al-Qaeda to hijack planes, but confused his accusers by constantly changing his testimony about his involvement. After first denying that he had played any part, he then signed a confession stating that he was 'the twentieth hijacker'. Asked why he did so, he replied: 'I did it because everybody used to call me that so it was a bit of fun.'

At his chaotic trial Moussaoui never shirked from declaring his allegiance to al-Qaeda, but he changed his story again, maintaining that his mission was to crash a hijacked plane into the White House in a second wave of attacks on America, though he didn't say when that was supposed be. As the guilty verdict was read out to him, he screamed: 'I am al-Qaeda, you are Americans, you cannot judge me,' adding that he didn't care what punishment he faced. When he was brought back to the court for the jury to decide whether he should face the death penalty or life imprisonment, he surprised everyone by suddenly claiming that he had been supposed to hijack a fifth plane on 9/11 and crash it into the White House with the help of a friend from his days living in south London, Richard Reid. There was no evidence to support this boast, and the jury spared his life, concluding that Moussaoui had overstated his standing in al-Qaeda.

The headlines concentrated on Moussaoui's hate-filled insults to families of 9/11 victims who were in court, and ignored the warning he gave that America had not asked what made men like him want to kill in the name of al-Qaeda. Staring at the jurors, he told them: 'You missed an opportunity here to find out why people like me and Mohammed Atta [who led the 9/11 attacks] have so much hatred. So we will come back again – if you do not hear it, you will feel it.'

As he was led from the court to spend the rest of his life in solitary confinement in America's toughest prison – the 'Supermax' in Florence, Colorado – Judge Leonie Brinkema told him: 'You will die with a whimper,' adding that there was no prospect of his ever being released. Moussaoui grinned, flashed a 'V' for victory sign to the jury, and used what will probably be his last ever public utterance to shout: 'God curse America. God save Osama bin Laden. You'll never get him.'

US intelligence knew Moussaoui was a product of Finsbury Park mosque, but during his nearly four months in court nobody asked him about his relationship with Abu Hamza, or about those who were at the mosque at the same time as him, and what became of them. Those secrets Moussaoui takes to his eight-by-five-foot cell, where he will be locked up for twenty-two hours a day. Among those held at the prison known as 'the Alcatraz of the Rockies' is Richard Reid, but Moussaoui is forbidden to speak to any other inmate.

By the time the verdict was reached in Moussaoui's case the CIA had enough al-Qaeda commanders in their custody, like the 9/11 organiser Khalid Sheik Mohammed, to know that Moussaoui was lying. Five years on from the worst terrorist attack on the American mainland, the authorities were still allowing the likes of Moussaoui to spread confusion.

In Khalid Sheikh Mohammed's fifty-eight-page written testimony from whatever secret detention centre the CIA were holding him in, he revealed that he didn't trust the likes of Moussaoui with a mission as important to al-Qaeda as 9/11. The US media largely ignored Mohammed's revelations about how he sent the hijackers to a different camp from other would-be suicide bombers like Moussaoui and Richard Reid. Moussaoui's essential worth to al-Qaeda back in those days was that he was one of the first Western-educated recruits willing to die. If he couldn't do it in the cockpit of a plane, then his performance in a Virginia courtroom showed that he was content to be strapped to a trolley in a federal prison in America and have lethal poisons injected into his veins. He was prepared to be al-Qaeda's first suicide witness.

While Moussaoui was always seen as a cocky figure during his time at Finsbury Park, Reid burned with a desire to prove himself. He felt that some of the regulars there looked down on him, as he knew little about the Koran and even less about the real suffering of his brother Muslims. Despite his size he was bullied and taunted at first at the mosque. It was Abu Hamza who would rebuke his tormentors and sit alone with him, encouraging him to pursue his faith. With nowhere else to stay in London, Reid joined the scores of other drifters who had moved into the Finsbury Park mosque, bedding down wherever he could find space at night in one of the offices or on the carpeted floors of the prayer rooms. One man there who always made time for him was an Algerian, Djamel Beghal. Calm and soft-spoken, Beghal would regale his young friend with stories of the horrific tortures being inflicted on true believers in Algeria, where civil unrest between government troops and Islamic radicals cost an estimated 100,000 lives in the years 1992 to 1998, many of the victims being killed in terror attacks. Reid had only ever read about such things, but Beghal breathed life into his idea of becoming a jihadi, a fighter in a real holy war.

The gently persuasive Beghal had another role that Reid was unaware of when they met in the spring of 1998. One of al-Qaeda's most highly regarded talent-spotters in Europe, he would spend hours coaxing reticent figures like Reid to sound off about their frustrations, trying to spot likely candidates he could mould into doing more than just ranting about their enemies. Beghal took his time identifying those he could manipulate, and there were rich pickings at Finsbury Park mosque whom he could send on to training camps in Afghanistan.

Beghal's task was to assemble a team of malleable volunteers who would not lose their nerve when they were called upon by al-Qaeda to sacrifice their lives. Timing was everything. The suicide raids he was planning for Europe had to wait until after the 9/11 plot was unleashed on Washington and New York. Osama bin Laden recognised that if the attacks on Europe came first, there was a risk that investigators might stumble on his plans for America.

His judgement proved right. The worldwide manhunt for those behind 9/11 uncovered a warren of terror cells in cities like Hamburg, Paris and London, and some of those arrested betrayed what was in store for Europe. Investigators noticed that many of these men had passed through Finsbury Park on their journeys, and wondered why.

Abu Hamza had the knack of making misfits like Reid feel good about themselves. Reid, who had never excelled at anything, was able to stomach the tough regime of the al-Qaeda camps in Afghanistan,

indeed he thrived. He was precisely what the handlers were looking for – zealous, stoical, uncomplaining and easily led. Brighter,
stronger, fitter candidates from Finsbury Park were begging to come
home after a fortnight, and Reid's mentors congratulated him on
being a better Muslim than such shallow men. Continue to do as he
was told, they said, and he would become a legend, and achieve the
glories that go with martyrdom.

This was the worst kind of manipulation. They were not creating
self-worth in Reid, but self-delusion, and this recruitment process
would end in the weakest of their volunteers giving the only thing of
value that they had – their own lives. Their training included ensuring that if men like Reid were captured, they did not betray who gave
them their orders. The exploitation worked, and several men sent
from Finsbury Park are either dead or went silently to prison without
implicating their mentors.

The trouble with picking misfits is that they make mistakes. Had
Reid used a cheap disposable plastic cigarette lighter to ignite the
fuse of his bomb, rather than a match that did not burn for long
enough, forensic experts are sure there was enough plastic explosive
in his boot to puncture the fuselage of Flight 63 and bring down
the aircraft.

Another of the class of 1998 at Finsbury Park being groomed as a
suicide bomber was Nizar Trabelsi. Tunisian-born, and as tall as
Reid, he had been a professional footballer in Germany until fame
tempted him into spending too much time in nightclubs, taking
drugs and partying with women who were only too eager to help
him squander his lucrative salary. Fortuna Dusseldorf, who signed
the promising striker in 1989, soon tired of Trabelsi's waywardness.
From posing with his distinctive dreadlocks in soccer magazines, he
soon had his picture on wanted posters as a drug dealer with a pen-
chant for violence.

Trabelsi gloated about meeting bin Laden while training in

Afghanistan, saying, 'I love him a lot, like a father.' He begged bin Laden to let him undertake a suicide mission in 1999, but was told, 'Be patient because the list of martyrs is complete' – supposedly a reference to the fact that al-Qaeda cells in Europe were already grooming the team chosen to hijack four aircraft on the east coast of America.

In September 2003 he was sentenced in the Palais de Justice in Belgium to ten years' imprisonment for planning to detonate a car bomb at a NATO base. At his trial Trabelsi, then aged thirty-three, broke the rules he was taught in Afghanistan, and instead of keeping quiet about his mission, puffed out his chest and proudly declared how he had been chosen to become Europe's first suicide bomber. The plan relied on his getting a job as a delivery van driver which served the NATO base at Kleine Brogel in north-east Belgium, where a couple of hundred US troops were stationed, along with a cache of nuclear weapons. Trabelsi was to pack his van with as much explosive as it could carry, and drive it into the base canteen at lunchtime.

He laughed when the judge jailed him for ten years, but his boisterous vaudeville performance in the dock obscured the fact that he had stubbornly refused to reveal his fellow conspirators who were simultaneously to blow up the US embassy in Paris and the European Parliament building and a Christmas street market in Strasbourg. All the men earmarked to carry out those attacks had spent time at Finsbury Park.

The intelligence agencies conspicuously failed to do anything about the legion of young men, like Reid, who had gone from north London to training camps run by bin Laden. Hundreds made that journey in the late 1990s, yet nobody was questioned or arrested when they got home. If they had been, perhaps MI5 and their foreign allies might have realised that these men had not been away on some macho camping holiday, but were at a terror academy where in extreme cases they were persuaded to turn themselves into human bombs.

Before Reid was supposed to blow himself up, his handlers had another task for him to perform. In July 2001 he was sent on a spying mission for al-Qaeda. His first chore was to acquire a new British passport, as the visa stamps in his existing document might make it difficult for him to get into Israel – one of the six stops he was to make. Reid put his passport in the washing machine, then presented its remains to clerks at the consular office in Brussels, who replaced it without question.

His travel diary, written in coded Arabic, was only discovered several months later, on an encrypted computer disk found by FBI agents at an al-Qaeda safe house in Kabul following the US-led invasion. Posing as a holidaymaker, Reid flew to Tel Aviv to test El Al's security. He complained that his tape recorder was ruined when his hand luggage was electronically screened. During the flight he watched how many times flight attendants opened the cockpit door, and jotted down in a notebook that the minutes just before the seatbelt signs were turned on for landing was the best time to strike.

In Tel Aviv he rode on buses and trains, photographed churches and tall buildings and strolled around shopping malls to determine which were the busiest. He recorded which bus routes had armed guards on board, and which stations carried out the most exhaustive bag searches, deciding that Haifa on a Saturday night offered a soft target.

Reid moved on to the tourist sites in Jerusalem, mingling with sightseers at the Western Wall, where he noted in his diary how astonished he was to find security remarkably lax. To cover his tracks he used tricks taught by his al-Qaeda tutors, such as taking empty alcohol bottles found in the street and leaving them in waste bins in his hotel room to allay any suspicions that he was a practising Muslim.

He has never said who funded his travels, which took him next to Egypt, then on to Turkey, where he was delighted to be singled out for special attention by the security guards at Ankara airport, who scrutinised and X-rayed his passport, then let him go with profuse apologies for the delay. After a stop in Pakistan he came back to Europe, where he shuttled between Belgium and Holland, staying with the likes of Trabelsi, who found him part-time work in hotel kitchens.

Reid's passport shows that in November he was on his travels again, with a flight to Pakistan. This time he was not alone. He was joined by a Gloucester-born grammar-school boy, Saajid Badat, who was supposed to detonate a shoe bomb on another transatlantic flight, at the same time as Reid destroyed Flight 63.

While Reid was an underachieving, shambolic figure, the then twenty-two-year-old Badat was a model of middle-class respectability. His parents had come to Britain from Malawi, part of the wave of Asian migrants who left East Africa in the 1970s. Muhammad Badat worked in the Wall's food factory in Gloucester, and his wife Zubeidah concentrated on the traditional role of raising their four children. Saajid was the oldest, born in March 1979, and went to a Church of England primary school before securing a place at The Crypt, one of Gloucester's most sought-after grammars. The headmaster, David Lamper, thought him an impressive scholar who passed ten GCSEs and four A-levels, and remembers him as 'punctual, cheerful and polite'. Outside school his absorbing passion was supporting Liverpool Football Club. He wasn't that skilled a player himself, but he was enthusiastic and regularly turned out for a local Sunday league team who called themselves the Asian Stars.

After a series of rows with his father, Badat left home at eighteen and moved to London, where he worked as a kitchen porter and a part-time security guard while deciding on his next move. Aimless and rootless, he began visiting mosques around the capital, and was moved by accounts he heard there of the ethnic cleansing of Muslim families during the civil wars that had torn apart the former Yugoslavia.

Abu Hamza had been there. He was animated in his depiction of the suffering he had seen, and his voice swooped and soared as he recounted a biased version of how it was only a band of mujahideen veterans from Afghanistan who had prevented the annihilation of the Muslim community. His performances prompted Badat to sign up for a trip to Sarajevo in 1998 to help out in relief operations for the thousands who were still homeless after the war. A timid, slightly awkward boy, he muddled around the city, resolving to do more to defend Muslim communities wherever they were being persecuted. The trouble was, he didn't know how best he could help.

He wasn't built to enlist in the foreign legions being sent to fight on the front lines in Chechnya and Kashmir, so his response was to turn himself into a religious scholar. He left Britain to study at madrassas in the Middle East and Pakistan, those bleak, disciplined institutions where pupils memorise verses from the Koran for hours at a time, until they can recite them in their sleep. This was not education, more brainwashing, and it was the ideal place for talent-spotters eager to manipulate naïve, obedient souls like Badat. MI5 later discovered that the very people who spirited Reid to training camps in Afghanistan had reportedly done the same for Badat in the early months of 1999.

On 11 September, as the world watched the staggering events unfold in two American cities, Badat was at the British consulate in Brussels, pulling the same stunt as Reid, claiming he had ruined his passport and needed an urgent replacement.

Police say that on 20 November 2001 the two Britons flew by different routes to Pakistan and slipped over to Afghanistan, where al-Qaeda's most celebrated bomb-maker, Abu Khabbab al-Masri, was waiting for them at his base at Darunta on the banks of the Kabul river, near Jalalabad. He had been working on ways to mould enough plastic explosive into a shoe to puncture a plane's fuselage, and seemed pleased with his handiwork.

Reid would claim at his trial that he paid £1,000 to buy the C4 military explosive over the internet from a neo-Nazi group, and then rigged up the bomb himself. The prosecutors pointed out that a hair and a palm print found on the mechanism were not his. There is no way of telling whether they belonged to the Egyptian-born bomb-maker, as Abu Khabbab was reported killed in a CIA missile attack in January 2006 on a hilltop village in north-eastern Pakistan, where he was supposedly arranging his wedding in the company of some of al-Qaeda's high command.

While Reid flew back to Britain on 5 December, determined to carry out his suicide mission, Badat was having second thoughts. Whether he suffered a fit of conscience or of fear he has never said, but nine days after flying back to Britain he sent a curt, coded, apologetic email to his handler in Pakistan saying he couldn't go through with the suicide operation. He hid the detonator in a green suitcase under his bed and wrapped the explosive in a rolled-up sock hidden in a cupboard on the first-floor landing of his parents' terraced home in Gloucester. By then he had already bought a ticket from Manchester to Amsterdam's Schiphol airport and then an onward flight to the US for 21 December – the day Reid was supposed to fly to Miami.

Badat saw the headlines about Reid's arrest, but decided to say nothing about his own involvement in the plot, hoping his al-Qaeda handlers would leave him alone and not seek their revenge. His specially adapted shoes were thrown in a dustbin, but agents investigating Reid uncovered Belgian telephone cards which Badat had used to stay in touch with the local contact they shared in Brussels – the erratic Nizar Trabelsi. Badat had also kept an incriminating letter he had written to his family explaining his suicide attack as 'a sincere desire to sell my soul to Allah in return for paradise'. Forensic tests would show that the detonator cords for Reid and Badat's devices were two parts of the same length of material.

Hoping to put his past life behind him, Badat enrolled in an Islamic college in Blackburn, unaware that he was being hunted by security forces on both sides of the Atlantic. He was arrested in an early-morning raid in November 2003, and even as he was being driven away the usually taciturn student began confessing that he didn't know how to get rid of the bomb under his bed.

There was surprise in April 2005 when an Old Bailey judge praised Badat's cooperation with the police, and rewarded his renouncing of terrorism by imposing a lenient sentence of only thirteen years. Prosecutors in the US immediately made it clear that they were not as forgiving, insisting that they would seek Badat's extradition once he had served his time in Britain.

After Badat had failed them, al-Qaeda put their faith in Reid to carry out his attack, but he made so many mistakes it is astonishing he wasn't spotted long before he boarded Flight 63. At a time when security was supposed to be at its most intense, he turned up at the British consulate in Brussels on 5 December 2001 to demand his second replacement passport in less than five months. He stayed at the Hotel Dar Salam in the city's Arab quarter, and spent most of his time in cheap internet cafés drinking thick sweet coffee and sending messages to his handlers. He took a train to Paris, and moved around the largely immigrant neighbourhood of Goutte d'Or, then on 18 December paid $1,800 cash for a flight from Paris to Miami and on to Antigua, telling the travel agent he was holidaying in the Caribbean over Christmas. When he turned up at Charles de Gaulle airport for the American Airlines flight on 21 December, check-in staff could not help but notice the dishevelled, surly character in foul-smelling clothes who was carrying no luggage for a supposed holiday trip.

On 11 December the Federal Aviation Authority in America had issued a security bulletin warning that terrorists might try to smuggle weapons or explosives onto flights in their shoes. Reid was never asked to hand over his scuffed ankle-high boots when he was searched. Had he done so, it would have been immediately obvious that there were holes drilled into the soles.

Security officers spent so long questioning him that Reid missed his flight. They told him he could book for the following day, and

A stash of knives and army-surplus field-kitchen equipment was hidden in the mosque. Police believe it was used in jihad training camps in the Brecon Beacons and elsewhere in Britain.

After his mosque was closed in the January 2003 raid, Abu Hamza continued to preach to hundreds of his followers on the street outside the barricaded building. The street preaching and prayers enhanced his reputation as a radical, and allowed him to portray himself as a victim of religious persecution.

otland Yard's bill for policing Abu Hamza's Friday open-air gatherings came to most £900,000.

ehzad Tanweer, Jermaine Lindsay and Mohammed Sidique Khan at Luton railway ation on a reconnaissance mission just weeks before they carried out suicide ombings on London tube trains on 7 July 2005. All three had heard Abu Hamza each.

Hasib Hussain, eighteen, was the fourth 7/7 bomber; he detonated his suicide bomb on a number 30 bus in Tavistock Square.

BELOW: Jermaine Lindsay with his wife Samantha and their first child. Lindsay's suicide bomb on a Piccadilly Line train killed twenty-six people.

helped him make the necessary arrangements. Reid took a bus back into Paris, and went straight to an internet café to email his handlers about the unforeseen delay. They ordered him to try again as soon as possible. Reid has never said whether he was told that Badat had already backed out, but from the tone of the emails he received it is clear that his al-Qaeda contacts did not want to risk giving him time to sit around in Paris, where he too might change his mind. Reid assured them that his conviction to die a martyr was unshakeable.

He had already sent a farewell message on his Yahoo account to his mother, hoping she would not be too upset over what he was going to do. The email, sent via an intermediary, was littered with spelling mistakes. It also contained his will. He told her his reason for sending it was to show her 'that i didn't act out ignorance nor did i do so just because i want to die, but rather because i see it as a duty upon me to help remove the oppressive american forces from the muslim land and that this is the only way for us to do so as we do not have other means to fight them'.

Passengers lining up with Reid in the airport queue on 22 December felt uncomfortable standing close to the unkempt, noxious giant who was grinning manically at them, revealing his missing teeth. The airline staff remembered him from the previous day, but just nodded him through.

Nine hours later FBI agents were waiting for him on the tarmac at Logan Airport after Flight 63 had been diverted to Boston. Reid's first question to the officers who came on board to arrest him was whether the press and TV crews were waiting for him. As he was driven away a photograph was taken which showed how his nose was cut and swollen after his skirmish with the flight crew and passengers, and that one eye was closed and the other bloodshot.

From the start of his interrogation at Plymouth County jail Reid made no apologies for trying to kill over two hundred people in mid-air. He boasted how he decided to scream a prayer to Allah in the

moment before he detonated the shoe bomb, in the hope that it
would be the last thing heard on any voice recorder on Flight 63. He
told detectives that had he succeeded, nobody in America would dare
to get on a plane again.

When he appeared in a Boston court for sentencing in December
2003, Reid played to the public gallery and the watching press, describing himself as 'a soldier of Islam' and pledging his allegiance to
Osama bin Laden. There was a shouting match when Judge William
Young tried to interrupt his noisy protestations, telling him, 'You are
not a soldier in any war, you are a terrorist.' Reid refused to be
silenced, declaring that he had nothing to apologise for, condemning
the US for its actions in Iraq and for sponsoring the systematic rape
and torture of Muslims in countries like Egypt and Turkey. There
were no expressions of remorse or regret as Reid glowered across the
court at Judge Young, shouting that he didn't care what punishment
he was given.

He was sentenced to eighty years in jail and a $2 million fine,
though it is not clear how the judge thought the penniless Reid would
ever pay that amount. As he was being wrestled out of the courtroom,
the judge told Reid: 'The world is not going to long remember what
you or I say here. Day after tomorrow it will be forgotten.' He was
wrong. What Reid attempted to do remains one of the most chilling
demonstrations of how far terrorists were prepared to go in their so-
called holy war. More worrying was that his own account of his
recruitment by al-Qaeda revealed that there were scores more
Western recruits like him ready to die in bin Laden's name.

Reid's guilty plea meant that there was no full investigation into
the identities of all those involved in the plot to destroy Flight 63. For
all his theatrics in court, he was careful not to say what became of the
other squatters from Finsbury Park who went to Afghanistan to be
groomed as suicide bombers.

16
The Ricin Plot

'This is now what we ask the Muslims, to do that, to be capable to do that, to bleed the enemies of Allah anywhere by any means. You can't do it by nuclear weapons, you have to do it by kitchen knife, no other solution. You can't do it by chemical weapons, you have to do it by poison.'

Abu Hamza

The National Express NX333 coach beat its relentless path northwards along the motorways of England – from Weymouth to Bristol, then on to Birmingham, eventually turning towards Manchester. On board, the passengers behaved as the British travelling public usually does. They ignored one another. Huddled against the winter's day outside, they busied themselves with their newspapers and books, curled up in search of uncomfortable sleep or plugged their portable stereos into their ears.

One man seemed especially intent on keeping his own company. A thin, wiry figure with short dark hair and wearing a long, grubby white shirt, he was concentrating intently on the copy of the Koran that was the most prized among his few possessions. Occasionally he broke off from his reading to take or make a call on his mobile phone. There was nothing in his manner to indicate that this twenty-nine-year-old was on that day – 9 January 2003 – the most wanted man in Britain.

Four days earlier, anti-terrorist squad detectives had raided a flat above a pharmacy in Wood Green, north London, and discovered a kitchen-sink laboratory where a small group had been attempting to make poisons using crude recipes identical to those found in al-Qaeda houses in Afghanistan. Handwritten in Arabic, they were copied from right-wing American websites of instructions for the manufacture of lethal doses of ricin, cyanide, botulinum and nicotine poison. There were also circuit diagrams for the manufacture of detonators for bombs and other components of bomb-making equipment. In the bottom of a cheap wardrobe was a padded envelope containing £4,000 cash and eleven passport photographs. An address written on the envelope had been heavily scored out with ink, but when subjected to intensive scientific study it was revealed as the Finsbury Park mosque, St Thomas's Road, London N4, and the addressee was Kamel Bourgass, an Algerian who arrived in London in 2000. The man in the photo-booth pictures was also Bourgass.

Bourgass himself, however, was nowhere to be found when the flat was raided. He had been in the mosque, the place where he slept and spent much of his time. When news of the raid broke, he fled the mosque and London. Now he was on the NX333 on his way north and, he hoped, out of Britain.

Bourgass's photograph had been copied and circulated by Scotland Yard to every police force in Britain. He was identified as a dangerous terrorist suspect. He might be armed; he might be carrying lethal doses of toxins. The authorities simply did not know. What they did know was that this man was the key figure in a major anti-terrorist operation that had been in train – largely undercover and unpublicised – across Britain for four months.

Their prey had his mind fixed not on committing a last act of terrorism, but on slipping out of the country. Bourgass was hoping to use a tried and tested escape channel established by the North African al-Qaeda cell that operated out of the Finsbury Park mosque. Manchester was the first step. He could hole up there for a few days, maybe weeks, at a safe house run by Islamist sympathisers while his associates obtained a false passport and an airline ticket to enable him to leave the UK. The next staging point was Liverpool John Lennon Airport, from where he could catch a flight to Barcelona, where he would stay at the Citadenes Hotel on Las Ramblas before travelling once more, to Morocco.

The route was well-worn. Security at Liverpool airport was not as intense as at the London airports, and there were unlikely to be specialist intelligence officers watching for al-Qaeda 'faces' travelling to and from Barcelona. Mohammed Meguerba, a close associate of Bourgass in the ricin plot, had used the same escape route just a few months before. Another shadowy figure, a Tunisian who has been linked by the Spanish authorities to the 9/11 plot and the recruitment of young European Muslims to fight in Iraq, had also skipped Britain using the same route. But Bourgass would not get away. He was caught, by pure chance, while he was in Manchester. But before he was restrained he would kill one policeman and seriously wound three others. They would be the first casualties on British soil of the new 'war' on al-Qaeda terrorism.

Operation Springbourne, the nationwide police inquiry into the ricin plot, had not started as an investigation into an active terrorist cell. Its origins lay in a concerted attempt to smash the fraudulent fundraising ring – set up by the North African activists who congregated in Finsbury Park – which had raised millions of pounds for mujahideen campaigns in Chechnya, Algeria and Afghanistan. The investigation was to discover that the terror cell – part of an international network created by Abu Doha – had moved from supporting terror elsewhere to planning an operation in Britain.

After months of surveillance of key suspects, the first arrests had been made in a north London internet café where two men were caught in the act of wiring a five-figure sum overseas. On 18 and 19 September 2002 a series of further arrests were made across London

– from Tottenham in the north of the city to Ilford in the east. Among those arrested was Meguerba, a key figure in the ricin plan who had allegedly been trained alongside Bourgass at an al-Qaeda camp in Afghanistan to manufacture simple poisons. Police had no idea at this stage how important Meguerba was, and released him after a short period in custody after he was found to be prone to epileptic seizures. He was freed on bail and given a date to return for further questioning. The appointment was never kept, as Meguerba, apparently on the orders of a veteran Algerian terrorist at the mosque, slipped out of Britain along the Liverpool escape run.

Ignorant of Meguerba's significance, detectives were busily pursuing the dozens of leads that seemed to spring out every time they arrested someone or raided an address. Addresses, phone numbers, names and photographs were leading in many different directions, overlapping with other inquiries in Britain and overseas. A hugely complex web of connections was emerging.

At one flat in east London police uncovered several false French and Belgian passports – including one with the picture of the Tunisian al-Qaeda organiser – and names and addresses of other associates of the fundraising ring. One lead took them to the small market town of Thetford, a hundred miles north-east of London in the Norfolk countryside. David Aissa Khalef, an Algerian, was arrested there on 26 September 2002 in a flat on Ethel Coleman Way. Among his personal possessions police found a black holdall, the contents of which were to change the course of the investigation. In a zipped pocket inside it were several photocopied sheets of paper containing dense Arabic writing in a neat hand. When translated, one set of papers was revealed to contain recipes for the manufacture of ricin, cyanide, nicotine poison and rotten meat poison. The second sheaf appeared to include a list of the chemicals and other ingredients required to make the recipes. As with the 7 July 2005 bombs in London, the materials needed to launch this terror attack could be obtained over shop counters on the high street.

The discovery sent shock waves through the senior ranks of Britain's security and intelligence community. For the first time they had uncovered an Islamist plot to carry out a terrorist attack in Britain. The warnings had been there for years – not least in the content of the sermons and lectures delivered by Abu Hamza to his recruits – but had not been taken seriously. 'It was the first tangible evidence that we had come across something more than fundraising,' recalled a senior anti-terrorist officer. 'Imagine the impact of discovering that we had found people who were apparently interested in mounting attacks in the UK using unconventional weapons.'

The photocopied recipes were sent to the Porton Down Research Establishment in Wiltshire, one of the leading centres in the world for the study of chemical weapons. Scientists there followed the Norfolk recipes to the letter and declared them 'viable' for the creation of small quantities of poisons.

A range of terrifying scenarios began to course through the minds of senior officers. Khalef, the man arrested in Norfolk, had been working in a sausage-meat factory. Could he have been planning to poison the food chain? He was also living close to US Air Force bases in the east of England. Might personnel from those bases have been his targets? Those questions could not be answered, but the authorities believed they faced a race against time to find the people who had written out the recipes, and who might be preparing to use the deadly toxins.

In Whitehall, the heart of the British state, a secret summit was held in October 2002, and orders to attend were issued to two hundred officials from the security and intelligence services, senior civil servants and key personnel in the transport industry – especially the London Underground network. The possibility of a terrorist poison attack on the Tube was outlined to those present. The importance of vigilance and secrecy was stressed.

Intelligence agencies stepped up surveillance on the north London suspects, but also across Europe. The CIA was asked to examine all the traffic it monitored to try to identify any references to a poison attack. In late October Meguerba failed to answer his bail. London was still unsure of his significance, but an alert was issued requesting information about him or his whereabouts, and declaring him a person of interest.

For weeks the intelligence radar remained blank. There was no internet chatter, no significant movement of either suspects or money. Officers continued to chase down every lead in the fund-raising inquiry, but nothing brought them any closer to whoever was behind the ricin plot.

A possible breakthrough came in November, when French intelligence told London that a key suspect was on the move. The man, known as Toufiq, had re-entered Britain. Toufiq, whose real name is Rabah Kadre, had been identified in 1998 by intelligence agents inside Finsbury Park as an important figure in the cell that operated from the mosque. His name features prominently in reports written by Reda Hassaine, who worked for British and French intelligence at the mosque.

Toufiq had been second-in-command to Abu Doha, the studious, bespectacled architect of the pan-European Algerian terrorist network that had its operational headquarters in Finsbury Park mosque. Abu Doha was the man who struck a deal with Osama bin Laden to establish a training camp for North Africans – predominantly veterans of the conflict in Algeria – in Afghanistan, recruits from which then fanned out across Europe and North America. Toufiq had been arrested at Heathrow airport after Abu Doha was detained in February 2001. But while there was a US extradition warrant to enable the detention of Abu Doha, who continues to maintain his innocence, the British authorities felt they had insufficient material to justify holding Toufiq. He was released, and later left Britain.

MI5 has told the Special Immigration Appeals Commission, Britain's secretive anti-terrorist court, that Toufiq was 'Abu Doha's successor' as leader of the terrorist network. Intelligence reports suggested he had taken himself to Chechnya, via Georgia, and spent some time with Algerian units engaged in the conflict against Russia. But French agents located him in Bratislava, the Slovak capital, where he was living with two Muslim sisters. He was tracked as he moved across Europe and re-entered Britain. Now the British authorities faced a dilemma. Did they allow Toufiq to run, keeping him under surveillance and seeing where and to whom he might lead them? Or did that strategy carry the risk that he had come to direct the ricin plotters, and would authorise an attack?

Given the fear that Toufiq's arrival might be the catalyst for action, the decision was taken to arrest him. He was picked up in a north London flat in November. A security source says: 'We could have let him run. But he was too much of a risk.' In a linked operation in Paris, four men were arrested in a raid during which police found a recipe for making cyanide and a chemical warfare protection suit.

The raids on opposite sides of the English Channel sparked a flurry of newspaper stories about a cyanide attack on the London Tube. But Toufiq had not had time to make contact with the key plotters. He was an important scalp for the authorities, but he was not the one who brought them closer to solving the ricin case.

The breakthrough came a month later, shortly after Christmas 2002, when a twenty-seven-page memorandum from the Algerian intelligence services landed on a desk at MI5 headquarters. The document was a report of the interrogation of Mohammed Meguerba, who had disappeared from London following his arrest at the beginning of Operation Springbourne. Meguerba had been arrested in November after crossing from Morocco into Algeria in the company of a small band of terrorists belonging to a group called the Dhamat Houmet Daawa Salafia (DHDS), which is designated by the US State Department as having links with al-Qaeda. Since then he had been held incommunicado in one of Algeria's network of secret detention centres, where, human rights groups allege, terrorist suspects are routinely tortured and ill-treated.

It seems likely that Meguerba was beaten by his interrogators. He was not seen again in public until May 2005, when members of his family were shocked by his gaunt appearance as he appeared before an Algiers court to face terrorist charges. Meguerba's case was a stark illustration of the problem faced by Western democracies in fighting the 'war on terror'. He appeared to have been tortured, yet the information he provided during his interrogation led British police to the flat where Bourgass had been attempting to make deadly poisons.

Meguerba was born in 1968 in the Algiers suburb of Belcourt, the youngest of three children of a couple whose marriage ended acrimoniously. He was brought up by his businessman father and an aunt, and is remembered by former neighbours as a quiet, religiously devout young man. In 1995, with Algeria in turmoil, he left his homeland and travelled across Europe; he arrived in Dublin in 1996, and lodged an asylum claim.

The following year, calling himself 'Frank', he met and married Sharon Gray, a trainee beautician from the west of Ireland who had not long moved to the city. It was a whirlwind romance that led to a register office wedding, then degenerated into abuse and brutality. Meguerba, Miss Gray recalls, beat her, locked her in a room and demanded sex whenever he felt like it. He told her that his purpose in marrying her had been to obtain an Irish passport. After eight months she escaped their flat on Dublin's South Circular Road and fled back home to County Sligo. He pursued her, but she took action through the courts and won a non-molestation order against him.

Feeling increasingly alone in Ireland, Meguerba began to attend a Dublin mosque, where he fell into the company of a number of fellow Algerians. During 2000, Ireland had become a hiding place for a number of Islamists criss-crossing the Atlantic. Meguerba was encouraged to attend another mosque in Belfast, on the northern side of the Irish border. Here he was indoctrinated into the Islamist cause, and was persuaded to travel to London, where arrangements were made for him to go to Afghanistan for jihad training. He reached the camps in 2000 and, according to the 'confession' he gave to his Algerian interrogators, was trained at the al-Qaeda-run Khalden and Darunta facilities. He and another man, who he knew as Nadir, were trained in making poisons. Meguerba, the Algerian documents claimed, said that during 2001 he had been personally assigned a mission in the UK by bin Laden, and was given $600 and a false passport with which to make his way to London.

His journey was not without hitches. Less than a fortnight before the 9/11 attacks he was stopped by police at Amsterdam's Schiphol airport as he disembarked from a flight from Tehran. It has since become known that the service from the Iranian capital was heavily used by al-Qaeda operatives leaving Afghanistan to take up station in Europe before the attacks on New York and Washington and the expected retaliation. The Dutch detected Meguerba's false passport and held him for six months, rejecting five asylum appeals. Then, in February 2002, he was suddenly released. He travelled to Paris, where he had relatives, and obtained a legitimate passport in his own name at the Algerian embassy. He went on to Turin, and from there caught a flight to London on 10 March 2002. He went straight to Finsbury Park mosque, where he immediately sought out Nadir, his comrade from Afghanistan. Nadir, who claims he entered the UK hiding in a lorry that crossed from Calais to Dover, was using several names to facilitate his life as an illegal immigrant in London. One of them was Kamel Bourgass. His true identity remains unknown.

Bourgass and Meguerba were enlisted into the principal activity of the Finsbury Park cell – raising money for the mujahideen. Bourgass ran a shoplifting ring, which stole many items, but mainly clothes which could then be sold from a market stall which Meguerba and others ran. Using a false French identity, Meguerba even bought an off-the-shelf company, Seven Roses, to run his 'business'. In July 2002 Bourgass was arrested for shoplifting in east London, after he was caught stealing two pairs of jeans. He was taken to a police station, interviewed, charged and fined £70 by a magistrate. His immigration status as an illegal overstayer was not discovered, because on the night he was detained there were no immigration officers on duty in London with whom his name could have been cross-referenced.

During that summer, Meguerba and Bourgass began the task of compiling their recipes and gathering the ingredients needed to make the toxins. Two sets of photocopies of the recipes – hand-written by Bourgass – were made using the photocopier in Abu Hamza's office in Finsbury Park mosque. The would-be poisoners stored the equipment and ingredients (items as simple as castor beans, cherry stones, blotting paper and nail-polish remover) in the flat of a young asylum seeker whom Bourgass had befriended. Most of the time Bourgass slept at the mosque, but he stored some of his possessions in the apartment, and occasionally spent the night there.

Meguerba had visited the flat infrequently, and could not recall its address. But, crucially, he remembered how he had travelled there. Under questioning in Algeria he gave the details of his journey and a description of the exterior of the flat. Inside, he said, he and the man he knew as Nadir had made poisons, including ricin. They had stored quantities of one toxin in two empty Nivea face-cream jars. According to the Algerian memo, the intention was to smear the creams on car-door handles and restaurant and office doors – possibly causing death, but certainly spreading panic.

The receipt of the Algerian memo triggered immediate action in London. Meguerba's description of his journey to the flat led police surveillance teams to 352b High Road, Wood Green – an address above the Guardian Pharmacy – which was let by the local authority to two young asylum seekers whose rent was paid by housing benefit. On 5 January 2003 the flat was raided by police officers, forensic scientists and chemical weapons experts, all wearing protective clothing and masks.

After months of searching they had found the amateur laboratory where Bourgass and Meguerba had been attempting to make poisons. In addition to the raw ingredients there were funnels, packets of rubber gloves and digital scales. A Nivea jar was found containing a mixture which, when tested, was found to be an unsuccessful attempt at making nicotine poison. Besides the instructions for making poisons there were recipes for high explosives and wiring diagrams for a type of firing mechanism which experts had not seen before, but which has since been found in improvised explosive devices used in Iraq.

Scientists believed initially that they had found traces of ricin in the flat, but the test result was later shown to be a false positive. The search teams did, however, find quantities of stolen toiletries, including bottles of mouthwash and several toothbrushes which were still in their packaging. The plastic covers on the toothbrushes appeared to have been tampered with, raising fears that one plan might have been to put poison on the bristles, reseal the packaging and replace the brushes on shop shelves. A senior Scotland Yard officer said: 'It exploded some of the doubts in my mind about what we might have been looking for. We wondered if it might have been some sort of laboratory. But this was garden shed, kitchen chemistry, and all that was required was stuff that could be picked up on the average high street, requiring adolescent knowledge to put it into action.'

Banner headlines reported the discovery of a terrorist poison factory in a down-at-heel suburb of north London. But the master poisoner had not been found. The young Algerian asylum seeker who rented the flat crumbled quickly under interview, protesting that he knew nothing about chemical weapons. He identified the man in the set of passport photos recovered from the wardrobe as Nadir, his sometime flatmate. Nadir, or Bourgass, was usually to be found at Finsbury Park. He often slept in the mosque, in the basement.

But when news of the ricin raid broke, Bourgass had immediately realised that the police would soon be looking for him. Instantly he was on his toes. Carrying nothing but his Koran and the shirt he wore when praying, he fled London, dumping his keys to the Wood Green flat and obtaining a replacement SIM card for his mobile phone. His first destination was Bournemouth, on the south coast, where the cell had contacts. But he was turned away there, and was forced to spend the night in a hotel in nearby Weymouth. The following morning he caught the NX333 coach service to Manchester.

In Manchester Bourgass took refuge in a cramped bedsit in a large Edwardian house on Crumpsall Lane in the Cheetham Hill district. He spent four days waiting for the uproar over the ricin raid to settle down and for a contact to supply him with another set of false papers. Unfortunately for Bourgass, on 14 January 2003 one of his Manchester associates was certified by David Blunkett, then Home Secretary, as a terrorist suspect to be detained without trial. It was a stroke of misfortune for Bourgass.

The Greater Manchester Police team that descended on Crumpsall Lane was not expecting to become involved in a major incident. Britain was on a high state of alert, but the pre-raid briefing had been 'relaxed', no body armour had been issued, and no armed officers would be deployed. The unit swooped as darkness fell around 4.30 p.m., and found three men in the flat: the man they were searching for, who can only be named as 'M'; the Libyan tenant of the property; and a third man, who seemed to be tense. He had a strong, prominent jaw and short dark hair, and his name, according to the London Transport travelcard he was carrying, was Rami. Asked to identify himself, he indicated that he did not speak English, and wrote 'Kamel Bourgass', '5/5/75' and the world 'asylum' on a piece of paper.

A Metropolitan Police Special Branch officer who had been assigned to take part in the operation because of its terrorist connections was immediately suspicious of the third man. Days before, the officer had been shown the photo-booth photograph of the chief suspect in the ricin case. The man sitting in front of him on the low single bed in Manchester bore a resemblance; most noticeably, he had a distinctive mole above his upper lip. The Met officer went outside to call his superiors at Scotland Yard.

Time was dragging on, and the operation was descending into farce. Strangeways, the Manchester jail, said it could not admit 'M', and police had to begin making other arrangements to accommodate him. Then the message came back from London that the man with the mole was almost certainly the ricin suspect. The nature of the operation changed, but the Special Branch officers present did not communicate what they knew to the uniformed police. They were operating, the courts would later hear, on 'a need to know basis'.

Disastrously, a decision had also been taken not to handcuff any of the three men because of concerns that doing so might contaminate any traces of evidence on their hands and wrists. It was a judgement that was making the uniformed officers standing guard over Bourgass nervous. Bourgass was talking in Arabic to one of the other suspects, his voice loud and aggressive. One uniformed officer noticed that he was repeatedly clenching and unclenching his fists, taking deep breaths and tapping his feet in a nervous manner. Bourgass, whose training in Afghanistan had been extensive, was psyching himself up for an escape bid. Around 5.50 p.m. he sprang into action.

He lunged forward, punching one of his guards in the groin. In a split second he was down on the floor executing a combat roll which carried him into the kitchen. He sprang to his feet, plucked a five-inch knife from the draining board, flicked off the light switch and threw himself at the advancing police officers, slashing the air and any flesh that came within his arc. He plunged the knife into the upper arm of a Special Branch officer, who ran from the flat screaming, with blood spurting from his wound. Another officer thought he had been punched three times; in fact he had been stabbed in the chest, side and back. PC Paul Grindrod, who had been punched in the groin, was stabbed in the leg. There was blood on the walls and floors and on those involved in the struggle, including Detective Constable Stephen Oake, who was attempting to grapple Bourgass from behind and pull him to the ground.

PC Grindrod would later tell the Old Bailey: 'Bourgass was struggling with some determination, his focus was on trying to leave the flat, the knife was being waved wildly. Eventually we seemed to end up in a bundle on the floor as we were trying to restrain him.' An officer with a long baton disarmed Bourgass by striking his wrist with force several times, until he let go of the weapon. He was handcuffed. The injured PC Grindrod then noticed DC Oake slumped against the wall: 'There was no life in him, his face was grey. I tried to get a response from him – I shouted at him and pinched his earlobe. But there was no response. I laid him back and cleared his airway. I had to remove a piece of gum from his mouth and then began mouth-to-mouth resuscitation. Then someone else tried heart massage.' It was too late. DC Oake, a forty-year-old father of three children with twenty years' service in the police, was taking his last breaths. Bourgass had inflicted eight stab wounds on him. Four had plunged in right up to the knife hilt; three had punctured his heart and lungs.

Bourgass would be jailed for life for the murder, and he received further heavy sentences for the attempted murders of DC Oake's colleagues. At a second trial he was jailed for seventeen years for planning his toxic attack on London. But, to the 'amazement and dismay' of senior police officers, seven other men charged along with him in the ricin plot were acquitted of poison charges.

More than any other event, the uncovering of the ricin conspiracy and the murder of DC Oake brought the reality of the 'war on terror' to the streets of Britain for the first time. Until then, terrible events had taken place in America and Bali or in faraway places about which most people cared little – Afghanistan, Yemen. In January 2003, however, the sight of armed police and mysterious, almost alien, figures in pale blue protective suits became quite familiar.

The ricin story was to become horribly distorted. Politicians in Washington and London queued up to exaggerate the scale of the Bourgass plot and claim it as justification for tougher anti-terrorism measures or the forthcoming assault on Iraq. Later, in the aftermath of Bourgass's trial in April 2005, newspaper columnists would claim that the whole affair had been a political confection – there had been no ricin, there was no terrorist threat. They were wrong. There was a plan, albeit a ham-fisted one, which had been hatched by men who had been trained in al-Qaeda camps and had based themselves in north London. Other items discovered during Operation Springbourne – including a letter referring to the recruitment of martyrs, and dozens of false passports, some bearing the photos of wanted men – reveal that their plot was part of the wider al-Qaeda conspiracy.

Perhaps most crucially, the evidence that emerged from the ricin investigation convinced the authorities that the headquarters of the British arm of that conspiracy would have to be dealt with. The confrontation could not be postponed any longer.

PART III

The Reckoning

17

The Raid on the Mosque

'The police have violated the sacredness of the mosque.'

ABU HAMZA

Londoners are used to having their sleep disturbed by the life of the city. Their dreams are punctuated by the all-night wail of sirens, the roar and whine overhead of airliners seeking runways and the mundane squabbles of homeward-bound drunks.

But the helicopter clatter that dragged William Morrison from the warmth of his bed just after 2 a.m. on 20 January 2003 was different. For a start, it was damn close. Moreover, it was accompanied by a piercing beam of brilliant white light that swept back and forth across the street outside and made a mockery of his thick bedroom curtains. Mr Morrison went to the kitchen window of his flat, which overlooked St Thomas's Road, to see what was going on this time at the Finsbury Park mosque. He was so taken aback by the sight that greeted him that he called to his wife Elsie to come and see. At once.

The beam of the searchlight was concentrated on the mosque, lighting it up as if it were the middle of the day. 'The noise of the chopper was deafening,' said Mr Morrison, 'and it was hard to see because the light was so bright.' As his eyes got used to the glare, he saw that there were hundreds of police officers outside. Police in crash helmets and face masks, police in body armour, police with guns and truncheons and riot shields, police climbing out of vans and minibuses. They were pouring through the front door of the mosque, clambering down the steps into the basement and crouching on the roof. Inside the building the lights were coming on, one floor at a time.

After two days of hurried planning, and consultation at the highest levels in Scotland Yard and Whitehall, Operation Mermant – the raid on the Finsbury Park mosque – was in full swing. A few hours earlier, more than two hundred Metropolitan Police officers had gathered at New Scotland Yard for a confidential briefing. Until then the operation had been a closely guarded secret, and there were compelling reasons for the secrecy. Firstly, storming a place of worship with a large force of police, some of them armed, ran a very high risk of sparking a violent reaction on the streets. Secondly, and of greater strategic importance, the raid had become an operational necessity in the hunt for the terrorist cell that had been plotting to make ricin, cyanide and other toxins to use against London's population.

The envelope found in the Wood Green flat that placed Kamel Bourgass inside the mosque presented a powerful argument for the raid. There was also the information coming from Mohammed Meguerba, the supergrass who was being 'debriefed' in Algeria. He had frequented the mosque, and to date everything he had said had proved to be accurate.

Interviews with the dozens and dozens of suspects being scooped up around Britain were providing more leads and more detailed information. One of those arrested told police that the photocopier in the Finsbury Park mosque office had been used to make the copy of the ricin and explosives recipes written by Bourgass that had been found in Thetford, Norfolk. In addition, the majority of the hundred people they detained during the ricin investigation seemed to have a connection with Finsbury Park. Many had worked in the kitchens, slept in the basement, or picked up false papers and dodgy credit cards there.

In his office at New Scotland Yard, a senior detective had compiled an ever-expanding chart which spread across three walls and was starting to block out the view from his window; the Finsbury Park mosque was at the centre of the diagram. Two further suspects he wanted to detain were known from surveillance operations to be sleeping in the basement of the building.

The first priorities of the raid were to arrest those two men and to seize the photocopier. But the officers knew that this was also a vital opportunity in the fight against Islamist terror in Britain and Europe. British police had belatedly reached the realisation their counterparts in Europe and the United States had come to some time before, that the Finsbury Park mosque was an active al-Qaeda terror facility in the heart of London.

Despite the clear operational imperative, sensitivities remained. A heavy-handed police raid on a mosque at Lye, near Stourbridge in the West Midlands, to arrest and deport a family of Afghan asylum seekers the previous July, had provoked a furious backlash. A Church of England bishop denounced the cultural insensitivity of invading a place of worship, and a Conservative councillor said the tactic could never be justified.

Political approval from the very highest level would have to be obtained before Operation Mermant could go ahead. Tony Blair, the Prime Minister, David Blunkett, the Home Secretary, and Jack Straw, the Foreign Secretary, were consulted. Straw was in the loop not just because of his ability to anticipate the reaction of the Islamic world, but also for his views on public opinion in heavily Muslim constituencies like his own in Blackburn. Blunkett had just returned to work from major surgery, but had already been briefed on the ricin operation and the mosque, and was a robust supporter of any action against Abu Hamza's power base.

Blair also gave his backing. 'At the meetings we had with the security services in Downing Street Mr Blair was always asking why we weren't taking action specifically against these people – Hamza and three or four others,' said a highly-placed source. 'He was getting rather fed up with being told they were being monitored. It took the trigger of the ricin inquiry and the murder of DC Oake to actually do it. Even then people remained really nervy about what the reaction would be. There were still some who were reluctant to act.'

The main concern for the ministerial trio was that the raid should be entirely an operational police decision. The government did not want to be accused in its aftermath that the search was a politically motivated stunt designed to strengthen the case for war in Iraq or tougher anti-terrorist measures.

In the twenty-four hours before police moved in, public opinion was softened up for a dramatic anti-terrorist swoop. Sir John Stevens, then the Commissioner of the Metropolitan Police, said in a broadcast interview that many terrorist suspects were under surveillance and arrests were inevitable. Blunkett told another interviewer that he was happy for counter-terrorist units 'to take whatever steps necessary, controversial or otherwise, without fear or favour to take action to protect us'.

The raid would therefore be conducted with all necessary force – hence the deployment of two hundred officers. But because of the need to tread carefully, every possible precaution would have to be taken not to offend. All officers entering the mosque were issued with plastic overshoes to make sure their boots did not come into contact with the floor areas where worshippers prayed. In Islam, prayer requires touching the forehead to the ground while facing Mecca; visitors to mosques are asked to remove their footwear to keep the prayer areas free of dirt. Copies of the Koran in the building were to be handled only by Muslim officers, who were to accompany search teams and advise them on how to proceed. Local community leaders, including the trustees of the mosque who had been ousted by Abu Hamza, would be informed about the operation, but not until it was under way. As the most dedicated worshippers turned up for early-morning prayers they were to be met by police officers and diverted to smaller mosques nearby.

After the briefing at New Scotland Yard, a convoy of vehicles – some clearly marked police vans, others hired for the purpose from private companies – ferried the huge force of policemen and women the few miles north through the night to Finsbury Park. Back in the third-floor control room, the tension was palpable. Senior commanders stayed up through the night to watch and hear the first reports from the scene. The control room was packed with people watching as roadside CCTV cameras relayed live pictures of the enormous convoy of vehicles snaking along the almost deserted city streets. No one knew what the reaction to the raid would be. The Met might find itself with a riot on its hands.

Slowly, engines just ticking over, the vehicles edged into position in the side streets around St Thomas's Road, and the first wave of officers emerged. This team was charged with gaining entry, subduing and arresting everyone inside, and securing the building. In the darkness, and in near silence, they fanned out, surrounding the darkened hulk of the domed building, identifying possible escape routes and climbing up assault ladders onto the roof. Close to the front door was Detective Superintendent Colette Paul, Silver Commander for the night. This was going to be a memorable birthday for her.

In his autobiography, *Not For the Faint-Hearted*, Sir John Stevens stated that Operation Mermant carried 'very high risks'. But his claims that officers expected to encounter armed terrorists, and possibly suicide bombers, have been questioned by former colleagues. Close surveillance of the mosque meant that Scotland Yard was well informed about how many people would be inside and where they would be when the raid took place. At 2 a.m. those in the mosque would be asleep.

When all her officers were where they were supposed to be, Detective Superintendent Paul gave the radio signal. Four officers swung a heavy metal battering ram and cracked open the front door of the North London Central Mosque. Downstairs, another ram broke open the basement door, and all around the building windows were smashed in. Police officers in body armour and helmets, wielding nightsticks, made straight for the darkened figures huddled on the floor and grabbed them roughly. Not knowing what was happening, some men raised themselves to their feet and ran towards stairs, doors, wherever. At every turn there was an adrenaline-charged police officer. The occupants of the building were wrestled to the ground, handcuffed and quickly led outside. A line of police vans was already drawn up to take them to different police stations around the north of the city.

Upstairs, on the first floor, the door of Abu Hamza's office was forced open and the room quickly searched for people. No one was there. The cleric himself was tucked up in bed miles away at his home in Shepherd's Bush, oblivious to the invasion of his headquarters. Other ante-rooms along the corridors beside the big prayer rooms were also checked; the doors had been taken off most of them, and there was evidence that some had been used as makeshift bedrooms. But, except for the basement, the mosque was unoccupied.

The first phase of the raid was over within minutes: seven men had been arrested with no significant resistance; no one was injured, and the building was firmly in police hands. The follow-up operation which could now begin was to last a week.

The search began in earnest at daybreak. Even before dawn, the first knots of curious onlookers had gathered outside. Also in position was the initial wave of what would become hundreds of reporters, photographers and cameramen who would relay news of the raid on Abu Hamza's infamous citadel to the world.

Morning also brought the revelation of just how far the building – which was less than ten years old – had been allowed to fall into disrepair under the stewardship of the London mujahideen. The basement, which was supposed to house the women's prayer room, was little more than a squalid doss-house that had been used for years by hundreds of unhygienic men. It was a chill, damp January day, but the place was fetid with the smell of unwashed bodies. Mouldy sleeping bags, rolls of carpet and dirty blankets lay scattered around. There were piles of old clothes and towels, hardened remnants of soap bars and squeezed and flattened toothpaste tubes. A rough breeze-block wall had been built down the middle of the room to provide some privacy for the handful of sisters who still chose to come there. The main sources of the stench, however, were the kitchen, toilets and washrooms. Abu Hamza had not paid the mosque's electricity and water bills. The bathrooms were in an appalling state; still in use but never cleaned. To leave a mosque in such a condition was particularly offensive to followers of a religion which places great stress on cleanliness.

'The Muslim police officers who went into the mosque were really shocked; they could not believe that Muslims could have treated a mosque in this way,' a senior police source recalled. 'It was squalid and filthy and in a dreadful state. The washrooms were dirty and the lavatories were disgusting.' Some weeks later, when control of the mosque was handed back to the former trustees, they took an immediate decision to close the building for reasons of public health and public safety.

Not having paid any utility bills, it was not surprising that Abu Hamza had given no attention to the upkeep of the physical structure of the mosque. As a qualified engineer, however, he must have known that it was falling into a decrepit state. The trustees announced with 'regret, sadness and a heavy heart' that they had to make an urgent charitable appeal for £70,000 to repair the building, and gave their assessment of its condition in a statement which was distributed to local Muslims: 'The building has deteriorated to such an extent that the roof is leaking in several places causing damage to main walls. The dome is leaking and has cracked and the possibility of its collapse cannot be ruled out. The front wall adjoining the minaret is damaged by rainwater and the wall plaster is collapsing.

On the ground floor and lower floor the washroom and toilet areas have all deteriorated and are now unfit for use. They are a health hazard. The lower ground floor area was used for sleeping and for illegal and commercial activities. It is in a terrible state and fungus is growing on the walls.'

Evidence of those illegal activities emerged in January as the specialist police search teams set about looking into every nook and cranny of the five-storey building. On the top floor, hidden close to where Abu Hamza used to deliver his Friday sermons, they found a hoard of amateurish military-style equipment. Some of it appeared comical: for example, there was a wooden cut-out revolver. Other finds – given that the raid was triggered by the search for the ricin gang – were much more sinister, including three nuclear, chemical and biological warfare protection suits.

The rest of the cache was clearly not the kind of material normally found in a mosque. There were three blank-firing handguns, a range of hunting knives, a stun gun, gasmasks, combat clothing including balaclavas, maps, and military camping and field equipment including hand-held radios. A counter-terrorist chief said: 'We went in there looking for material links to the ricin inquiry – we did not expect to find anything like this sort of stuff. The fact that they were happy to keep this sort of stuff in the building is an indication of how safe and secure they felt they were inside.'

Much of this equipment would have been useless to any serious terrorist operative planning to carry out an attack in the UK. But Scotland Yard commanders believe it was used by Abu Hamza's young recruits when they were sent on survivalist training weekends in the Brecon Beacons and the Welsh countryside, or was taken out of hiding for use in the series of 'Islamic Camps' that were held in the basement of the mosque. These were supposed to be the first stage for recruits who, Abu Hamza dreamed, would go on to undergo serious training in Yemen, Oregon or Afghanistan.

Elsewhere in the mosque, search teams were uncovering more

incontrovertible evidence of terrorist support activity. On the ground floor an officer was patiently and methodically pushing a tall stepladder along a corridor, stopping every couple of feet and climbing up to remove polystyrene tiles to examine whether anything was hidden in the cavity between the ceiling and the floor of the room above. One tile seemed a little heavier than the others, and as he pushed it upwards around thirty passports cascaded down on top of his head. He kept going along the corridor. Nothing under the next tile, or the next one. Then a jackpot again: another flood of documents from the ceiling.

Hundreds of forged and stolen documents were found in the ceilings, dumped in bins and hidden under floors and carpets around the mosque. There were passports – including a substantial number of blank Portuguese documents – credit cards, identity cards primarily from France and Belgium, driving licences and chequebooks. There was also laminating equipment, essential for the production of forged passports. Every single item could be used in the racketeering that raised money for terrorism, or by terrorists who needed to cover their tracks.

Strips and strips of passport photographs were discovered. One suspect had kept an album of photo-booth snaps of himself taken over a period of several years which could be used to falsify a range of identity documents. If he had a stolen passport which was three years old, he had a picture of himself from three years before to affix to it. If an ID card required a photo from nine months before, he had that too.

This was exactly the kind of material that informants like Reda Hassaine had told the intelligence services about years before. It was precisely the type of terrorist support activity that television documentary-makers and newspaper journalists had alleged was going on inside the mosque. Finally it was being collected into plastic bags as evidence.

But it was not to be used as evidence. High-ranking police officers believed that, given where they were found, it would have been impossible for Abu Hamza not to have known about both the false documents and the military-style equipment, and what uses they were intended to be put to. But the cleric was neither arrested nor interviewed. The haul of evidence was not produced at his trial, which followed three years later. At the series of trials of Kamel Bourgass and his associates charged in connection with the ricin plot, only the mosque photocopier was alluded to by the prosecution.

The discoveries made at the mosque in January 2003 are said by Scotland Yard to have led to police inquiries in twenty-six countries around the world – a clear indication of the reach and influence of the terrorist networks operating out of Finsbury Park. But there was no major terrorist trial in Britain. To the 'immense frustration' of the police who ordered and executed the raid, they could not put on show what was found inside Finsbury Park mosque for three years, until the end of Abu Hamza's Old Bailey trial. The obstacles to trumpeting the success of the raid and informing the public of the true nature of what was going on inside Abu Hamza's mosque were Britain's aged and increasingly anachronistic *sub judice* laws. By preventing the discussion or publication of any material which might be considered prejudicial to a forthcoming criminal trial, these laws skew the entire debate on the extent of the terrorist threat in Britain.

Nervy government lawyers would not countenance the police publicising their discovery of guns, knives, chemical warfare suits and hundreds of forged documents at Finsbury Park. Any such triumphalism, they cautioned, could unfairly influence the upcoming trials of a range of terrorist suspects connected to the mosque. The details of what police found as they searched the mosque had to be kept secret.

There was no such restriction on Abu Hamza, who emerged to claim that the raid on the mosque was yet more evidence of the victimisation of Muslims by the British state. 'It's disgusting,' he railed. 'The police have violated the sacredness of the mosque. They have been allowed to come in before for meetings, to search and to see each room. They could have just given us a call and come. They haven't done that against churches or synagogues. Why are they harassing us? Have you ever heard of somebody's church being raided because they had pornography or drugs?'

Far from having been conclusively identified as the threat he was, Abu Hamza was able to portray himself as the victim of religious oppression. Around the Algerian cafés and patisseries of Finsbury Park, his views were quickly echoed. 'This is panic,' said one man angrily. 'It makes me feel bad and it makes people here angry. They would never do something like this at a synagogue.'

Even those Muslims who had little time for Abu Hamza and his ilk were made to feel – in the absence of the production of evidence to the contrary – that their religion was under attack. Karim, a local Muslim with an Arsenal FC bobble hat on his head, was confused as well as concerned: 'I am proud to be British but I feel sad and angry about what has happened at the mosque. I think we are all being made out to be terrorists. I pray at the mosque, I hear Abu Hamza preach. But the mosque does not belong to Abu Hamza, it is for any Muslim.'

Such opinions gained credence and currency among the Muslim community. The Islamic Human Rights Commission echoed Abu Hamza's claim that the mosque had been violated. In an open letter to British Muslims, Massoud Shadjareh, its chairman, wrote: 'How many of us realise the precedent that has been set by the raid at Finsbury Park mosque? Regardless of the views we hold as Muslims, we needed to take a clear stance that the violation of any mosque is unacceptable, just as a raid on a church or any other place of worship would be. Instead we have allowed the British authorities to feel complacent that they can attack our sacred places with impunity.'

Abu Hamza had few friends in mainstream Islam in Britain. Most

Muslims regarded him as a dangerous fringe element whose rhetoric and actions only brought trouble for the rest of the community. But the failure of the authorities to capitalise on the success of Operation Mermant reinforced his status as victim and hero, increased his influence over alienated youth and provided him with a dangerous new platform.

William and Elsie Morrison would soon be treated to a new spectacle as they looked out of their kitchen window onto St Thomas's Road.

18
Street Preacher

'I do not order people. I do not have followers.
I have listeners.'

ABU HAMZA

The showman in Abu Hamza was never going to allow the closure of his citadel to stop him performing for his adoring supporters. Within hours of the police raiding the mosque he summoned his lieutenants to a strategy meeting at his home to plan their response. Squatting on the edge of his armchair, he was in truculent mood. He was gesticulating so wildly that he knocked over the cup of tea one of his aides served him. 'Whatever we do,' he shouted, 'we make them pay.'

His entourage was not sure who he had in mind for his revenge – the police, the mosque's former trustees, newspaper editors who had published unflattering stories about him, or Tony Blair, who he claimed was behind this plot to silence him. Abu Hamza was hurling threats and accusations at such a pace that the assembled group knew better than to interrupt. A foam of spittle had formed on his lower lip, his arms were flailing and his face was getting redder. 'They are out to get me,' he cried, and then, apparently drained by his spasm of rage, he slumped back into his chair, his chin resting on his chest. Occasionally he would ask one of the group to peer behind the curtains to see if the police were outside, keeping him under surveillance.

The invasion of what he saw as 'his' mosque clearly caught Abu Hamza by surprise. He was already irritated. The Charity Commission, the body charged with making sure charities behaved within the law, was attempting to strip him of his post (see page 286), and he was determined to defy it by continuing to preach at Finsbury Park. A couple of days earlier he had stood defiantly on the steps of fortress Finsbury and eased aside some of his bodyguards so the television crews had room to film him as he compared himself to the Archbishop of Canterbury. Even his aides looked momentarily puzzled at that remark. He had explained that both he and the archbishop were religious leaders, soulmates with a duty to 'make political statements'. 'The archbishop talks about Iraq from the pulpit. I do the same, so why don't the commissioners close down Canterbury Cathedral?' he asked.

His supporters spilling out onto St Thomas's Road lapped it up as he dismissed the commissioners as 'nagging nobodies' and dared the commission's director of operations to be man enough to come to north London to enforce the ban. 'I'll keep going until they arrest me,' he pledged, raising his voice to be heard above the din of his sycophants. Lifting his arms to appeal for quiet, he continued: 'This is not the last time you will see me here. I intend to carry on preaching. That is my right. The Charity Commission does not have a plug big enough to gag my mouth. They have to stop a lot of churches and synagogues before they stop this here.'

For all the bluster, in private Abu Hamza brooded about his future. He told close confidants that he feared arrest. Ministers were loudly condemning his behaviour, and tabloid newspapers that had the government's ear increasingly vilified him on their front pages and called for the authorities to act against the notorious preacher of hate.

Some of his friends suggested he should flee the country and establish another base for himself. But where, he asked, could he go? No government would want him, and he had no desire to move to the sort of primitive badlands where outlawed Muslim groups with which he had contact had their camps. His disabilities, and his liking for the comforts of Western living, ruled out his hiding in some freezing cold cave in the Afghan mountains. England might be 'a toilet', but it was quite a comfortable one which had a free health service. He drew solace from the thought that as a British citizen he could not be rounded up under the emergency terror laws that had led to seventeen foreign militants – including Abu Qatada – being interned without trial. Surely, as such an influential figure in the Muslim community, he was untouchable.

Fortified by telephone calls of support on that January morning as he watched the news coverage showing forensic officers tramping in and out of 'his' mosque, Abu Hamza settled on his counterattack. If Scotland Yard would not let him into the mosque to deliver his weekly sermon, then he would do it on the street outside.

On the morning of Friday, 24 January, a cavalcade of supporters in their cars followed Abu Hamza's old Mercedes across London as he descended on St Thomas's Road, where two dozen uniformed policemen and a phalanx of journalists were waiting. Traffic was diverted as the road was sealed off and Abu Hamza, the stumps of his amputated limbs in the pockets of his coat, stood gazing up at the heavy padlock on the mosque's iron gate. He stepped onto the traffic island in the middle of the usually busy junction, twisting and turning so the photographers could capture the best image of him with the barricaded mosque behind him.

His sermon, delivered alternately in Arabic and English, was 'typical Hamza', angry, self-righteous and provocative. Some of the police on duty had to smile as he gestured towards them, describing them as 'agents of Satan'. Muslim leaders who had refused to join his protest that morning were decried as 'monkeys in three-piece suits, stupid people, they are just a joke'. Some demonstrators held up banners that warned: 'British government, you will pay'. Other placards proclaimed that Tony Blair had declared 'war' on British Muslims. When it was time to pray, his supporters laid their coats on the road, or used black dustbin liners to kneel on. Their shoes were piled on the kerbside. In the coming weeks, as these protest rallies became more organised, sympathisers brought sheets of blue tarpaulin and carpets to cover St Thomas's Road.

Local complaints about the nuisance these weekly gatherings caused were set aside by the police, who argued that there were strong public order reasons for stewarding them. Far-right groups occasionally threatened to break up these Friday assemblies, trying to goad Abu Hamza's Supporters of Shariah into a street battle by chanting offensive slogans about their hero, or waving packets of bacon in the air. Police were forced to step in when one group brandished a copy of the Koran and threatened to set it on fire.

Bystanders were fascinated by the behaviour of the cleric's minders. These young men had clearly watched too many gangster movies. They stood to attention at the shoulder of their leader, scanning the crowd and whispering to one another out of the corners of their mouths. They dressed in combat gear, bought from high street army surplus stores, and sought inventive ways to mask their faces. Palestinian headscarves were a favourite disguise. No matter what the weather, they sported designer sunglasses.

When prayers and preaching were finished the street theatre continued. Abu Hamza's bodyguards would clear a path through the crowd and carry a large, wooden armchair into the street for their boss to host an open-air advice session. Petitioners would line up to humbly seek his guidance on the Koranic rights and wrongs about a wayward daughter, a work problem or a marital difficulty. Most of those in the queue were warm admirers, but Abu Hamza's guards were in their element sorting the genuine supplicants from the potentially dangerous.

These Friday street gatherings at Finsbury Park attracted an exotic audience. Foreign embassies, which had been monitoring Abu Hamza for years, occasionally sent along a junior diplomat to take notes. Moderate Muslims who had no sympathy for Abu Hamza sometimes attended out of a sense of anger that police had invaded, closed and locked down a mosque. And minibuses of sympathetic demonstrators made the journey from all around Britain to show their solidarity and vent their anger at the police.

There was also a weekly sprinkling of curiosity-seekers who made the fifteen-minute trip on the Underground from central London to gawp at the street preacher who was making headlines across the world. For some tourists, this was London's cheapest matinee. Abu Hamza liked to entertain. He would castigate the police officers present, telling his audience he was intrigued about whether they were there to protect him, or to eavesdrop on his sermons so they could prosecute him.

The police taped his every performance. They also filmed the faces in the congregation. Those who tried to hide their identity would be watched until they drifted away to drink coffee at nearby cafés, where they would drop their guard and peel off their masks, and could be photographed by undercover teams. Some were familiar faces. Intelligence agents struggled to work out the identities of the rest. At the time, most meant nothing to them. Some, though, would come back to haunt the security agencies.

Three men, Mohammad Sidique Khan, Shehzad Tanweer and Jermaine Lindsay, who would detonate bombs hidden in their rucksacks on London Tube trains on 7 July 2005, were occasionally among the crowds listening to Abu Hamza's exhortations to wage holy war. Two of them, Khan and Tanweer, had first heard him speak at a mosque near where they lived in the Beeston area of Leeds. They were so impressed that they travelled south from Yorkshire to hear more. Khan, at thirty the oldest of the bombers, first went to Finsbury Park in 2002, and is said to have spent the night in the basement on some of his visits.

Before he brought carnage to the capital, few men were more respected on the streets of Beeston than Khan. Hard-working and helpful, he was a family man with a young daughter, Maryam. His wife Hasina, who worked with the disabled, was expecting their second child. Her mother Farida Patel attended a Buckingham Palace garden party in 1998 in recognition of her efforts in the community, and received a civic honour at a Downing Street ceremony attended by Tony Blair.

Beeston is a cramped maze of working-class Victorian housing with a largely British-Pakistani population, a transient sprinkling of students and occasional influxes of asylum seekers. The new arrivals had particular reason to thank Khan who, in his role as a teaching assistant, helped their children find their feet during their first, nervous days at Hillside Primary School. Government school inspectors had made a point of praising his work.

Families who had watched this scarred and deprived inner-city district slide into delinquency and street violence admired Khan for being prepared to devote his spare time to coaxing their teenagers back into the education system and taking them out of their ghetto on camping trips to the Yorkshire Dales. He was something of a local hero, and many urged him to stand as a councillor. Modestly he refused, saying he was just happy to help youngsters from the same Pakistani background as himself.

Khan was a first-generation Briton, as were many of the teenagers who had drifted into shoplifting and drug-taking, and who looked up to him as someone they could confide in. Although raising his family on a salary of just £17,000, he spent his own money treating the youngsters to paintballing trips and football matches. He also organised them into teams for tournaments at nearby Cross Flatt's Park.

Khan renovated a basement gymnasium tucked away amid the red-brick terraces of south Leeds and started a martial-arts club. Jermaine Lindsay, a young carpet-fitter who met him at a mosque, was persuaded to come along. There he met Shehzad Tanweer and another Beeston teenager, eighteen-year-old Hasib Hussain, who would become the youngest of the 7/7 bombers.

Khan encouraged his recruits to go to their mosques, and told them of his visits to hear radical figures like Abu Hamza explain the way Muslim boys of their age should be leading their lives. Those who knew him recall how after his trips to other mosques Khan was eager to share what he had learned with his younger 'brothers'. There was a sense that he was trying to make up for lost time. He was older than everyone else in the group. He resented the poverty of his neighbourhood, and became depressed about the fact that his parents' generation had little to show for their years of hard work.

Admission to Khan's training sessions, and to the talks he held afterwards at the government-funded multi-faith Hamara Living Centre, was soon restricted to those youngsters prepared to live by his code of self-discipline and religious observance. He enjoyed being a leader. Be it white-water rafting trips, hill climbing or cricket matches, Khan was in charge. Former acquaintances say he was always looking to prove himself. One Finsbury Park veteran who played football with him remembers him as 'naturally aggressive': 'He wanted to win at all costs, but you could tell he wanted to hurt people. When he tackled, he went for the man. You could see it in his eyes. He was up against bigger men, but he would never flinch. It was an honour thing for him.'

Khan regarded Tanweer as his protégé, and took him along on a trip to Finsbury Park when Abu Hamza was still preaching inside his stronghold. For the recruiting agents lurking about the mosque these men were ideal recruits; Khan was clearly leadership material, and frustration oozed out of both of them. At the mosque the indignation they felt about getting a raw deal out of life in backstreet Leeds was stoked by religious figures telling them it was all because they were being persecuted for their faith. They were shown gory videos and DVDs portraying the suffering and slaughter of Muslims in hotspots around the world, and were urged to make common cause with the people of Chechnya, Iraq and Afghanistan. Copies of the films were given to them so they could be shown to other young men back in Leeds. They were urged to keep a lookout for visits to their area by other radical preachers, particularly students of Abu Hamza like the Jamaican-born preacher Abdullah al-Faisal.

Born William Forest to a Salvation Army family, he changed his name to al-Faisal, converted to Islam and came to Britain in the early 1990s, living in east London with his wife and five children. Abu Hamza was al-Faisal's mentor. They shared speaking platforms, and the Jamaican asked Abu Hamza to testify at his trial in 2003 when he was charged with inciting murder and racial hatred.

Al-Faisal made a name for himself touring around Britain, conducting religious study circles for small groups like the one run by Khan. The self-styled sheikh went on at least three such trips to Beeston, and witnesses remember Khan peppering him with questions at their meetings. The Jamaican had a prolific collection of his taped sermons on sale, and Khan became an avid collector.

The fast talking al-Faisal branded non-Muslims as 'cockroaches' ripe for extermination. He claimed that the royal family would burn in hell, and said: 'The only way forward is for you, the Muslims, to kill the kuffars.' The rhetoric echoed that of Abu Hamza, and Khan was entranced.

Instructors at Finsbury Park would have spotted that in Khan they had a small-time street boss who was an ideal candidate to organise his own cell. Their job was to fire up the likes of Khan, fuel him to radicalise his friends and followers. Another advantage was that Khan ran his own youth club, which he could turn into a mini-Finsbury Park. Behind closed doors, he could pass on to his 'brothers' in Beeston the skills he had picked up in north London.

Tanweer was a gift. He did everything Khan told him, and saw himself as a sort of second-in-command in the gym. Regarded as a promising student, he was bored with Beeston. He dropped out of his sports science degree course at Leeds Metropolitan University, and would occasionally help out at his father's fish and chip shop, though he hated doing so. Friends called him by an Urdu nickname, 'Khaka', meaning baby. In common with many of his age in the neighbourhood, he had been in trouble with the police, who cautioned him for disorderly conduct for running with street gangs.

One group of Asian youths called themselves 'the Mullah Crew', and their regular meeting places included the Iqra Islamic bookshop, which was among the first properties the police raided in the days after the 7 July attacks. Khan lectured the Crew on how they had to stop Muslim boys taking heroin, which was giving the Asian community a bad name. Locals told how the gang would kidnap drug-takers, lock them in a room for days at a time and put them through a tough regime of 'cold turkey' to beat their habit. The police knew about this, but were encouraged not to interfere by local Muslim officials, who thought the Mullah Crew were a force for good.

The Crew expected their members to be physically fit, hence the long weekends devoted to outdoor activities, as well as nights working out under Khan's supervision. The gang members regarded themselves as the guardian angels of Beeston's Asian community, patrolling the streets on the lookout for skinhead gangs, who Tanweer blamed for smashing the windows of his father's shop. This simmering feud led to a street fight in April 2004 in the course of which a local mixed-race sixteen-year-old, Tyrone Clarke, was murdered. Up to twenty attackers are said to have cornered him and beat him with baseball bats and metal poles. He was also stabbed three times in the back in what his mother believed was a racist attack. Four Asian youths, aged from seventeen to twenty-two, were convicted of murder and sentenced to life imprisonment. Tanweer was seen with the youths that evening, and while murder squad detectives questioned him, he was not charged.

Tanweer's family thought it a good idea that he spend some time away from Leeds, and agreed to his plan to visit relatives living near Lahore in Pakistan. He travelled with Khan, and the pair used the journey to seek out the militant groups they had been encouraged to contact. This was another crucial step in the Finsbury Park indoctrination course. Travel broadened recruits' minds, particularly when their journeys took them to military training camps in Pakistan and Afghanistan.

Police investigating the 7/7 bombings have heard evidence from former trainees at a camp in Mansehra, a remote area near the Kashmir border, run by the banned terror group Harakat-ul-Mujahideen (HuJ). For years, agents for this 'Movement of Holy Warriors' had taken British-born recruits from the pool of volunteers hanging around Finsbury Park. In April 2004, when the Home Office tried to strip Abu Hamza of his British citizenship, one reason cited by lawyers was that he had sent men to join up with outlawed Kashmiri groups to 'fight jihad' and take part in terrorist attacks. The cleric frequently hosted leaders from Kashmiri groups at the mosque, inviting them to deliver recruitment speeches at the end of his sermons. On one Friday he introduced 'a brother friend of mine who is the leader of some of the mujahideen in Kashmir and he was looking after me when I was injured … he is running a training camp in Kashmir'.

Tanweer's uncle, Bashir Ahmed, blames Abu Hamza and his network for brainwashing his nephew, who blew himself up on a packed train at Aldgate underground station, killing seven people and wounding scores more: 'No child could have thought of 7/7 by themselves. My nephew was influenced by someone spreading the wrong message. The people who made Shehzad do the things he did are influencing thousands of other young men to hate and kill and they need to be stopped.'

In the aftermath of the London bombings, the authorities contacted every friendly foreign intelligence agency and visited every known or suspected militant in Britain in their efforts to piece together how these young Yorkshiremen came to commit murder. Crucial clues have come from America, where officials are holding an informant, originally captured in Pakistan, who has given evidence that he spent time in the same training camp as Khan and Tanweer. Like the bombers, he had also been to Finsbury Park, and at mealtimes and during breaks from military training the three spoke together of mutual friends in north London. They all shared an abiding admiration for Abu Hamza. Other information about Khan and Tanweer has emerged from detainees held at Guantánamo Bay, and from investigations into foiled terror attacks in Britain.

Britain's intelligence services have been forced to admit that they had Khan and Tanweer under surveillance more than a year before the 7 July bombings, but did not appreciate that they were active, operational terrorists. Restricted documents indicate that surveillance teams taped and filmed the pair in the company of others subsequently suspected of terrorist offences. Finsbury Park mosque and overseas training camps were a common thread between the gangs. The security services in the UK filmed and recorded conversations involving Khan, Tanweer and other suspects, but allowed the men from Leeds to drop off the radar. They judged that Khan seemed more exercised about devising fraudulent schemes to fund militant groups than about undertaking a terror mission. Yet, hemmed in by commuters on a Circle Line train deep underground at Edgware Road on 7 July, he detonated a rucksack bomb, murdering six innocents.

In his street performances outside the mosque, Abu Hamza often played to the cameras. His speeches would veer off in all sorts of erratic directions. One minute he would be fulminating about the need for his followers to grow their beards and not trim them, designer style, as footballers do, then without drawing breath he would lambast Tony Blair for running a cabinet full of homosexuals. He would delight in suddenly breaking into Arabic, then pausing and mischievously asking the police and MI5 agents present whether he was going too fast for their translator to keep up. His supporters loved the theatrics.

Islamic scholars, however, despised the way Abu Hamza mangled the Koran to support his warped teachings. He would miss out chunks of verses to suit his purpose, and he was accused of adopting a 'pick'n'mix' style of pirating rival schools of Islamic thought.

There was a puritanical strain of the two-hundred-year-old Salafist movement about Finsbury Park. The core of the Salafi ideology is that Islam has strayed from its origins, and secular Muslim society has grown decadent and heretical. Modern standard-bearers, like Osama bin Laden, embraced the idea of holy struggle – jihad – to achieve their religious and political objectives, saying it was permissible to kill those who stood in their way. Abu Hamza copied this, and finessed the doctrine to appeal to inner-city British youths.

While there were many who showed up on Fridays to be entertained by Abu Hamza's histrionics, the more studious like Jermaine Lindsay came to listen to his message. Increasingly, the topic of martyrdom operations was part of that message, and young men like Lindsay were particularly intrigued by this. There was no higher calling in Islam than martyrdom, Abu Hamza preached.

Nineteen-year-old Lindsay triggered his device on a Piccadilly Line train as it pulled out of King's Cross station on 7 July. His was the deadliest attack of the day, with twenty-six passengers slaughtered. His family had moved from Jamaica to a town close to Huddersfield when he was just a few months old, and Lindsay converted to Islam as a schoolboy in Rawthorpe. Keen to learn more about his adopted faith, he joined Khan's gym and instruction classes, which were twenty minutes' drive from his home.

Lindsay was shy and soft-spoken, and was seen, like Khan, as a devoted family man. He had married the teenage daughter of a British soldier, Samantha Lewthwaite, who he met through an internet chatroom in 2002. Ulster-born, she was a year older than him, and the couple had a son, Abdullah, who was seventeen months old when his father killed himself. Eight weeks after the 7/7 bombings Samantha gave birth to a daughter, Ruqayyah.

Jermaine Lindsay's widow condemns the influence of militant preachers like Abu Hamza for 'poisoning' her husband's mind. She described him to the *Sun* newspaper as 'innocent, naïve and simple' until friends took him to Finsbury Park and other radical mosques.

These visits, she said, would last for several days at a time.

Lindsay had moved to Aylesbury in Buckinghamshire a few months before the attack, and made several trips to London, catching the Thameslink train from nearby Luton to King's Cross, the same route the bombers would use on the morning of 7 July. His visits to north London were few, but significant. He revelled in being part of the defiant Friday crowd gathered in protest outside Finsbury Park mosque to listen to Abu Hamza.

Thousands of grainy images from surveillance cameras have been scanned to determine if the youngest of the bombers, eighteen-year-old Hasib Hussain, ever joined the congregation on St Thomas's Road. The difficulty is that Hussain's appearance changed remarkably in the last months of his life. Friends say he was unrecognisable from recent school photographs, having 'bulked up' as a result of the intensive weight-training regime Khan put him on, and his prodigious capacity for junk food (he was caught on CCTV in a McDonald's near King's Cross station after the first bombs had exploded). On the morning of the attacks he appears either to have lost his nerve or to have been thwarted by delays on the underground heading north. His mobile telephone showed that he tried to ring the rest of the group, but by then all three of them were dead. An hour after their attacks he climbed onto a number 30 bus stuck in traffic in Tavistock Square, detonated the bomb in his rucksack and slaughtered thirteen passengers.

One of those who regularly attended Abu Hamza's outdoor lectures recalls how the cleric urged his followers to watch programmes on Arabic satellite television channels such as al-Jazeera, where religious thinkers would debate the efficacy of suicide attacks. 'He talked about the examples of Hamas and Hezbollah, and the suicide bombers targeting British and American soldiers in Iraq,' this former sympathiser said. When worshippers headed off to cafés after prayers some of Abu Hamza's lieutenants would accompany them, handing out leaflets with details of websites where they could learn more about being a 'shaheed' (martyr). These websites carried video footage of car bombers hurtling towards unsuspecting American and British army patrols manning checkpoints on some anonymous road in Iraq. The men responsible for creating these web pages lived only a couple of miles from the mosque.

While Abu Hamza liked to claim that barring him from Finsbury Park had no effect on his operation, the reality was that his Supporters of Shariah were hampered by not having a sanctuary where they could go about their business unmolested. They now held their meetings at private houses, and kept in touch by email with novices, including some who had gone abroad to train and to fight. But they missed the mosque and the privacy and security it had provided, not to mention the reservoir of raw talent for them to work on. Some of Abu Hamza's acolytes were sent to other mosques to replicate the Finsbury Park model on a smaller scale. For those who could not catch his performances in person, he had volunteers selling tapes of his sermons outside mosques, Islamic bookshops and colleges. There were newly recorded extracts from his street sermons, in which he expounded some of his more lurid conspiracy theories, such as that the British government and its secret agents were planning to assassinate him. At a rally in Trafalgar Square in August 2002 he claimed that the Twin Towers were destroyed because of 'an American-Zionist plot to blame the Muslim world'. He said: 'There is no way these buildings could collapse in that manner after three hours. Al-Qaeda may have ambitions to do that, but I don't believe they did. I'm a trained civil engineer and I know from what I have seen those buildings collapsed from the inside.' He later changed his stance, claiming that the hijackers acted in 'self-defence' and that the towers were 'the centre of evil'.

Critics of the way Whitehall was handling the troublesome cleric complained that the authorities seemed paralysed into indecision over what to do with him. In the early months of 2003 legal moves were stirring – to officially expel him from Finsbury Park, take away his British citizenship and deport him. Legal writs were shuffling through the courts, but here he was, lording it in front of his Friday gatherings, closing roads and taking over an entire street in a north London suburb, while being given police protection at vast expense to the taxpayer. Scotland Yard was reluctant to reveal how much this operation was costing until forced to do so under the Freedom of Information Act. The total bill for the period from January 2003 to November 2004 came to £874,387. Sir John Stevens, the former Metropolitan Police Commissioner, defended the cost, describing it as 'a challenging operation' which he thought had been handled with 'appropriate sensitivity'. His critics argued that taxpayers were paying the price for Whitehall's timidity in tackling Abu Hamza.

When the mosque was handed over to a new board of management in February 2005, and work began on repairing the damage done under Abu Hamza's occupancy, his Supporters of Shariah made a final attempt to keep control. In foot-high letters in black and red, a banner over the entrance announced 'A New Beginning', and quoted a passage from the Koran: 'Whoever kills an innocent soul … it is as if he killed all mankind.' As the new trustees arrived, a reception committee was waiting for them. Around forty men, led by one of Abu Hamza's well-known thugs, announced that the SoS were 'taking the mosque back for the people'. They were forced to retreat in the face of far superior numbers, but as they left they vowed to return with thirty times more men, and shouted that they would rather see the mosque burn down than allow it to fall into the hands of bad Muslims.

The response of the new management was to post guards around the building to prevent another takeover. Not for the first time in the troubled history of Finsbury Park, the Muslim community was left to combat the menace of Abu Hamza and his forces on their own, and to wonder when the authorities would make good their threat to deal with the preacher of hate.

19

The Untouchable

'Many times they try to entrap me, and they are still trying. They bring people to testify against me, but I have nothing to hide. What I say is what I do. I am a cripple and I use their country to spread good, exactly like they [the British] use it to spread corruption.'

ABU HAMZA

The knock on the door that ended Abu Hamza's liberty came before 3 a.m. on Thursday, 27 May 2004. Roused from his sleep, the cleric appeared at his door in Aldbourne Road, Shepherd's Bush, in a long nightshirt, clearly shocked to find police officers brandishing warrants for his arrest and the search of his home. 'You can't do this, you can't do this,' he complained. But his protests were futile. He was ordered to dress and was led, still arguing, to an unmarked police car waiting on the street outside.

His older children shouted protests and complaints that woke the neighbours. In their bedrooms the locals – who included journalists, authors and government ministers – grumbled about 'bloody Hamza' causing a commotion, drew the curtains tight and returned to their beds. These respectable middle-class folk had always found it hard to match the usually courteous man, who had made an appearance at their street party to celebrate the Queen's Golden Jubilee in June 2002, with the godfather of terror they read about in the newspapers. Little did they realise that this was the last time they would see him on their street.

The car took Abu Hamza the short distance to Paddington Green police station, drove around the back of the building and disappeared down a ramp to the fortified basement unit that houses the cell block where terrorist suspects are interviewed. As Abu Hamza was taken away, his wife and children were left to watch as a team of specialist search officers scoured their home for evidence, confiscating documents, books and hefty boxes of video and audio tapes.

Mudassar Arani, Abu Hamza's solicitor, learned of his arrest around 6.30 a.m., when she switched on her television to watch the breakfast news bulletins. Her client contacted her soon afterwards, and told her not to worry. He was in Paddington Green, he explained, being held under an extradition warrant issued by the United States of America. 'Take your time, come whenever you can,' he said calmly.

Abu Hamza had been picked up by Scotland Yard detectives, and had been taken for questioning to London's most secure police station, but this operation was nothing to do with Britain. The only reason he had been detained was because United States prosecutors had issued an eleven-count criminal indictment alleging his direct personal involvement in terrorist recruitment, fundraising and kidnapping.

Less than a week before, Abu Hamza had led Friday prayers on the street outside the barricaded and shuttered Finsbury Park mosque. As usual, a substantial force of London bobbies was standing just a few feet from him to ensure he was left in peace to preach. Six days later he was a category 'A' prisoner, indicted by the Americans as a serious international terrorist with direct links to al-Qaeda.

Within twelve hours of his detention Abu Hamza was on the move again, this time inside an armoured police van as it rushed across London in a high-speed convoy. Patrol cars, blue lights flashing and sirens screaming, led the way, slicing through the traffic and heading east. The destination was Belmarsh high-security prison, a grim concrete edifice on London's south-eastern edge, and just about as isolated a spot as one can find and still be in the capital city.

The convoy swept into the prison compound at 2 p.m., and Abu Hamza was taken through the reception area for his induction as one of Her Majesty's prisoners. His hook was taken away because of the danger that he might use it to harm himself or attack others. At 4.30 p.m. he was readied for his first court appearance as a defendant since 1981, when he had stood before the Great Marlborough Street bench as an illegal immigrant. This time he was being accused of crimes that, if he was convicted in the United States, could lead to the death penalty.

A phalanx of guards led the new inmate through 'The Pipe', the tunnel which leads from Belmarsh prison to the adjoining secure court complex, where armed police were stationed at every door. At precisely 4.47 p.m. Abu Hamza emerged in the dock and took his seat behind thick panes of armoured glass, the stumps of his arms in the pockets of a grey coat. Asked by the court clerk if he was Abu Hamza, he replied: 'Known as, yes.' He answered 'yes' twice more, to confirm his date of birth as 15 April 1958 and to say he understood that the US government had sought his extradition. He was then formally asked by the court if he wished to consent to being sent immediately to the US. 'If you consent you could be returned to the United States this afternoon,' the clerk helpfully informed him. Abu Hamza shook his head. 'I don't really think I want to,' he replied with a mirthless laugh. Paul Hynes, his defence counsel, provided the more appropriate legal response: 'Consent is not forthcoming.'

Abu Hamza sat sullenly in the dock as the American allegations were detailed to the court. They accused him of involvement in the kidnapping of hostages in Yemen in 1998; the recruitment of young Feroz Abbasi to attend a training camp in Afghanistan; and conspiracy with the brash James Ujaama in attempting to set up a jihad training camp in Bly, Oregon, in 1999.

Then a lawyer used the kind of language about Abu Hamza that a British criminal court had never heard before. Despite his unmistakably English accent, the barrister Hugo Keith was representing the US government, and spelling out its reasons for opposing bail for Abu Hamza: 'The charges indicate he has engaged in a systematic pattern of terrorist activity since at least 1998. Even after his arrest in 1999 he continued to lend support to terrorism by engaging in the plot to set up a training camp in Oregon, and of course he sent CC2 to Afghanistan.' CC2 was code for Abbasi, the Croydon computer student. Keith paused for a moment to ensure that the impact of his words registered, then continued: 'Having immersed himself so deeply in these activities, we think it is highly unlikely he will renounce them now. He is no less than a supporter and facilitator of terrorism. He has been in contact with and provided support for terrorist groups and people associated with terrorist groups ... He has had contact with high-ranking terrorists in the Taliban and al-Qaeda.'

On the other side of the Atlantic, as Abu Hamza was being refused bail and led away to spend his first night in a prison cell, senior personnel in the Washington administration were heralding his arrest as a triumph in their 'war on terror'. The Americans were jubilant, so much so that they insisted that daytime soap operas were interrupted to carry live television coverage of a press conference hosted by John Ashcroft, then Attorney General in the Bush administration. Ashcroft was joined on the platform by a crowd of smiling deputies, federal prosecutors, FBI officials and police chiefs. Just in case the public did not quite grasp the message, there was a huge portrait of Abu Hamza alongside them, caught in mid-rant, his one eye glaring, the steel hook raised.

Everybody in turn got their chance to speak, using their moment in the spotlight to explain what a catch they had made in Abu

Hamza. Assistant Attorney General Christopher A. Wray denounced him as 'a terrorist facilitator with a global reach'. But it was left to Raymond Kelly, the New York Police Commissioner, to sum up the drama of the day in a no-nonsense soundbite. 'He's the real deal,' said Kelly. 'Think of him as a freelance consultant to terrorist groups worldwide.'

If the Americans considered Abu Hamza 'the real deal', the question that hung uncomfortably in the air in Whitehall that after-noon was why Her Majesty's government and its agencies had not appreciated the danger he posed, and done something about it. The unpalatable answer was that Britain had missed, or had chosen not to take, at least a dozen opportunities to act against Abu Hamza.

There was considerable unease among the Cabinet that day over what was happening to Britain's most infamous Islamic militant. Some ministers argued that the government should be grateful to the FBI for 'doing Britain's dirty work'. Others felt Britain came out of the affair looking like America's poodle. David Blunkett, Home Secretary at the time, was more circumspect. He had seen some of the intelligence material on Abu Hamza, and was later angered to discover that MI5 had not shown him everything it had about the cleric's terrorist connections. But there had been enough for him to introduce legislation to attempt to strip Abu Hamza of his British citizenship and have him deported or interned as a foreign terror suspect. 'I set about the task with a vengeance,' recalled Blunkett. No sooner had Parliament passed his Bill, in April 2003, than he went on the BBC to proclaim that the imam of Finsbury Park had 'over-stepped the mark'. He went on: 'I want to deal with people who our intelligence and security people believe are a risk to us. If you encourage, support, advise, help people to take up training, if you facilitate them, then of course that takes you right over the boundary.'

Blunkett thought the whole process would take three months at the most. But he failed to factor in the snail's pace at which British justice crawls along. Abu Hamza appealed against the revocation of his hard-won citizenship. Then he delayed the appeal by simply not filing a defence, and claiming that the hold-up was the state's fault because it would not pay his legal fees. It was a further twelve months before the case came before a judge in the bombproof basement in Holborn where the Special Immigration Appeals Commission, Britain's anti-terror court, sat.

At the long-awaited hearing on 26 April 2004, Ian Burnett, QC, appearing for the Home Secretary, accused Abu Hamza of turning Finsbury Park into 'a centre for extremism' and 'a safe haven' for terrorists. He spelt out evidence of his long record of 'support and advice' to at least five terrorist organisations. Abu Hamza, said Whitehall's lawyer, worked with the Islamic Army of Aden (IAA), the Yemen kidnappers; he was also involved with the Armed Islamic Group (GIA), Algerian terrorists who had massacred thousands; Egyptian Islamic Jihad (EIJ), whose many atrocities included the Luxor massacre in 1997; Kashmiri terrorists who would later help to train some of the 7 July bombers; and of course there were his long-established links with al-Qaeda.

For all the newspaper headlines and unsubstantiated accusations made by foreign intelligence agencies about him, this was the first time the British authorities had detailed specific allegations directly linking Abu Hamza with terrorists. The court heard that he had 'encouraged and supported the promotion of individuals in physical acts of jihad fighting overseas and engaging in terrorist acts'. This was a month before the FBI made its move to charge Abu Hamza. If intelligence agencies already had a dossier like this, why was the cleric not in the dock of the Old Bailey, instead of arguing about whether he could hang onto his British passport?

Despite the welter of allegations, Abu Hamza's defence team successfully argued for the case to be adjourned until January 2005, so they could stage a separate fight for Legal Aid to fund his defence. This request for public funds infuriated Gordon Brown, the

Chancellor of the Exchequer. Abu Hamza was a designated international terrorist, subject to United Nations sanctions, and was not
entitled to a penny of taxpayers' money. All his welfare benefits had
been stopped. The Department for Work and Pensions had written
to him a year before announcing that he was to lose his disability
living allowance of £56.25 a week, mobility allowance of £39.35,
severe disability allowance of £56.95 and income support of £42.25.
Yet now the courts were giving him extra time to ask for money to
pay for expensive lawyers.

Money and Abu Hamza had always been a mystery. 'I don't care,
God will provide for me,' he once quipped. In fact, it was the state
that continued to provide, paying out hundreds of pounds each week
in benefits to Nagat, his wife, even after his own allowances had been
terminated. And in September 2004 – despite the facts that he was in
jail and his assets were supposed to have been frozen – he sold a
former council flat and made a tidy £128,000 profit. The authorities
have no idea where the money went.

The Treasury was not the only department being taken for a ride
by Abu Hamza. At a lower level of the state apparatus, the Charity
Commission was inquiring into his reckless stewardship of Finsbury
Park mosque, registered as a charity in the name of the North
London Central Mosque Trust. The commission, which regulates the
conduct of all the registered charitable organisations in Britain, first
began to examine the mosque's affairs in 1998, after complaints from
the trustees. It was hardly an urgent investigation. Since taking over
the mosque, Abu Hamza had submitted no accounts and had
amassed a string of unpaid bills. Yet it was not until after 9/11 that
the commission took a serious look at his abuse of the mosque's
charitable status.

In April 2002 the commissioners suspended him, but he again
exercised his right of appeal. He was supposed to respond within a
month, but predictably he ignored the ruling and continued to run
the mosque. It was eight months before his lawyers sent a letter

denouncing the commissioners for being Islamophobic. By the time Abu Hamza had been removed from his role as an agent of the charity, the mosque was shut down and he was preaching on the street.

No one seemed willing to take responsibility for tackling the Abu Hamza problem. Government departments pointed the finger of blame at one another. Politicians complained that the police and the spymasters did not investigate him properly. Scotland Yard moaned about MI5 and vice-versa. Detectives felt that lawyers at the Crown Prosecution Service let them down, and the CPS moaned that the system in the courts was stacked against them. The judges retorted that they did not make the laws; if anyone was to blame it was the civil servants and politicians at Westminster. The blame game went round and round in circles as Tony Blair banged the table in exasperation.

Every chance there had been to pursue Abu Hamza seemed to have been wasted, not spotted, or blocked. For more than twenty years there had been a catalogue of bureaucratic foul-ups and a lack of resolve by the British authorities to tackle him even when they were presented with a clear opportunity to do so.

The first occasion arose in 1980, when Abu Hamza was arrested as an illegal immigrant and brought before the courts for overstaying his visa. Had his case been subjected to a proper investigation, potential offences under the Marriage Act, the Births and Deaths Registration Act and the Forgery and Counterfeiting Act could have been discovered. But the validity of his marriage to Valerie Traverso, and the truth about his claim to be the father of her baby daughter, were not examined.

He came to the attention of the police again in the mid-1980s, when his bullying behaviour began to alarm the imams and trustees of a number of mosques. Members of the Muslim community in Brighton approached Sussex police, and at Regent's Park mosque in London trustees took court action to keep him away from the building. When he returned from Afghanistan and Bosnia in the mid-1990s there was further trouble in Luton. But he was left to carry on with his activities and to seize control at Finsbury Park. Abdulkadir Barkatullah, one of the management committee ousted by Abu Hamza, said he and community representatives went to the police on seven occasions to complain about assaults and the extremist nature of the activities being conducted inside the mosque. No action was taken. Tony Blair had urged the Muslim community to do more about the scourge of extremism within its own ranks, but, Barkatullah said, 'When we did do precisely that with Abu Hamza, we were ignored.'

If those who raised the alarm at home were overlooked, then foreign intelligence agencies were discounted. Those of France, Spain, Germany, Italy, Belgium and the Netherlands all accused Abu Hamza of being the ringmaster of a terrorist operation. The French and the Algerians had spies inside the mosque, and were horrified at what they uncovered. Egypt wanted to swap a British prisoner for Abu Hamza. All shared their findings with Whitehall, but again, nothing happened. The French were so infuriated by British inaction that their agents contemplated assassinating some of the London-based jihadis and kidnapping Abu Hamza. Senior sources now admit that the British response was coloured by a belief that the French were wildly overreacting to the Islamist threat. These same sources agree that Britain underestimated the real menace of Abu Hamza, and did not devote enough resources to investigating him and his network until 9/11 jolted every Western power.

It seems a lame excuse that British security authorities needed to see skyscrapers collapsing in New York to realise the danger of Islamic fundamentalists, when they had damning proof of Abu Hamza's direct involvement with terrorists in Yemen as long ago as 1998, when Abu Hamza had bought a satellite phone and supplied £500-worth of airtime for the kidnappers of sixteen Western holidaymakers. Irrefutable evidence of his calls to and from the kidnappers' leader was gathered by GCHQ, the British government's intelligence listening post. But under British law, telephone intercept evidence gathered in the UK or by domestic intelligence or police services cannot be produced as evidence in the criminal courts.

A leading investigator in UK counter-terrorism says today he has no doubt that if such phone tap evidence was admissible, Abu Hamza would have been prosecuted for his role in the Yemen abductions and deaths. Scotland Yard did send a file to the Crown Prosecution Service in March 1999 but it was rejected, marked 'insufficient evidence'. The FBI thought differently. To Whitehall's embarrassment, US investigators have announced that they will use the evidence harvested by GCHQ and other British agencies should they get the chance to prosecute Abu Hamza in an American court.

The tragic events in Yemen did lead to Abu Hamza's brief arrest for four days in March 1999. During that operation his home was thoroughly searched, and a large number of audio and video recordings of his sermons were confiscated. They included three videotapes of sermons that, the Crown would say in 2006, amounted to the offence of 'soliciting to murder'. Back then, the police took no action. Among the recordings was one in which Abu Hamza told his followers that they had to fight, kill and die, because 'no drop of liquid is loved by Allah more than the liquid of blood'. Detectives only examined one of the tapes, and decided that no offence had been committed; they explain this by saying that the focus of their inquiry at the time was Yemen, and not the cleric's sermons. The content of the sermons did not form part of the report that police prepared for the Crown Prosecution Service, and the videos were returned to Abu Hamza in December 1999. He insists that he took this as a clear signal that nothing he was saying in his sermons could be deemed to be illegal. Also taken from him in that search in 1999 were the eleven volumes of the *Encyclopaedia of Afghani Jihad*. Seven years later these would be described to an Old Bailey jury as a terrorist manual. They too were returned to

Abu Hamza, and no charges brought in relation to his possession of them.

The police signalled their concern about his activities by permanently confiscating two passports found in his home during the raid. One, in his own name, had expired; the second, in the name Adam Ramsey Eaman, had been used by Abu Hamza to travel to Bosnia, where he met Arab mujahideen fighters in 1995. No prosecution ensued from his possession of this document, because he obtained it legally after changing his name to Eaman by deed poll.

If Abu Hamza used sleight of hand to change his identity, others at the mosque engaged in naked fraud to purloin identities and money, and to falsify benefit claims. Surely someone should have thought it strange that so many young men, of similar ages, were turning up with near-identical claims for welfare and housing, and using the same address? Islamist militants were jailed for massive credit card frauds which could be traced back to London N4, but Abu Hamza was not even questioned. The British authorities were clearly aware that he was involved in fundraising for terrorism – not least because he confessed it to his contacts in the intelligence services.

Some of his emissaries were stopped leaving Britain carrying large amounts of money. James Ujaama, who has struck a deal to testify against Abu Hamza in the US, was questioned at Heathrow airport with a suitcase full of cash just days before the 11 September attacks. He told the British officials that he was flying to Pakistan and then crossing into Afghanistan to deliver the funds for the establishment of a Taliban school.

US investigators claim to have obtained further evidence that Abu Hamza was directly bankrolling al-Qaeda's Darunta camp, which specialised in explosives and poisons training. Some of his followers have testified that the cleric gave them cash from mosque funds for their travels to Afghanistan. Despite all of this, he was never charged with financing terrorism.

Abu Hamza was not simply a fundraiser for terrorist camps. He provided a production line of recruits for al-Qaeda and others to train as jihadi fighters and suicide bombers. In the camps, his name was well-known; he was someone who could refer candidates to the highest echelons of al-Qaeda's leadership. When Ujaama fell ill on a visit to Afghanistan he was treated by Dr Ayman al Zawahiri, who as well as being Osama bin Laden's personal physician was second-in-command of al-Qaeda.

British law enforcement agencies say they knew about Abu Hamza's activities, but argue that they were powerless to stop him. It was not until late 2001, when the controversial Anti-Terrorism Crime and Security Act was passed into law, that sending someone abroad to undergo terrorist training and instruction became a criminal offence. Yet even after the new laws were introduced, Abu Hamza's followers continued to disappear off to camps run by outlawed groups, and still nobody in authority laid a finger on him.

David Blunkett, out of government since November 2005 and with time to reflect on his stewardship of the fight against terrorism, believes that the sinister nature of Abu Hamza was not appreciated. 'There was still an assumption when I took office as Home Secretary [in 2001] that he was a bigmouth and was worth tracking but wasn't at the centre of events,' he says. Blunkett is angry to have learned since that the intelligence services never showed him 'the detailed trail' of networks, the personal history and the high-level contacts that would have indicated that Abu Hamza was 'a real threat and a danger'. He freely admits that the British authorities at all levels were nervous about taking action against Abu Hamza. They saw the preacher not as a terrorist suspect but as an outspoken religious leader of a minority faith, and feared that any action against him would be labelled as Islamophobic and an abuse of human rights.

'It is also clear that for all sorts of reasons ... there was a reluctance in our society to believe that it was possible for a faith to be misused in that way,' says Blunkett. 'That is strange given the experience in Northern Ireland, where Christian Churches had been used and abused. But of course when you're dealing with a minority faith in a free, liberal society, people are even more reluctant in terms of what they will be accused of and the ramifications. We were struggling with that. I was one of those who was probably more robust in recognising that these things had happened historically here and across the world, and you had to be sensitive to it, but you also didn't have to be naïve. Other people weren't really naïve, but they were more jumpy about what the consequences may be. You heard it over and over again in Parliament and outside, people saying that if you alienate the faith community then what you did would be counter-productive. They said it over and over again and it created an atmosphere. And it was understandable, we had to take account of that, and you would be very foolish not to in terms of the ramifications for civil disorder and fracturing of our community. But the pressure that that brought to bear, in terms of the psychology that was being adopted, was actually tipping the balance the wrong way.' But he adds: 'It is clear now – and I think that those close to this would acknowledge it – that there were opportunities for having taken action. By putting the jigsaw together, it is possible for us to realise that this man was a danger because he was at the heart of organising, glorifying and persuading.'

The links between Abu Hamza, Finsbury Park and active terrorists around the world are much better understood now, and high-ranking counter-terrorist officials admit errors in countering the threat from the mosque in London N4. But they contend that things were never as simple as they seem with the benefit of hindsight. Before 2001, no one considered that Islamist terror was a threat to Britain, and up until that year the anti-terrorist effort in the UK was still directed at fighting the dissident elements of Irish Republicanism bent on a never-ending armed struggle for a united Ireland. It is easily forgotten now, but the Real IRA waged a destructive bombing campaign in London during 2000 and 2001. Bombs were planted at BBC Television Centre and a rocket fired at MI6 headquarters. Two devices were defused on the Underground in July 2000 – five years before suicide bombers struck the network. And just five weeks before 9/11 a Real IRA car bomb exploded on Ealing Broadway, west London, injuring several people and causing considerable damage.

Counter-terrorist officials point out that France's problems with Algerian terrorists seemed to have as much to do with her own colonial past as with the new threat of Islamist terrorism. Britain, meanwhile, was still preoccupied with its colonial legacy across the Irish Sea. Until 9/11 there had appeared to be no such threat to Britain. Indeed, what discussion there was about Islamist dissidents living in Britain was largely self-congratulatory. Britons were proud of the fact that their country continued to give safe haven and a platform to political refugees who, in all likelihood, would be arrested and tortured if they were sent back to their native lands. Dissidents seeking refuge from dictatorial regimes in the Middle East were following the tradition of nineteenth- and early-twentieth-century political refugees like Marx and Lenin who plotted revolution and sedition while living in London.

Even in the aftermath of the 9/11 atrocities there were still prominent voices among politicians and the media which questioned whether there really was a threat to Britain or the rest of the Western world. Voices which said that 11 September was a one-off, that it was all to do with American foreign policy and that politicians were exaggerating the danger in order to create a more authoritarian state apparatus. The same voices continued to claim – even in the aftermath of bombs in Bali, Madrid and Casablanca, and clear evidence of a poisons and explosives conspiracy in London – that al-Qaeda didn't exist, that there was no Islamist menace. After the suicide bombers struck in London in July 2005, those voices complained about security clampdowns and Islamophobia, then began to play a game of blame and recrimination. It was all due to the war in Iraq, or the alienation of Muslim populations, or the failures of the police and intelligence services. It never appeared to be the fault of the bombers, or those who inspired and incited their acts.

The British debate on terror is desperately ill-informed, not least because British *sub judice* laws create legal constraints which prevent the public from being made fully aware of the reality of what anti-terrorist forces are dealing with on a daily basis. But there is also a widespread unwillingness to understand what al-Qaeda is. Too many people believe that it can be negotiated with, infiltrated or dismantled through investigation. But how do you negotiate with a suicide bomber? Al-Qaeda is not the IRA or the Red Brigade or the PLO. It is a constantly mutating global phenomenon which is driven by a fascistic ideology of religious fundamentalism, martyrdom and world domination. Central to its ability to continue spreading are men like Abu Hamza, skilled orators who speak with a chilling certainty of their own correctness, firing their listeners with a sense of injustice and offering them a utopian vision of revenge, sacrifice and reward in paradise.

This debate raged on not just in the media and among the chattering classes, but at the heart of Britain's government. It left American investigators aghast. They were sick of handing over information to British agencies about Abu Hamza, only to see him being allowed to continue preaching hatred in front of the cameras. One senior official in the US Department of Justice said: 'We just did not understand what was going on in London. We wondered to ourselves whether he was an MI5 informer, or was there some secret the British were not trusting us with? He seemed untouchable.' Exasperated US security agencies decided that if Britain was not going to act, then they would. Hence the warrant handed over by FBI agents stationed at the US embassy in Grosvenor Square in May 2004.

Some in the British government continued to dither. Lord Goldsmith, the Attorney General, thought it would look bad for Britain to hand over a British citizen to the Americans without making any effort to try him in Britain. This argument won the day. Britain would not hand Abu Hamza over if it could be proven that he had committed serious crimes here. The police were instructed to build a case, and to do it swiftly. The obvious place to look again for evidence was in the thousands of recordings of his sermons recovered in the search of his home on the day he was arrested. The authorities had successfully prosecuted one of his radical protégés, Abdullah el-Faisal, who was convicted and jailed for seven years for inciting murder in 2003. Surely Abu Hamza was guilty of the same?

In August 2004, Abu Hamza was formally arrested inside Belmarsh jail and taken back across London to be interviewed at Paddington Green police station. Two months later he was charged with using his sermons to incite murder and stir up racial hatred against the Jews. His lawyers pointed out that police had examined some of this evidence before and handed it back to him. He himself said: 'If I was not already in prison, I would have laughed.'

America wanted to put Abu Hamza on trial for recruiting, financing and directing terrorism, charges that could see him jailed for up to a hundred years. But British prosecutors chose to intervene and to accuse him of lesser offences, mostly under a century-and-a-half-old Victorian statute. The central charge was that he had crossed the boundaries of freedom of expression – the criminal equivalent of ignoring the park keeper's 'Keep off the grass' sign. Somehow Britain managed to make it look as if Abu Hamza was getting off lightly again.

20
Abu Hamza in the Dock

'Every court which is ruling other than by Allah's
law is a target.'

ABU HAMZA

When his trial finally began in earnest on 11 January 2006 at
London's Central Criminal Court – better known around the world
as the Old Bailey – the jury of seven men and five women was treated
to the spectacle of not one, but two Abu Hamzas. On four large
flat-screen televisions, for all the world like alien invaders in the
hundred-year-old wood-panelled courtroom peopled by men and
women in wigs and gowns, the firebrand held forth day after day.

This was the familiar Abu Hamza, the angry preacher. He raged
against the decadent West, the treacherous Jews, the waywardness of
women, the accursedness of homosexuals, the corruption of Muslim
rulers and the idleness of ordinary Muslims who had not yet gone to
wage war for Allah. He was frothing and shouting and pleading with
his congregations to fight, to give their lives, to rouse the Muslim
nation by spilling their blood. The man on the screen was wild, his
one good eye bulging, sweat pouring from his brow, the hooked
hand prodding the air.

In the raised dock another Abu Hamza, a much more subdued
figure, sat expressionless, watching and listening to the more animated, younger version of himself. This was an altogether different
man. His hair and beard were noticeably greyer than those of the

man on the screen. Indeed, they were almost white. He looked heavier and older, an impression reinforced by the reading glasses on his nose. When not in use, they hung around his neck on a silver-coloured chain.

Each day of the four weeks of the case he would climb ponderously up the steep stairs from the Old Bailey cells into the raised dock of Courtroom Number Two. Four prison officers accompanied him. As a category 'A' prisoner Abu Hamza was deemed to be a potentially dangerous man who must be under guard in court.

But there was no trouble from the prisoner. He smiled wearily at his guards as if to say, 'Here we go again,' and shared a few words of small talk with them. He was the model inmate. With little else to do the prison officers slipped paperback books from their pockets, bent the covers back, held them low on their laps out of the judge's sight and quietly passed the long hours in court by reading thrillers.

Their charge, Abu Hamza, was a big man, tall and broad-shouldered. He seemed to have gained weight in prison. But in the cavernous courtroom, with its high ceilings, tiered rows of green leather seats and a judge peering down at him from the bench, he appeared dwarfed and defeated by his surroundings. All around him – lawyers, police officers, journalists – were attired in legal black or sombre greys and browns. He arrived in court each day wearing either a pale blue or a beige shalwar kameez. Somehow the splash of colour emphasised his otherness and relative smallness. Occasionally a follower or supporter appeared in the public gallery, an ornately carved wooden balcony suspended over the court. One of Abu Hamza's sons attended on a few days. There were glances and nods of acknowledgement. But mostly the man who had preached to thousands, and cast himself as a leader of the mujahideen, was alone.

Mudassar Arani, Abu Hamza's solicitor for several years, conceded from the beginning that her client was not optimistic. Whichever way the Old Bailey trial went, it would not be good news for Abu Hamza. If he was acquitted of the fifteen charges against him, he was highly unlikely to be released. Even if declared innocent by the jury he would remain in prison, and the United States would immediately resume its case for his extradition to stand trial on the other side of the Atlantic. The British government's attempt to strip him of his citizenship would also be restarted; if he no longer had the protection of being British he faced the threat of deportation or of detention without trial under a terrorist control order.

In the face of inevitable defeat, there appeared to be little fight left in Abu Hamza al-Masri. He restricted his belligerence to a small show each day when he routinely refused to recognise the authority of the court. Traditionally in English courts every person present stands when the judge rises at the end of the day's proceedings. It is one of the small ceremonies that preserve the museum-like character of the British legal system. The court clerk, a man or a woman in a black robe and wearing a horsehair wig, stands and announces the end of the day and the requirement for all to attend court the following day. Like a town crier he or she proclaims: 'All persons having anything further to do before My Lords the Queen's Justices may now depart hence and give your attendance at 10 o'clock tomorrow morning. God Save the Queen and My Lords the Queen's Justices.'

When the words were uttered in Court Number Two everyone automatically rose to their feet, glad of the end of another day. Everyone, that is, except Abu Hamza, who remained firmly on his wooden chair in the dock. There was no declaration, no turning his back, no staged rebellion in the manner of the IRA prisoners of the 1970s, who made a great show of refusing to recognise the British courts. But this was his protest. Although he would gladly have accepted thousands of pounds in Legal Aid, he would not recognise a court that did not practise Shariah law. Following the same principle, when he took the witness stand to give evidence, Abu Hamza made a secular affirmation to tell the whole truth and nothing but the truth. He would not swear an oath on the Koran in an infidel court. This daily gesture of defiance was tolerated without comment by the trial judge, Mr Justice Hughes, one of the trio of learned lawyers who ran the case in the civilised, bookish and gentlemanly way that British justice conducts itself at the highest level.

In the rarefied atmosphere of these courts, no case seems capable of starting without a day or two (indeed sometimes weeks) of procedural wrangling. The arguments are often circular and self-defeating, and are frequently conducted with the air of an exercise in scholarly curiosity rather than any sense of purpose. Many may have been capable of being resolved weeks in advance with an efficient exchange of paperwork.

For example, in all cases where the defendant has acquired some kind of public notoriety, the defence counsel will invariably attempt to have the entire prosecution thrown out, on the grounds that his client cannot possibly receive a fair trial because he or she has been the subject of adverse press coverage. Highly-paid barristers stand for days reading aloud from thick files of press cuttings to show that no juror could possibly approach the case without prejudice towards the defendant. Oddly, these same lawyers are usually the most impassioned defenders of the sanctity of trial by jury, who say that the right of a man to be tried by his peers must be preserved at all costs.

Any layman sitting in the court is left to wonder if the judge is an illiterate imbecile who cannot read, or whether the whole process could not be speeded up by simply handing the files of press reports to the judge to examine for himself. The process inevitably ends with the judge ruling that the trial must go ahead, because juries have shown their independence for centuries. He also agrees to warn the jurors, as the judge always does, that they must try the case on the evidence they hear in court, and ignore anything they have read in the newspapers, heard on radio or seen on television.

This legal pantomime was performed in Abu Hamza's case on and off over a series of months before the case was eventually opened before the jury. The preamble done with, the jurors were sworn in; eleven took the jury oath on the Bible, and one affirmed. Abu Hamza waived his right to object to the selection of any of the jurors. The long-awaited trial, postponed from its original start date because of the climate of public opinion in the immediate aftermath of the 7 July London suicide bombings, was under way.

Presiding over the court was fifty-seven-year-old Sir Anthony Hughes, a former law lecturer at Durham University who became a barrister in 1970 and a Queen's Counsel in 1990. He sat alone on the bench, robed in red, beneath the royal coat of arms and with the sword of the Old Bailey mounted above his head indicating his status as the highest-ranking member of the judiciary in the courthouse. As a man who in his spare time enjoys the precise and rhythmic pastimes of mechanics and bellringing, the judge was to betray more than a little impatience with the pace of proceedings – especially when Abu Hamza came to the witness stand and attempted to preach rather than to answer questions.

The cleric's defence counsel, Edward Fitzgerald, QC, was no stranger to defending infamous clients. In the past he had represented Mary Bell, the child killer, Jon Venables, who murdered the Liverpool toddler James Bulger, and Maxine Carr, former girlfriend of the Soham murderer Ian Huntley, when they sought anonymity after being released from custody. But Fitzgerald is no celebrity lawyer. He is a courageous and respected international advocate whose studies and cases have moulded the law on extradition and changed the outlook on the use of the death penalty in former British colonies. A bespectacled and cheerful man, he is also known as one of the more enthusiastically verbose members of the English Bar. When he indicates that a speech or argument may take up an hour of the court's time, most experienced observers allow for two hours.

The jury heard first, however, from David Perry, whose title of senior Treasury counsel indicates that he is one of the Crown's first-rank prosecutors. In 2002 he had successfully prosecuted another hot-headed Muslim cleric on similar charges to those faced by Abu Hamza. Abdullah al-Faisal, a friend of Abu Hamza, was jailed for incitement to murder for preaching sermons that encouraged his listeners to kill Hindus, Jews and non-Muslims. With such experience, and a reputation for dedication and incisiveness, Perry was the first choice to take the Abu Hamza case. His cross-examination of Abu Hamza was to be a one-to-one courtroom duel that lasted more than three days and left both men visibly exhausted.

In his opening speech, Perry laid out the Crown's case before the jurors. Britain, he reminded them, was a country that was proud of its tradition of free speech and freedom of expression. But those freedoms carried responsibilities as well as rights. They did not entail the freedom to incite murder and hatred. The alleged abuse of those freedoms led to thirteen of the fifteen criminal charges against the accused. Arraigned under his real name of Mostafa Kamel Mostafa, and his alias Abu Hamza, the imam of Finsbury Park faced nine counts of soliciting to murder under Section 4 of the Offences Against the Person Act 1861. Three of those charges alleged that he specifically encouraged the murder of Jewish people; the other six that he had encouraged the killing of 'a person or persons who did not believe in the Islamic faith'. Another four charges, brought under the Public Order Act of 1986, alleged that Abu Hamza used 'threatening, abusive or insulting words or behaviour with intent to stir up racial hatred'.

The evidence against the cleric on all of these charges was contained in video and audio recordings of sermons he had delivered between 1997 and 2000, thousands of copies of which were found at his home when he was arrested in May 2004. The possession of the tapes led to another charge under the Public Order Act of 'possession of threatening, abusive or insulting recordings of sound' with a view to distributing or displaying them.

The final charge was the only count on the indictment which mentioned the word terrorism; it related to the discovery of the eleven-volume *Encyclopaedia of the Afghani Jihad* in Abu Hamza's home. This was described on the charge sheet as 'a document which contained information of a kind likely to be useful to a person committing or preparing an act of terrorism'. The charge was brought under the terms of the Terrorism Act 2000. The encyclopaedia was, Perry informed the jury in his well-spoken tones, nothing more or less than 'a manual, a blueprint for terrorism … It contains anything anyone would ever need to know if they wanted to make home-made bombs or explosives.'

But it was the issue of Abu Hamza's words, rather than his reading material, that dominated Perry's speech. Words were 'a powerful weapon', he said, and Abu Hamza had used them to preach violence in a way that was 'destructive and corrosive' of a free society. The barrister reminded the jury that Abu Hamza was not a simple rabble-rouser. As the imam of a large London mosque he preached to thousands of Muslims, and had influence over many aspects of the lives of his congregation: 'As a person delivering a sermon in a holy place and as a person holding a position of responsibility in the Muslim community, a spiritual leader, you might expect talks delivered by such a person would contain expressions of hope, charity and compassion. In fact the speeches contain very little of that. Sheikh Abu Hamza was preaching murder and hatred in these talks.'

The jurors, listening with rapt attention during these first hours of the trial, were told that they would see and hear hours and hours of Abu Hamza's sermons on tape: 'You will hear Sheikh Abu Hamza encourage his listeners, whether an audience at a private meeting or the congregation at the mosque, to believe it was part of their religious duty to fight in the cause of Allah. It was part of that religious duty to kill. The people his audience were encouraged to kill were non-believers, those who did not believe, anyone who was not a follower or even a true follower of Islam as perceived by the defendant.' The jury would hear intolerance and bigotry, particularly directed against the Jewish people and the unbeliever, or kuffar. Perry's slow, careful and ever-so English pronunciation of the Arabic word – he said 'koo-far' – was in stark contrast to the guttural aggression invested in the word by the defendant.

Abu Hamza, Perry told the silent courtroom, 'accused the Jews of being blasphemers, traitors and dirty. This, because of their blasphemy, and because of their filth, was why Hitler was sent into the world. He also tells his audience that the Jews control the West, by which he means Western liberal democracies such as this country. He says the Jews control the West and must be removed from the earth.' In the opinion of the Crown, there was no ambiguity in Abu Hamza's words. 'The words used by the defendant do not require any fine-grain textual analysis for their meaning to become clear. They are ordinary words and their meaning is beyond doubt,' stated Perry. 'This prosecution is not brought to criticise Islam or criticise the teaching of the Koran. It is brought because of what the defendant says. No religion condones the murder or killing of innocent men, women and children or the dissemination of hatred and bigotry. Any suggestion that hatred and bigotry can be wrapped in a cloak of righteousness and justified on the basis of the great religion of Islam and its great book, the Holy Koran, is simply incorrect.' Neither, added Perry, could the Crown case be described as an attack on Britain's liberal traditions: 'The pluralism, tolerance and broad-mindedness reflected in our right to freedom of expression and freedom of speech do not extend to opinions which amount to racial hatred or encouragement to murder.'

His speech completed, Perry sat down, and for several days the court watched the recordings of Abu Hamza's sermons – the crucial evidence in the trial. There was little attempt to explain or editorialise or comment. The jury watched most of the recordings in their entirety. The sound quality was poor, distorted and muffled, and the onscreen Abu Hamza often rambled wildly and incoherently. But the jurors were equipped with hundreds of pages of transcripts to enable them to follow every decipherable word, and with a six-page glossary of Islamic phrases and terms used in the sermons. In the dock, Abu Hamza was also given the transcripts, which piled up on a low table in front of him. Because he was deprived of his prosthetic hook for security reasons, a young female member of his legal team was permitted to sit beside Abu Hamza and act as his page-turner.

After just a week, the prosecution case was over. It was now Fitzgerald's turn to try to find flaws in the edifice built by Perry, to sow doubt in the minds of the jurors and to question the very basis of the prosecution case. He began by handing six brand-new copies of the Koran to the twelve jurors, each book to be shared between two of them. The holy book, he explained, was the source of all Abu Hamza's words. The 'offensive' statements he preached were contained in the Koran, which, like the scriptures of the other great monotheistic religions, contained 'the language of blood and retribution'.

Fitzgerald directed the jurors to two verses from the Koran which he said his client, and other clerics who preached about the doctrine of physical jihad, relied on. The first came from sura (chapter) two, verse 216: 'Fighting is ordained for you, though you may dislike it. You may dislike something although it is good for you, or like something although it is bad for you: God knows and you do not.' His second selection was sura nine, verse 111, and read: 'God has purchased the persons and possessions of the believers in return for the Garden – they fight in God's way: they kill and are killed – this is a true promise given by Him in the Torah, the Gospel, and the Koran. Who could be more faithful to his promise than God? So be happy with the bargain you have made, that is the supreme triumph.'

Ironically, at the same time that Abu Hamza was using the Koran as the basis of his defence, the leader of the far-right British National Party, Nick Griffin, was on trial in Leeds, and also citing Islam's holy book to justify comments that were alleged to amount to incitement to racial hatred.

Fitzgerald claimed that the case against Abu Hamza was 'simplistic', and amounted to a denial of the right of preachers to repeat what was written in one of the great religious texts: 'It is said he was preaching murder, but he was actually preaching from the Koran itself. The Koran imposes a duty of jihad and that involves a duty of fighting in defence of the Muslim community and their religion. It is a big ask to say that quoting the words of the Koran amounts to incitement to murder … Can it be an incitement to murder simply to remind you of a duty laid down in the Koran?'

Furthermore, he continued, speeches in which Abu Hamza appeared to be calling on Muslims to kill Jews were direct quotations from the Hadith – the collected sayings of the Prophet Mohammed, which are also regarded as holy texts by Muslims. The passage the cleric had used on a number of occasions was a quotation from a prophecy. It was 'bloodthirsty language', but far from being an incite-ment to do anything, the words were a prediction drawn from the scripture.

Beyond that, Fitzgerald continued, the jury should consider the context of the times at which Abu Hamza delivered the sermons that were under consideration. His words had coincided with the con-flicts in Kosovo and Kashmir, and with the Palestinian intifada, in which many Muslims were suffering and dying. And the jurors should not forget that when the mujahideen began fighting against the Soviet Army in Afghanistan they were supported by the West. Why, there was even a James Bond film – *The Living Daylights* – in which 007 fought alongside Afghan guerrillas. Abu Hamza's words, said his lawyer, were directed at those situations, and were not about fomenting terrorism in Britain: 'It is not all as simple and obvious as they [the Crown] say. Hamza has said things which most people will find deeply offensive and hateful. But he is not on trial for describing England as a toilet or denouncing democracy or dreaming of a caliph in the White House. There is no crime of simply being offen-sive.'

Both lawyers had set out powerful cases. Perry argued convinc-ingly for a conviction, while Fitzgerald raised enough doubts to make the jurors wonder whether it would be more appropriate to acquit. Much would hinge on how Abu Hamza came across when he took the witness stand, which he did on 19 January. For five days he would walk from his seat in the dock to stand in the witness box in the corner of the courtroom, between the judge and the jury. Two prison officers walked with him, and stood close behind as he gave his evidence. He declined the offer of a seat, choosing to stand; his legal assistant sat close by, ready to turn pages in the bundles of paperwork provided.

Within five minutes Abu Hamza was treating the witness box as if it was a pulpit. He recited Koranic verses, directed the jury and lawyers to the relevant passages and sought to dictate the direction of the discussion. But this was not a debate. It was a court of law, and Abu Hamza's desire to control it smacked of an attempt to avoid answering difficult questions. Four times Fitzgerald lobbed him tame questions about his personal attitude towards Jewish people. Not once did he receive a straight answer, and within minutes Abu Hamza had launched into a tirade against the 'abomination' of the existence of the state of Israel. Under a much tougher cross-examination by Perry, he was goaded into revealing more of his real attitude. He believed in the conspiracy theory that the Jews controlled the banks and the media, and had a controlling hold over Western political leaders. 'I can justify what I am saying scientifically,' he claimed.

Abu Hamza was, according to his recall of his life, not responsible for anything. He was a humble and insignificant preacher who was merely repeating the words of the Koran and citing the views of more learned men. 'I'm not a Pope,' he said. His association with the murder squads of the GIA in Algeria was merely peripheral. Yes, he edited their newspaper, but he never really knew what they were up to, and was constantly phoning the leaders to find out. When he realised that they had carried out massacres he disassociated himself from them. Yes, the *Encyclopaedia of Afghani Jihad* was on his bookshelf, packed with information about bomb-making and warfare.

But Abu Hamza had never read it; he was not a military man and had kept the books 'as a piece of history'. He had no idea that tapes of his sermons – thousands of which were found in his home – were being sold and distributed; it was no concern of his. Nor did he have any idea what parts of Britain he had travelled to to preach his message; he was not an A–Z. MI5 knew all about his preaching and his activities, and had told him it was OK to carry on. He himself had not been interested in Islam until his first wife Valerie, an Englishwoman, had become curious.

By the end of each day of cross-examination, any semblance of reasonable exchange between Abu Hamza and Perry had disappeared. Things were fraught and tense. The prosecutor was tired of attempting to bring the defendant back from his meanderings to the matter of the court case, while Abu Hamza was unhappy at being pushed on subjects he did not want to face. He snapped when asked a series of questions about the radical group al-Muhajiroun. Did he know where it was based, and who controlled it? He retorted: 'Has this case gone so hollow and so low? You are asking me questions you can ask any postman. You can call 118 and say, "Give me the number." I am a sick man, I am tired, I am standing here for everyone to do their job. Now ask me some questions or just lock me up.'

As well as the tantrums, there were moments when the two men simply misunderstood one another. 'My house is not a terrorist house,' Abu Hamza fumed when Perry, asking questions about the police search of his home, asked if it was terraced.

When Abu Hamza's evidence was finally over, he appeared drained. Similarly, Perry had an appearance of total fatigue. But the long, meandering exchanges had given the prosecutor ammunition for his closing speech before the jury. He roused himself for the chance to force home the Crown's case in the closing days of the trial, describing Abu Hamza as a terrorist recruitment agent. He pointed out to the jurors, in case they had not noticed, that while in the witness box Abu Hamza 'did everything in his power to avoid answering questions ... Not only that, you may also think that he betrayed his true nature and his own recognition of the fact that in his talks he was preaching terrorism, homicidal violence and hatred.'

Abu Hamza, Perry told the jury, had abused his position as a religious leader to promise his followers spiritual reward in return for carrying out acts of violence: 'The defendant was a recruiting sergeant, a recruiting officer, for terrorism and murder. In addition to his role as a recruiting officer for homicidal violence we say he was also preaching hatred. Through his threatening, abusive and insulting words, he preached hatred against Jews as a racial and ethnic group – not limited to Zionist Jews or Jews in Israel, if that would not be bad enough. He preached hatred unqualified of the Jews.'

Closing the case for the defence, Fitzgerald repeated that although his client's remarks might be deeply offensive, that did not necessarily make them criminal. 'He has told you repeatedly that he never intended to incite murder, and the prosecution have not proven any such intention,' Abu Hamza's barrister told the jurors. 'We are dealing with generalisation, with religious language and unspecific statements. There is a gulf between what he talks about and what he intends ... If he was intending inciting murder, why was he willingly talking to police and MI5 at the same time?'

Finally it was down to Mr Justice Hughes to sum up all the evidence in the case, despite the fact that his home had been burgled the previous weekend, and a laptop computer on which he had made trial notes stolen. He had already told the jury to put aside any thoughts of conspiracies. Now he reviewed the evidence methodically, and cautioned the jurors to put aside their personal feelings about Abu Hamza's words. They must reach their verdicts on the evidence alone. At 3.30 p.m. on Wednesday, 1 February, the jury retired to its room to begin consideration of its verdicts.

While the jurors talked, the rest of the cast in the courtroom drama began the waiting game of hanging around, speculating pointlessly about when the jury might return, making unnecessary phone calls and drinking too much coffee. The judge's impatience showed through on the Friday, when both sets of counsel had to dissuade him from trying to hurry the jury up by telling them he was prepared to accept majority verdicts of ten–two, rather than unanimous decisions.

The jury went home over the weekend, and did not sit the following Monday because one of their number was ill. On Tuesday, 7 February they again retired to their room to resume their deliberations, offering the court no indication of their progress. There was no inkling of how close they were to reaching verdicts until three minutes before 1 p.m. Just as those waiting were putting on their coats to leave the court precincts for a breath of air and a bite of lunch, the Old Bailey Tannoy system spluttered into life: 'All parties in Hamza to Court Two.' Court staff whispered that the jury had reached verdicts on all fifteen counts. The frustration of waiting and not knowing was immediately transformed into the dramatic tension of realising that the decision was imminent.

The jury filed into the packed courtroom, and its foreman stood at the clerk's request to reveal that unanimous verdicts had been agreed on all the charges. Asked in turn about the verdict on each of the first five counts on the indictment, the foreman responded with the one-word answer: 'Guilty.' On charges six, nine, eleven and twelve – three of soliciting to murder and one of inciting racial hatred – the jurors had decided that Abu Hamza was not guilty. But on four other charges – including the possession of the Afghan encyclopaedia – he was also guilty.

In the dock Abu Hamza appeared to be talking quietly, perhaps praying. There was no other display of emotion from him. The judge announced that the defendant would be sentenced at 2.15 p.m. After lunch. Abu Hamza was led back down to the cells while Mr Justice Hughes retired to his room to eat and ponder his sentencing remarks.

After four weeks of being the even-handed ringmaster, the judge now had the opportunity to tell Abu Hamza forcefully what he thought of him and his conduct. He said the cleric had been 'evasive and specious' in the witness box. He did not accept his claims to speak for Islam; it was 'perfectly plain' that he did not. But the preacher's position at Finsbury Park meant that he had spoken with authority and influence. 'You spoke with great anger, it was directed at virtually every country and a very large number of people,' the judge said, his gaze fixed firmly on the grey-bearded figure who remained seated in the dock. 'You are entitled to your views, and in this country you are entitled to express them up to the point where you incite murder or incite racial hatred. That, however, is what you did. You used your authority to legitimise anger and to encourage your audiences to believe that it gave rise to a duty to murder. You commended suicide bombing, you encouraged them to kill in the cause you set out for them.'

No one knew how many people had listened to and been influenced by the thousands of copies of Abu Hamza's recorded sermons that had been made and distributed. The harm his words had caused around the world was 'incalculable'. The judge concluded: 'No one can say now what damage your words may have caused. No one can say whether your audience, present or wider, acted on your words. I am satisfied that you are and were a person whose views and the manner of expression of those views created a real danger to the lives of innocent people in different parts of the world.'

After such a ringing condemnation, the actual sentence was expected to be harsh. On paper it sounded just that. Abu Hamza was sentenced to seven years' imprisonment on each of the six counts of soliciting murder of which he was found guilty. For the three charges of inciting race hatred, he was given twenty-one months each. The offence of possessing offensive tapes with intent to distribute them attracted a term of three years, and the possession of the jihad encyclopaedia three and a half years. Added together, the sentences amounted to a jail term of fifty-three years and nine months. But the judge ordered that the sentences should run concurrently, not consecutively. Abu Hamza would be jailed for seven years.

He was taken down the Old Bailey steps for the last time. Two supporters acknowledged him from the gallery overhead, one shouting, 'God bless you, Sheikh Abu Hamza.' The cleric replied, but he was already out of sight, below stairs, and his response was muffled.

It was left to his solicitor Muddasar Arani to utter words of dissent on his behalf outside the court. How could he possibly have had a fair trial after the 'massive campaign' that had been waged against him? Some of the verdicts were 'absurd' and would be appealed. Abu Hamza had done nothing other than 'stand for his principle of the right to preach jihad against the oppression of the Muslim community worldwide'. He had never intended harm to the British people. Most importantly, her client was adopting a role which would continue to give him power and influence in the world of jihad. He was still the servant of Allah, prepared to do whatever was wished. God knew better.

'Sheikh Abu Hamza wishes to thank God Almighty for what has been decreed for him,' said Arani. 'We may have lost one battle, but there are many more to be fought yet for Sheikh Abu Hamza. So much for freedom of expression. Sheikh Abu Hamza is a prisoner of faith. The sentence that has been decreed on him constitutes nothing more than slow martyrdom.'

Epilogue: The Legacy

Martyrdom is not turning out to be as glorious as Abu Hamza envisaged. There are the physical discomforts he must endure in prison. He suffers with diabetes and high blood pressure; he has a painful skin condition and requires regular medical attention for his damaged eye. Without his metal hook, deemed a dangerous weapon under penal regulations, he cannot fend for himself.

Incarceration has been a leveller. He has discovered that despite his reputation he is entitled to no special privileges. He has been refused permission to preach to Muslim inmates or to conduct prayer circles.

Signs of paranoia are creeping in. Abu Hamza has been predicting that he will be murdered, claiming that his cell is bugged and that MI5 has bribed a fellow inmate with the promise of early parole, to arrange a fatal accident. He has staged a very brief hunger strike because, bizarrely, he complained he wasn't getting enough to eat. But he has remained utterly unrepentant as he faces years of court appearances in connection with his appeal, his battle to remain a British citizen, his fight against extradition and possibly another high-profile trial in New York.

While not kind to him personally, prison has enhanced his reputation in extremist circles beyond the walls of Belmarsh jail. On 5 December 2005 London's *Time Out* magazine named Abu Hamza as number five in its list of the 'movers and shakers' of the year, even though he had been in prison for the whole of it. He was placed ahead of Tony Blair (tenth) and the Metropolitan Police chief, Sir Ian Blair (sixth). The magazine said the cleric continued to 'cast a long shadow' over life in London, especially in the wake of 7/7.

His reach, of course, extends far beyond London. Thousands upon thousands of copies of his recordings – DVDs, videotapes, audiocassettes – are circulating around the world, spreading his words and influencing young minds. And the internet site for Supporters of Shariah is still online. In its Q&A section is the question: 'Are suicide attacks haram [forbidden]?' The answer, in Abu Hamza's name, is: 'If it is done as a tactic of war because there is no other strong means to resist the enemies then it is of course one of the highest and noblest form [sic] of shahadah [martyrdom].' Mohammed Babar, an al-Qaeda supergrass who gave evidence at another terror trial at the Old Bailey in 2006, said he was inspired to pursue jihad after listening to Abu Hamza's taped sermons and internet preaching.

The former trustees of Finsbury Park mosque say they still receive death threats, and the new managers of the building – who are busily reconstructing its image and renovating the physical edifice – are constantly alert for any return by Abu Hamza's disciples. Some have attempted takeovers at other mosques, but Muslim leaders are exasperated at the meek response from the authorities after all they had gone through with Abu Hamza. In the wake of the closure of Finsbury Park a group of radicals tried unsuccessfully to seize control – by threat, intimidation and indoctrination – at Stockwell mosque in south London. Trustees there complained to the police, who assisted them in putting in security cameras but took no action against the invaders.

When the Pentagon recently declassified hundreds of documents regarding the detainees at Guantánamo Bay, they included files from Defense Department investigators which revealed that far more of their prisoners passed through the doors of Finsbury Park than they had at first imagined. A number of Finsbury Park graduates are among the sixty men in British jails currently awaiting trial for terrorist offences. According to Peter Clarke, the head of Scotland Yard's Anti-Terrorist Branch, the allegations against those waiting to be tried 'include conspiracies to murder, to cause explosions, to cause a public nuisance by means of radiological devices and possession of automatic weaponry'.

Addressing a London conference on politics and terrorism only weeks after Abu Hamza's conviction, Clarke said: 'The terrorism we are now combating has its roots in this country. We're seeing many, many British citizens engaged in it … We know that the terrorists we are facing in the UK are well trained, highly motivated and confident of achieving their goals.' Clarke, a man who always measures his words carefully, has dismissed notions that the West will get to grip with al-Qaeda terrorism within ten years as 'hopelessly optimistic'. In other words, the genie is out of the bottle, and no one has any firm idea how to squeeze it back in there.

There are no reliable estimates of how many young men passed through Abu Hamza's hands. Thousands attended the mosque and heard him preach around Britain. Some have perished on faraway battlefields in wars they knew little about, or in suicide attacks in Baghdad, Kashmir and Kabul; some are in jail cells or interned behind razor wire at Guantánamo Bay; some have been inspired to become preachers and recruiters themselves.

There are hundreds of others. Shorn of their leader and their sanctuary in Finsbury Park, they have dropped out of sight, but not necessarily out of action.

Acknowledgements

Since Abu Hamza became a public figure in 1997, we have written thousands of words in newspaper articles about him and the suspected terrorists who passed through the doors of Finsbury Park mosque when he was in control there. His trial at the Old Bailey in early 2006 presented an opportunity to pull these threads together and compile a detailed and comprehensive account of his role in the global jihad.

Much of the material we have drawn upon is available from public sources. The US Freedom of Information Act, for example, provides access to a range of legal documents that puts the corresponding British legislation to shame. Britain's secret anti-terrorist court – the Special Immigration Appeals Commission – does, however, publish limited judgements on cases involving terrorist suspects which are packed with information about the activities of the Finsbury Park mujahideen. A series of lengthy terrorist trials – such as those concerning the murder of Detective Constable Stephen Oake and the London ricin plot – have also disclosed previously secret information about the presence of Islamic extremists in the UK.

We were fortunate to have access to courageous individuals who long ago realised the menace of Abu Hamza, and who spoke out despite the risk to themselves and their families. At their own request a number of these sources have not been named, but they know who they are, and we thank them for sharing their experiences with us.

It is the Muslim community that has been the most forceful at raising the alarm, and we thank Dr Abduljalil Sajid in Brighton, and former trustees of Finsbury Park such as Shafiullah Patel and Abdul Kadir Barkatulla for their assistance. Men like Reda Hassaine infiltrated Finsbury Park mosque and repeatedly warned the authorities of the activities of Abu Hamza and his cohorts.

Many other sources, involved in counter-terrorism and intelligence-gathering, have generously allowed us to tap their resources. Although their identities have to be protected, they have shown themselves to be people who think long and hard about the fight against terror, and who understand that every decision, and potential error, they make can have enormous consequences.

We have also spoken at length to men who continue to regard Abu Hamza and other leaders of the jihadi movement as scholars. These are followers who once stood alongside Abu Hamza and have been inspired by him to travel overseas and follow the path of jihad.

It is highly unlikely that any of these people, from either side, will agree with all of the conclusions we have reached in examining the phenomenon of the Finsbury Park mosque. We are, however, indebted to them for their time and their insights.

We must also thank fellow journalists for their invaluable help, especially John Wellman, Paul Sanders and colleagues at *The Times* for their indulgence and tolerance. We owe debts of gratitude to Chris Buckland, Deborah Davies, Sandra Laville, David Williams, Simon Hughes, Rajeev Syal, Richard Ford, Paul Grover, Peter Nicholls and Chris Evans. Thanks too to David Taylor for a moment of wisdom, and to Maeve Boothby O'Neill.

We are especially grateful to Bill Hamilton at A.M. Heath for his belief, support and one particular flash of inspiration, and to Richard Johnson and Robert Lacey at HarperCollins for their speed, skill and constant encouragement.

Sean O'Neill and Daniel McGrory, April 2006

Index